WINE
DYNASTIES
OF EUROPE

To Kate

WINE
DYNASTIES
OF EUROPE

PERSONAL PORTRAITS OF
TEN LEADING HOUSES

HARRY EYRES

Lennard Publishing
1990

Lennard Publishing
a division of Lennard Books Ltd
Musterlin House
Jordan Hill Road
Oxford OX2 8DP

British Library Cataloguing in Publication Data
is available for this title
ISBN 1–85291–088–7

First published 1990
© Harry Eyres 1990

Text designed and phototypeset by
Nuprint Ltd, Harpenden, Herts AL5 4SE
Cover design by Pocknell & Co
Reproduced, printed and bound in Great Britain by
St Edmundsbury Press Ltd, Bury St Edmunds, Suffolk

Contents

List of Illustrations

Acknowledgements

My main thanks are due to the ten families for patiently submitting to my questions, and in some cases even answering them. I am especially grateful to Anthony Barton Esq, Baron Henri Le Roy, MM. Jean and Etienne Grivot, M. Christian de Billy, M. Christian Pol-Roger, Mme Odette Pol-Roger, Erwein Graf Matuschka-Greiffenclau, the Lingenfelder family, the German Wine Information Service, Marchese Piero Antinori, the Torres family, Catherine Scott, Sr Alberto Fornos, H. Sichel & Son, Sr Javier Hidalgo, Michael and Elizabeth Symington, James and Penny Symington, Paul and Janey Symington, Bill Warre MW and Tim Stanley-Clarke, Esq.

Introductions were facilitated by: Dr Peter Hallgarten, Anthony Hanson, Bill Gunn MW, Stuart Pigott, and Richard Tanner. Giles MacDonogh kindly allowed me to consult his unpublished work on Irish and English families in Bordeaux. Finally thanks to Dieter Klein, who provided the initial impetus for the book; to my editor Duncan McAra, and to Roderick Brown of Lennard and his hard-working assistant Arabella St John Parker; to Valerie Roden for typing two chapters; and last but not least to Kate Stuart-Smith for constant help and encouragement.

Maps reproduced with the permission of Michelin from their maps, nos. 988, 989 and 990.

Introduction

FOR THE CONSUMER, that late-twentieth-century version of humanity whose name begins to sound sinister as the planet becomes shop-soiled, this is a golden age of wine. Scientific and technological advances have immeasurably improved standards of wine-making all over the world. The long-established preeminence of the classic wine-producing regions of Europe has been challenged, to stimulating effect, by the emergence of new great powers in the wine sphere—notably California and Australia—impatient of many of the shibboleths of the Old World.

The influences now work in both directions: techniques such as cold fermentation developed in the New World have transformed wine-making in parts of southern Europe; fermentation in new oak barrels, a version of a traditional European technique adopted and developed in the New World, has now been used to create a new style of wine in the Graves region of Bordeaux. Italy, for so long profligate with her huge resources, in wine as in many artistic areas, is being galvanised by a new generation of dedicated young wine-makers. The slumbering, isolationist giants of the Iberian peninsula, Spain and Portugal (fourth and ninth respectively in the world league of wine producers), are showing signs, albeit infuriatingly slow, of waking up and coming to terms— now that they are members of the EEC—with an international market. Even nature has helped, contributing a splendid run of vintages in the 1980s.

In the midst of this euphoria, there is a danger of losing sight of some elementary facts about the production of wine. Just as many Americans are apparently horrified to discover that the meat they buy in a supermarket was once a live animal, so the new-style wine consumer may not be aware that he or she is drinking a product of husbandry, a fruit of the earth worked by human hands. Wine is not just another mass-produced standardised thing—or rather it need not be. The vinous equivalents of a McDonald's hamburger or a packet of cornflakes exist: they are, say, Piat d'Or or Gallo's Hearty Red. They serve a useful function: they give pleasure. This book is not about wines of that sort, however, because they offer no challenge or stimulus either to our sense organs or to our imaginations.

We must not take the production of fine wines—its wonderful continuity and diversity—for granted, though; it is the result of hundreds of years of hard work on the part of dedicated individuals, committed to an idea of excellence, of the exceptional—an idea which is constantly being renewed and which therefore represents a living tradition. Fine wine, like music or literature or other arts, is the result of skills being passed on from generation to generation, together with the sense that what is being pursued, in the face of hostile weather, wars, disease, has a worth which transcends the life of the individual. That may sound excessively grand, but fine wine will not be made where there are not individuals who are prepared to sacrifice their lives to its making.

Wine is a local product, wedded not just to the soil and the climate, but also to ways of doing things long established in a particular place, yet constantly undergoing refinement. This book is about ten families in Europe who have been committed to fine wine-making, in particular places, for several generations, who seem to me to have achieved a judicious balance between tradition and innovation. The word dynasty needs a little gloss. The original Greek sense of 'power' is apposite in some cases (Torres, Antinori) but not in others (Lingenfelder, Grivot). The point is family continuity. All the wine producers in this book are still predominantly family concerns—though in some cases only by a whisker (the Antinori family have 51 per cent of the shares in their 600-year-old wine business, Whitbread have 49 per cent).

One may have mixed feelings about family businesses—it would hardly be human not to. Most of the younger generation featured in the book have had doubts about joining the family firm: most have been through periods when it was the last thing they wanted to do with their lives (Rainer Lingenfelder wanted to be a pilot, Javier Hidalgo wanted—perhaps still wants—to be a naturalist).

This is a time when there is much hypocritical celebration of family values. Families mean conflict as well as continuity. One of the sub-themes which kept cropping up in the writing of the book was the tension between old and young pretenders. In the case of Anthony Barton it was uncle and nephew—an uncle, Ronald, who kept promising to hand over the reins but could never quite bring himself to do so. Meanwhile the nephew saw the twin family properties gradually accumulating the dust of a reputation for being old-fashioned, not up with the new rising stars. The conflicts in the Torres family have been widely publicised: the brilliant wine-making son actually left the firm at one point because the autocratic father did not allow him to have his way. All the same these are families which have successfully negotiated their conflicts. But success breeds its own dangers. The most obvious is the temptation to sell out. This is a temptation which affects all the larger concerns. The most dramatic examples are in Champagne. Take the firm of Pommery et Greno, called by a recent writer 'one of the most glittering inheritances in Champagne'. The Polignac family sold it in 1979 to the entrepreneur Xavier Gardinier, who sold it in turn, in 1983, to the giant conglomerate BSN which owns the champagne house of Lanson as well as manufacturing Kronenbourg beer and yogurt. BSN is run by marketing people whose tactics include the 'repositioning' of Pommery up £2 a bottle in price above Lanson in one market and £2 a bottle below it in another. Once family control is lost, the destiny of a company is in the hands of other forces, the freewheeling forces of money and profit. Giles Clarke of Majestic Wine Warehouses, the company he bought, made famous, then nearly bankrupted by the acquisition of the much larger Liquor Barn chain in the United States, summed up his philosophy in the wine trade journal *Wine and Spirit*: 'I am a dealer: everything I have is for sale at any given moment.' If you think like that, you are unlikely to remain in the same line of business for generations. To build up a company to the size of Torres or Antinori, and to hold to a distinctive philosophy of quality, is a valuable achievement and a perilous one. It may well be that by the time this book is published one of the families included will have sold out to a multinational corporation.

But why is this long-term family continuity in the wine business necessary, or indeed desirable? The answer is that wine is a long-term business. A vine, for a start, will not produce grapes for three years. It will not reach optimum maturity for ten, fifteen or even twenty years after that. The world's best wines take a similarly long time to reach maturity —fifteen years in the case of *cru classé* claret and certain Californian Cabernets, twenty years in the case of vintage port of a top vintage.

That is only the beginning. In the classic wine-producing regions of northern Europe, the selection of sites for vineyards, the matching of grape variety to vineyard and the refinement of wine-making techniques are processes which have gone on for centuries. In central France and Germany, very near the northern limit for the cultivation of the vine, these processes are conditioned by a harsh climate. In Germany vines will thrive only on south-facing slopes, and the steeper the slope, the greater the exposure to the sun and therefore the riper the grape. The astonishingly steep, rock-face vineyards which line the Mosel and, in places, the Rhine, and the Douro in Portugal, are perhaps the most dramatically impressive pieces of cultivated land in Europe. They match the Inca terraces of Peru and the paddy-fields of South-East Asia. They bear witness not only to centuries of toil but also to pride and belief. In a world increasingly dominated by accountants, they would never have been created.

The *vigneron* (vine-grower) also has an interest in safeguarding the long-term future and fertility of his land. Any sort of impoverishment, erosion or contamination means ruin. Not many of these families may yet be producing 'organic' wine, but correct viticulture implies a care for the earth which would satisfy any ecologist.

In the early days of the Californian and Australian wine industries, it was proudly (or arrogantly) asserted that the emphasis on different types of soil and particular slopes, on which the whole French hierarchy of *Appellation d'Origine Contrôlée, premiers crus* and *grands crus* is based, was just European snobbery: 'soil', as the Californian Bill Jekel put it succinctly, 'is dirt'. Californian or Australian sunshine produced ripe fruit which a skilled wine-maker, using computerised technology and new French oak, turned into great wine. Now the wheel is turning. The Californians and Australians have realised that even in their sunny climates the matching of grape variety to vineyard location is a tricky, absorbing business. The Napa Valley, not a large patch of land, is in the process of being divided into several sub-regions.

If the Californians and Australians are becoming more 'European', they are merely acknowledging that Europe was where the production of fine wine started. It is Europe's great cultural and political diversity which has created the world's wine styles. As the new Europe which has emerged since the last war moves, however uncertainly (and the recent unshackling of Eastern Europe raises a new set of questions) towards some kind of federal structure, one of its struggles will be to maintain cultural identity and diversity in the face of very powerful homogenising forces.

This is also the struggle which wine faces. What has been well described as the international jet-set of Cabernet and Chardonnay has been extending its domination over the world's vineyards from Chile to Bulgaria. At the same time, though, there have been encouraging moves back towards indigenous styles and grape varieties, especially in Italy. Vintage port, a unique wine grown in unique conditions, is enjoying an unlikely boom. Sherry lags behind but must soon be appreciated for what it is, one of the world's most complex and rewarding wines. Perhaps the most threatened of the world's fine wines are the estate-bottled Rieslings of Germany. A crisis looms in the river-valleys of the Nahe, Mosel and Rhine, because the young generation are simply not prepared to continue their ancestors' back-breaking work in the vine-yards.

Wine is a business: if it ceases to be profitable in any place, it will cease to be made. But it is also a magical substance, intimately bound up with human culture from the earliest times, and something which expresses our culture as fully as almost anything else human beings have made. It is worth remembering that wine itself has a culture, or many different cultures: a selection of those is the subject of this book.

H.E.

The Bartons

of

Château Langoa

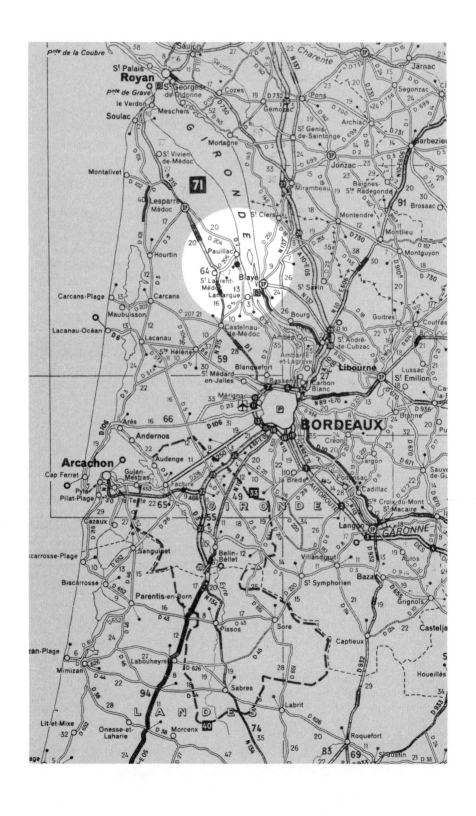

'YOU KNOW CHÂTEAU LANGOA-BARTON?' I asked the bus driver. 'Oui, oui, Léoville-Langoa: on arrête juste là.' The journey from Bordeaux—that perfect, honey-stone, eighteenth-century city whose rich sobriety some find repellent—up-country into the Médoc peninsula, which juts a hundred kilometres north between the widening Gironde and the Atlantic, is bound to give a *frisson* to anyone with the remotest interest in wine. It is far from being one of wine's most romantic routes—not a patch, scenically, on the train journey up the Douro, the valleys of the Moselle, Rhine or Rhône—but it concentrates more of the great names in wine than any other comparable stretch, except possibly the Côte d'Or in Burgundy.

The first part of the journey is through scrubby land, dotted with bungalows, leading to a stretch of pine forest. It seems as if we are going down a cul-de-sac, or one of those French roads marked 'sans issue'. The Médoc does indeed lead nowhere, and until the eighteenth century was nowhere. When the first major plantations of vines were made there in the late seventeenth century, the swampy Médoc was considered wild, rough country—'terre sauvage et solitaire'.

Signs start appearing off the main road: the first that makes me look round states CHÂTEAU CANTEMERLE, and points to an elegant, ghostly-white building hiding among trees. Cantemerle is, with La Lagune, the southernmost of the sixty-two estates, known in Bordeaux as châteaux, sometimes with a pretension to grandeur they do not possess, selected in 1855 as *grands crus classés*—the aristocracy of the wine world then and now.

The signs indicate Margaux, but Château Margaux itself, one of the four original first growths, and one of the Médoc's most splendid buildings, is not visible from the main road. The second most famous château of the Médoc's largest and most straggling appellation does stand right by the road: two flags, British and Dutch, fly from the nineteenth-century turrets of Château Palmer, representing the château's dual ownership. The vineyard stretches up to the château garden: I am surprised to see bunches of grapes lying on the ground. They are rotten ones rejected by the pickers in this wet harvest.

The villages, as opposed to the châteaux, are small and undistinguished: a post office, a church, a few shops; they seem afflicted with something more withering than the normal dozy inertia of rural France.

After Margaux, we head back into the woods, away from the river. We enter the parish of Moulis, not classed growth country but home of some of the best of the *crus bourgeois*, the order below the *crus classés*: signs point to two of them: Chasse-Spleen and Maucaillou. Small patches of vineyard look moth-eaten in forest clearings.

The woods thin out: the broad, muddy river comes into view, with the more varied, hilly landscape of the Côte Blaye unfolding on the far bank. The gentle vine-covered slopes leading to the Gironde on our side are the gravel-banks of St Julien, the heart of the Médoc. We pass a beautiful low cream-stone château, with proud wrought-iron gates: this is Beychevelle, built in the eighteenth century in the chartreuse (hunting-lodge) style characteristic of Guyenne: a fourth growth in classification, a second in reputation and airs. A little further on, another château with rather pompous, square end towers tacked on to a graceful trunk, can be seen among cedars to the right near the river: Ducru-Beaucaillou, one of the best of the Médoc's second growths. The road dips down and crosses a stream: half-way up the other side the bus stops. 'Léoville-Langoa, monsieur.'

There are imposing farm buildings on the right; a wide gateway on the left leading to a cobbled yard. Further up the road, and set back from it, I can see a fine eighteenth-century chartreuse, not unlike Beychevelle, but more discreet in style.

I proceed into the cobbled yard to find a tractor trailer full of small deep purple grapes with thick green stalks, which are being fed into a destemmer; there is also a coach with Dutch number plates in the process of disgorging about three dozen rubicund senior citizens. A tall, dark-haired, elegant man, dressed in a check tweed jacket, charcoal-grey trousers, Hermès tie, gold tie-pin, is greeting the visitors. Anthony Barton looks younger than his late fifties: his style is what people on the Continent think of as English, but a traditional English country gentleman would consider a little too dapper to be quite respectable.

Mr Barton spies me and comes over. 'Good to see you. We're going mad here—I'm afraid we've got another invasion. Lillian, would you mind looking after the Dutch.' The senior citizens are left in the hands of his tall, blonde daughter.

Talking of national styles, there is a further surprise when Anthony Barton opens his mouth: he speaks with an unmistakable and engaging hint of an Irish brogue. He also has a most infectious Irish humour: 'We had a party of Danes here the other day. I was explaining the method of vinification and suddenly I realised that there were only three left out of forty. I had to go and round them up: some were peeing behind the bushes in the garden, some were climbing up ladders into the fermentation vats, children were drowning. Others were putting their fingers into the destemmer and chopping them off. We thought, this is the end. But of course we can't turn them away.'

We head through the buildings on the right of the yard: in the first I just catch a glimpse of great vats of varnished oak, with thick rubber pipes trailing from them. Four or five people are working but the atmosphere, considering it is the middle of the vintage, is calm and orderly. We pass through a double door into the next building: this is dark and silent, filled with long, low rows of the 225-litre oak casks called *barriques*. Maturing inside is the 1986 vintage of Anthony Barton's twin classed-growth properties, Châteaux Léoville- and Langoa-Barton. Tastings later will confirm that this is a vintage of exciting quality. 'I'll show you all this properly later,' Anthony Barton comments.'What we need to do now is decant the wine for lunch.' We emerge from the barrique *chai* on to a circular lawn in front of the château. The main range, whose tall windows have claret-coloured shutters, is only one storey high, but it is raised above the lawn on a plinth, through which two flights of steps fan up to the front door. The long plinth is not just decorative: as the wooden door at its base, wide enough for a barrique to pass, might suggest, it is the cellar. We enter the house through a side door and find ourselves in a green-painted hall hung with Irish hunting prints, the floor littered with gumboots, fishing-rods, guns. We seem to have crossed an invisible border: outside, eighteenth-century France, inside eighteenth-century Ireland. Beyond the hall there is a splendid kitchen with a spectacular array of copper pans, and, covering one entire wall, the mother and father of all Agas.

Here we collect Anthony's red setter, Brenda, and proceed to the cellar. 'I'm afraid all this needs reorganising—it's just as my uncle left it. In a terrible mess, in other words.' There is a butler's pantry with assorted candles, corkscrews, empty bottles, cobwebbed iron racks and two doors leading to other parts of the cellar. 'What shall we have for lunch? We need some champagne, and some white wine.' Roederer '73 and Hugel's Sporen, from a single vineyard in Alsace, are selected. Anthony Barton is a devotee of Alsace wines. 'As for claret, I don't know what vintage would be best. Some of the '71, that's drinking quite well; the '64; and we'll try a spot of '55.' Two bottles of each vintage are carefully decanted by the proprietor of two grands crus classés: the butler is instructed to bring them through to the dining-room.

Anthony Barton, with a hospitality more Irish than either English or French, holds an open table at lunch for the two weeks of the vintage. On this occasion, two other cru classé château owners are expected: the Taris of Château Giscours, third growth, Margaux, and the Bories of Château Grand-Puy-Lacoste, fifth growth (but with a reputation higher than its class), Pauillac. They have in common with Anthony Barton the still unusual fact of being owner occupiers rather than absentee landlords. The other guest is the American proprietor of the cru bourgeois (but the 1945 vintage, picked up for a song in London, tasted excellent at nearly forty years old), Château Sénéjac.

The table is a splendid long refectory one in the spacious, open-beamed new dining-room on one side of the chai courtyard, designed and rebuilt by Anthony's Danish-born wife, Eva. The predominant colour is light beige, reflecting the stripped pine of most of the furniture. There are copper carriage lamps, a couple of Roman amphorae, and an antiquated machine for steam-cleaning barrels, and on the walls a series of prints depicting different species of fish. It is all light, tasteful and cool.

The other guests arrive, the men dressed in the English style of tweed jackets and grey trousers, the women in expensive-looking coats and skirts. The champagne, ripe, butter-yellow and mature, is served by the Bartons' Moroccan butler.

As we drink our aperitif, a procession of cars, mud-splashed old Citroën Amis, battered Renault estates, pulls into the yard and unloads its colourfully dressed, talkative contents: the team of *vendangeurs*, nearly all locals, who have been picking grapes since eight in the morning. The pickers, laden with thermos flasks and cagoules, pile into the great kitchen/dining-room on the level below ours—but visible through a large semicircular window to the châtelain and his guests. They sit at four trestle tables, warmed by a great open log fire in the middle of the far wall. The stone fireplace in our dining-room, by contrast, is purely decorative.

'They eat the same food as we do,' says Eva Barton, an immaculate-looking Nordic blonde. Today it is a hearty soup followed by casserole. 'They don't drink the same wine, though,' her husband adds. Our '71 Léoville-Barton has smelled of cedar and sealing-wax, but the fruit has faded on the palate; the '64 has been rich and ripe, a great success for the vintage when only the wines picked before the rains came out well; the '55 bricky, rather short and acid—not one of the better bottles, according to Anthony Barton. 'What they drink is a bit of a blend—a light *vin de table* spiced up with some of our press wine (the wine made from pressing the skins and pips left at the bottom of the fermentation tanks), which is good, deep-coloured, sturdy stuff.'

Conversation on the high table is relaxed. The poor weather—it seems that I have arrived on the first sunny day for a week, and more rain is to follow—is discussed and lamented, but without despondency. Not surprising, perhaps, since five out of Bordeaux's six previous vintages—'81, '82, '83, '85 and '86—have been good to exceptional in quality, and large in quantity. It is a run of successes almost without parallel in this region of uncertain Atlantic weather. A mediocre '87, while disappointing in itself, could be a necessary breathing-space for a replete market incapable of absorbing another good, keeping vintage. The unprecedented run of good vintages has certainly brought great wealth to the château-owners: Pierre Tari, the energetic owner of Château Giscours, has constructed a polo park in its grounds. Langoa, less flashy perhaps, exudes the air of a well-cared-for estate.

This very conspicuous prosperity, however, is a recent phenomenon, as my long discussion with Anthony Barton after lunch about the history of the Barton family makes clear. One fact alone is telling: Léoville and Langoa-Barton are the only châteaux, apart from Mouton-Rothschild, not to have changed hands at least once since the classification of 1855.

At that time the twin estates had been in Anglo-Irish hands for thirty years: it is something of an irony that the Bartons, who have never taken French citizenship, are the oldest-established cru classé château owners in Bordeaux. Thomas Barton, son of a sheep-farmer from Curraghmore, County Fermanagh, and great-greatgrandson of a member of the expeditionary force sent by Elizabeth I under the Earl of Essex to suppress the rebellion of O'Neill, Earl of Tyrone, arrived in Bordeaux around 1715. A thriving trade, prohibited by England, had grown up between Ireland and Bordeaux, to supply the necessities of life to a region newly and heavily planted with vines, but not much else. The vessels which arrived from Ireland with wool needed cargo for their return journey: they took back the obvious commodity, wine. Tom Barton's brother-in-law James Boyd (the Boyds became another notable Protestant Irish dynasty in Bordeaux, owning the third-growth Château Boyd-Cantenac in Margaux) was caught disguising wool as salt-beef.

Bordeaux had produced wine since Roman times, and since the Middle Ages (the marriage of Henry II to Eleanor of Aquitaine brought Bordeaux under English rule) it had supplied England with the lightish-coloured wine called claret. We would now call it rosé, and probably turn our noses up at it. The late seventeenth century saw a momentous change to the production of dark red wines, capable of ageing, especially when bottled (the Verrerie Royale founded by the Irishman Mitchell moved to the quai des Chartrons in Bordeaux in 1720). The founding father of the politics of quality was Arnaud de Pontac of

Château Haut-Brion, and perhaps its chief, paradoxical stimulus was the penal duty imposed on French wine by England from the late seventeenth century through to 1786. Only very high-priced, high-quality wine could withstand a rate of duty which was double the price of the finest wine of the time. Only in England, and to a lesser extent Scotland and Ireland, were there connoisseurs prepared to pay such prices. The English, partly through their connoisseurship but also through their Customs and Excise, created the new fine wines or grands crus from the thin gravel plateaux of the Médoc, which quite quickly sold for as much as ten times the price of ordinary Bordeaux, as they still do today.

The Irish community in Bordeaux thrived, shipping wine to Irish and Scottish ports to avoid the high rate of English duty. In 1747 Tom Barton bought the estate of Château Le Boscq in the most northerly of the Médoc's important communes, St Estèphe, then more or less virgin territory. He also bought the Grove estate in County Tipperary, for which he paid the substantial price of £30,000. In 1756 he is known to have had land in Léognan, an important wine-growing commune in the Graves area just south of Bordeaux.

At that time Tom Barton was perhaps the most powerful shipper on the quai des Chartrons, the riverside district just outside the old city walls of Bordeaux where foreign, mainly Protestant merchants began to establish themselves from the late seventeenth century onwards. There was a powerful Irish mafia, largely though not entirely Protestant, in Bordeaux, including families such as the Boyds, Dixons, Woodwards and Skinners. Two of Tom Barton's partners were Abraham Lawton, from whom descends a still-important broking family, and Dennis MacCarthy, most prominent of the Catholic Irish shippers. Religion seems to have meant less to these expatriate traders than nationality. All the same, there were 4000 Protestants living in Bordeaux in 1780, the year Tom Barton died aged eighty-four, representing 5 per cent of the population.

Most dynasties, on close investigation, reveal certain patterns: a repeated peculiarity of the Bartons has been the omission of alternate generations, made up for by the longevity and business acumen of their predecessors and successors. Tom Barton's son William was, says his descendant, 'a bit of a no-gooder. He took to the bottle, got involved in law-suits, took little interest in the business.' He was certainly a wealthy man. When, as one of the very first consequences of the Revolution in 1789, contributions for the relief of the poor were levied, William Barton paid 3000 livres, out of an annual income estimated at 5000, one of the city's highest contributions.

By that time Tom Barton had found a worthy successor in his grandson Hugh, who was born in Limerick in 1766, and went out to Bordeaux to be taken into partnership in 1786. In that same year Hugh Barton formed an association with Daniel Guestier, a French Huguenot of Breton origin, son of the steward of the Marquis de Ségur, who at one time owned Châteaux Lafite, Latour and Mouton, and after whom the St Estèphe third-growth Château Calon-Ségur is named. Guestier became a ship's captain, and made enough money to buy his own ship.

The repercussions of the Revolution took quite a while to affect commercial life in Bordeaux. The most immediate effect was that a good deal of property, confiscated from aristocrats and the church, came on to the market, though Hugh Barton presumably did not feel confident enough to take advantage of the situation, for he did not buy his château until thirty years later. In 1792, after the execution of Louis XVI, the port of Bordeaux was blockaded, and business became difficult. In 1793 all the Bartons were arrested and incarcerated in the Carmelite convent in Bordeaux, at the order of the notorious deputy Alex Ysabeau. The story, much embellished no doubt and at least partly apocryphal, is that they made a dramatic escape. One version has it that Hugh Barton made off with the key of the local guillotine. He was fortunate on two counts: he escaped with his life, unlike the owners of Lafite (President Pichard) and Margaux, and was able to leave his business in the trust-worthy hands of his associate Guestier. Hugh Barton reverted to the other half of his dual existence—that of a wealthy Irish landowner. He bought a vast new estate at Straffan, County Kildare, in the early years of the nineteenth century, but by 1802 was back in Bordeaux at least part of the time.

The Anglo-Irish merchant dynasties of Bordeaux seem to have been in no hurry to buy vineyards. It was only in 1821 that Hugh Barton (aged fifty-five) completed the purchase of Château Langoa (for 550,000 francs, £22,000 at the then rate of exchange, well down on the 1818 asking price of 700,000). This was followed, as can still be seen in the original ledger kept at Langoa, by the purchase of about a quarter of the great Léoville estate once owned by the Marquis de Las Cases, in 1825. The two other portions of the estate are now called Châteaux Léoville-Las-Cases and Léoville-Poyferré. The price for the Barton portion was 242,550 francs (no château this time, though a growth classed second rather than third in 1855). It is interesting to see, immediately below these two momentous purchases, two dates in the Revolutionary calen-dar, 17 Ventose An 13, 27 Germinal An 13, for two transactions made in 1805. Another telling set of figures is Hugh Barton's 1825 accounts: Langoa is valued at £30,000 out of a total estate of £526,000. That is a sizeable fortune by the standards of most people—excluding Rothschilds. Even his descendant wonders if it could all have been made out of wine.

As well as his interests in Bordeaux, Hugh Barton managed the wine-importing firm of French & Barton in Dublin. At the same time, he was interested in maintaining a position in the English social scene: in 1828 he rented Battle Abbey for the season. In 1830 Hugh Barton turned his back on Bordeaux, leaving his interests in the hands of the ever-dependable Guestier, and returned to Straffan to spend most of what remained of his long life hunting. He died in 1854, at the age of eighty-eight.

After the Napoleonic Wars, the wine business did not pick up as quickly as many hoped. The fine vintages of 1814 and 1815 (not the last to coincide with the end of a great war) were followed by the disastrous 1816. In the early 1820s not much money was being made. Daniel Guestier became the first President of the Banque de Bordeaux, an institution which specialised in making loans to wine-growers.

It was in 1855 that the President of the Chamber of Commerce of Bordeaux signed the list of the top sixty-two Châteaux of the Médoc, arranged in order of 'merit', in other words price, in five classes. It was, in the words of Hugh Johnson, 'an inspired publicity stunt, aimed at the Paris International Exhibition of the same year'. However opportunistic its inspiration, it has proved almost as durable as the Ten Commandments. Only one change, the elevation of Mouton from second to first growth, has been allowed in over a century. The Barton properties remain as they were classified, Léoville-Barton a second-growth and Langoa-Barton a third. Few today would quarrel with this placing.

After the death of Hugh, there is something of a hiatus in the story of the Bartons as a wine dynasty. The following generations were more interested in leading the lives of country gentlemen, riding to hounds, consuming rather than trading in claret. Hugh's eldest son Nathaniel (he had eleven children in all) was a J.P. and, like his father, High Sheriff of County Kildare.

Nathaniel's fifth son, Charles Thomas Hugh, resided both at Château Langoa and at rue Pavée de Chartron in Bordeaux. When he died young, at thirty-seven, he possessed only ten fewer decanters than his years. Nathaniel's grandson Bertram, son of his third son, also Bertram, bought out his brothers' and cousins' shares in the business, but his interests lay more in socialising. 'Grandad did the London season,' Anthony Barton says, 'took a house in Half Moon Street, and just quietly walked through the money. The story is that if he'd lived a few months longer the banks would have foreclosed.' Anthony's father, as the elder son, inherited the Irish property; his uncle Ronald, third in the great line of wine Bartons, inherited Langoa and Léoville.

Ronald Barton ranks with Baron Philippe de Rothschild as one of the longest-reigning and most dedicated of twentieth-century Bordeaux châtelains. Whatever else they did not have in common (Ronald was by all accounts the opposite of the flamboyant, publicity-hunting Baron), they both reacted against the Médocain norm of absentee ownership. Because he was, like all the Bartons, a countryman at heart, Ronald did not find living in the quiet—not to say moribund—Médoc a penance. 'It all depends on what you are used to,' says his nephew. 'If you're accustomed to the sound of buses then the sound of starlings must come as something of a shock.'

Ronald Barton went out to Bordeaux in 1927 following the death of his father in a hunting accident, initially in order to run the broking house of Barton et Guestier, since at that time the vineyard properties were not profitable. He must have discovered a great affinity with the land and the vines, for the next decade, the 1930s, following the great depression and further depressed by a string of rotten vintages, was one of the most disastrous in two hundred years. Yet Ronald Barton stuck at it, spending as much time as he could spare at Langoa.

When the Second World War broke out he stayed in Bordeaux, running Barton et Guestier practically single-handed, leaving the office at lunch-time on Saturday and driving to Langoa to spend the weekend overseeing the vineyards. With a greatly reduced staff, and the horses then used for ploughing requisitioned, he managed to keep the properties running reasonably smoothly for the war's first winter and spring. He made a point of drinking a good bottle of Léoville or Langoa every evening—'one less for the Germans if they won, one less for my heirs if we did.' Langoa had by that time become home also for twenty refugees from eastern France.

It was in May 1940 that Pétain signed the armistice with the Germans which put all citizens from the British Isles in immediate danger. Ronald had to leave abruptly, with a maximum of one suitcase and three days' rations. When he arrived in England a cousin greeted him and said, 'This is marvellous! You are repeating the story of your ancestor Hugh who had to leave Bordeaux in 1793, made a fortune and bought Langoa and Léoville thirty years later.'

Whether Ronald felt quite so thrilled at history's way of repeating itself is doubtful. He wrote a moving account of his sombre farewell to Langoa in the afternoon before his ship left, 'wondering whether I would ever see it again, and if so in what condition'.

After a few months looking for work Ronald got himself commissioned in the Royal Inniskilling Fusiliers in September, but very shortly after he was offered a job with the Spears mission in the Middle East. He spent some time in Beirut (where he was distressed to find a fraudulent bottle of white 'Léoville-Barton', and even found time to prosecute the fraudster), then was transferred to the 1st Free French Division, with which he spent the rest of the war, in the Desert and in Italy.

In 1944, when the Division was involved in the recapture of Marseilles, Ronald was able to return briefly to Langoa, where he held an emotive reunion party for all the estate employees, before returning to Italy. It was not until late 1945 that he returned home for good.

The 1945 vintage was small in quantity and magnificent in quality, but deceptive as an augury of the years ahead. Ronald Barton was faced with a gruelling private battle in the vineyard which had been left virtually untended for five years. The temptation was for vineyard owners to uproot and replant wholesale, but Barton knew that the loss of all the old vines would mean a disastrous drop in quality. So he set about preserving as many as possible of the old vines and replanting on the system of complantation—replacing only dead or dying vines.

The effort may have been, as Ronald Barton himself put it, 'uneconomic', but his properties produced some magnificent vintages in the late 1940s and early 1950s, while many competitors languished. I was lucky enough to drink the 1952, not an especially renowned year, while visiting Langoa: it was beautifully balanced and complete, the finest of all the wines from the Barton estates which I sampled. It was very nearly not made at all. After the appalling 1951 harvest, Anthony Barton told me, if the next vintage had been bad, his uncle would have sold up. No fortunes were being made in the Médoc in those days: Ronald Barton sold the very fine 1953 vintage for the same price as the 1945, while in the meantime costs of labour and materials had risen dramatically. Things seemed to have stabilised somewhat by 1955, then the exceptionally hard frosts of February 1956 wiped out a quarter of the vineyard.

Ronald Barton was, however, a completely dedicated wine man. He was perhaps so wedded to his vines that other kinds of marriage were precluded, at least until late in his life: he became engaged more than once in middle age, but married only in his seventies. His thoughts regarding the continuation of the dynasty turned to his younger nephew. Anthony Barton went out to Langoa for the vintage in 1948 while still at Cambridge. He did not know his uncle particularly well, but an offer to join the family firm out in Bordeaux the following year was not unattractive.

'The thing was that I'd gone down from Cambridge without a degree. I didn't really see the point of education at that time. I was encouraged to read Modern Languages because I knew some French—though I couldn't speak it at all then, it was all literature, and I had no interest in the set texts. I might rather enjoy the letters of Madame de Sévigné now, but in those days I was completely bored. One day I received a letter from the university authorities which said: "In view of the lack of interest in your academic studies shown by your performance in the recent examinations we do not feel it appropriate to hold your place open for a further year." I must say that the only thing I regretted at the time was the loss of a possible rowing blue.'

Anthony Barton did the milk round without any great enthusiasm and went to Bordeaux rather, as he admits, *faute de mieux*. 'My father wasn't at all enthusiastic about my going into the wine business. But I was the younger son; my brother was expecting to inherit the Irish property. He would have done if my father had not sold it.'

Barton et Guestier in 1950 was, Anthony Barton says, 'ticking over'. He found Bordeaux society difficult to penetrate at first, but things gradually became easier. He met his wife in 1954 when she was over from Denmark on a language course. In the same year Seagrams took a 50 per cent share in Barton et Guestier; although Anthony continued to work as export director through the 1970s, he knew the firm would not continue under family control.

The 1960s and 1970s were probably rather difficult working decades for Anthony Barton. Ronald had promised to hand over the running of Barton et Guestier and the estates to his nephew in 1962, but in 1960 Danny Guestier was killed in a car accident. Ronald had second thoughts about retiring; and as it turned out he never retired at all. It was not until 1982 that Anthony was able to take control.

A number of changes needed to be made, for some of the attitudes which had kept the property going in hard times were less suited to a period of expansion. There is no doubt that people had got the idea that Léoville-Barton was a place with a wonderful old English atmosphere, but which had been left behind the times.

'My uncle, quite understandably, was not keen on borrowing too much money. He replanted and bought new barrels when he had the cash available, rather than making an investment and doing it systematically.'

There were also some slightly old-fashioned aspects to the wine-making. 'He was against chaptalisation [the perfectly legal addition of sugar to the fermenting grape must, which does not sweeten the wine but increases its alcoholic strength]. Now chaptalisation can be overdone, but I think that below 12.5 degrees the wine tends to lack body. The cooling system for fermentation was archaic. My uncle also had a *laissez-faire* attitude to malo-lactic fermentation—you left it to nature. We now use sulphur to stop premature malo-lactic fermentation, which can cause excessive volatile acidity.'

Beneath the charming Irish exterior, Anthony Barton is as shrewd and committed a wine-maker as you will find in the Médoc. He is typically deprecatory about the influence a man can have on his wine. 'Wine-making is just a whole lot of small details. The soil fixes the potential: it is just up to the wine-maker to realise that potential.'

One important decision has been to change the *régisseur*, the man in charge of the technical side of wine-making. 'My old régisseur was becoming too set in his ways. We had a machine for cleaning the barrels, but he wouldn't use it. He was also a bit lazy about *remontage*— the system of pumping the fermenting must over the cap of skins and stalks which forms at the top of the vat.' Other decisions have to be taken by Anthony Barton himself. 'The most important is selection. We had to sacrifice about 30 per cent of our crop last year, in order to achieve better quality.'

There is also the question of oak. All good Bordeaux wine is matured, usually for about twenty months, in barriques bordelaises. These, as wine-makers all over the world, from Piedmont to New Zealand, well know, are expensive things (£250 each at 1989 prices). Anthony Barton puts half his crop in brand-new barrels every year, and this is a decision made not entirely on economic grounds. 'I don't like wines on which the wood stands out.' The consensus of critical opinion is that all this attention to detail is paying off.

The 1985 Langoa-Barton (which I tasted next day with the doyen of British claret experts, Edmund Penning-Rowsell) had a splendid deep colour; on the nose there was a combination of ripe, sweet fruit and the drier, cedary tone which is said to be the hallmark of St Julien wines. The first taste in the mouth was also sweet; the wine was already attractive, though tannin at the finish indicated that its development was far from complete. In Britain it is considered almost indecent to drink classed-growth claret at less than ten years old: the French are known to commit unmentionable acts of infanticide. The 1985 Léoville-Barton, as is usual, was far less developed than its precocious sibling; its deep, powerful meaty character requires several more years to show at its best. Incidentally, the differences between the wines of the two châteaux must be a question of minute variations in the soil composition of the various parcels of land. The figures for the grape varieties planted at the two properties are identical: 70 per cent Cabernet Sauvignon; 20 per cent Merlot; 8 per cent Cabernet Franc; 2 per cent Petit Verdot.

There was a heavy rainstorm centred just to the south of Bordeaux on 23 September 1986. It meant that the quality of the 1986 vintage was more variable than had been hoped during the exceptionally dry summer. It is generally agreed that the central Médoc communes of Pauillac and St Julien produced the best wines of the year. Having tasted them alongside a comprehensive range of other classed growths, I regard the two Barton wines as among the very finest of the vintage. Much more closed and backward both on the nose and on the palate than the 1985s, the 1986 Langoa- and Léoville-Barton nevertheless showed a concentrated ripeness of fruit, masked by tannin, but promising exceptional riches for the future.

These two very successful vintages, following on from the much-lauded 1982 (one of those vintages of the century which has passed into a rather awkward adolescence) and the fine 1983, have undoubtedly made a good deal of money for Anthony Barton. Since the late 1960s, the Bordelais have developed a system called *en primeur* selling. The wine is sold to the customer in the summer following the vintage while it is still in cask and will not be bottled for at least a year. In effect, the customer rather than the producer or the merchant is financing the maturation of the wine. This is perhaps inevitable in a time of high interest rates, at least in Britain: it is practically impossible for British wine merchants these days to mature wines for many years with the cost of money as high as 15 per cent or even 20 per cent. En primeur purchasing has proved beneficial to the investment purchaser too, when he has seen a good appreciation on his initial investment, as was the case with vintages such as 1966 and 1970. More recently, the benefits of the system have come to seem much more questionable. At the time of writing a person who had purchased 1983 clarets en primeur in 1984 stood to make a net loss by selling them at auction four years later.

Anthony Barton has considerable doubts about these developments. 'I think buying wine purely for investment is very dangerous,' he says. 'Clearly, for the wine to appreciate as an investment, somebody, somewhere, must be pulling the corks. As far as en primeur is concerned, my philosophy is that the customer should buy early to save money, not to make money.'

1987, Barton foresaw, was not going to be an en primeur vintage. Having bought copiously in the 1982, 1983, 1985 and 1986 vintages, customers would simply not have room in their cellars (if they had cellars) for 1987. 'I expect to make a loss on this vintage. In fact the next few years could be lean ones.' Perhaps he was being unnecessarily Cassandra-ish. With 1988 and again with 1989 Bordeaux seems to have resumed its charmed run of good vintages, eagerly sought by the market—however difficult it is for some observers, including the writer, to understand how a market can continue to absorb so much young wine when there is so much older wine still to be drunk. Confidence in Bordeaux remains immensely strong. When I asked Anthony Barton, by no means an arrogant man, if he was worried by competition for his wines coming from, for instance, Australian and Californian Cabernet Sauvignon, he replied, 'No, not at all. We have a product that is absolutely unique. There will always be a demand for it.'

One thing for which his customers at least can thank Anthony Barton is that he has not pushed his prices as high as some of his competitors. Châteaux such as Pichon-Lalande, a couple of kilometres up the road in Pauillac, and Barton's St Julien neighbours Léoville-Las-Cases and Ducru-Beaucaillou, decided to lever themselves up a notch nearer the 1855 first growths (Lafite, Latour, Margaux, Haut-Brion and the more recent recruit Mouton-Rothschild). They doubled their prices and set themselves up as a separate group, between the first growths and the rest of the seconds—a position already occupied by Château Palmer. A new name was coined for them—'super-seconds'. What they were really doing was turning their wine from a drink, albeit an expensive one, into an investment commodity. The process had begun a decade earlier with the first growths. Nicholas Faith recalls in *The Winemasters* the moment when Baron Elie de Rothschild saw a photograph of a bottle of Château Lafite sitting in a bank-vault: ' "I assembled my staff," he wrote later, "and told them, the crisis has begun." Indeed from the moment when you start to think of wine as an investment and not as something to be drunk, that's the end.' Unfortunately this did not prevent him from selling Lafite at prices no ordinary drinker could swallow.

Anthony Barton has not followed the path of the super-seconds. The price of Léoville-Barton in 1985 and 1986 was roughly half that of Léoville-Las-Cases, once part of the same estate. In quality, the Barton wine, in those two years, has conceded little or nothing to its larger neighbour. 'It's interesting', Barton comments, 'that in the Wine Society's en primeur offer, Léoville-Barton outsold Léoville-Las-Cases by ten to one.'

Even at half the price of Las-Cases, sales of the two Barton châteaux over the past few years have not been unprofitable. Apart from the chai and the new dining-room, a good deal of money has gone into restoration of the beautiful eighteenth-century château, left in a dilapidated condition at the time of Ronald Barton's death. The rooms of the central block are on a grand scale: now meticulously redecorated to the original colour scheme, with a vast new Aubusson carpet and tapestry, they still have a somewhat forlorn, uninhabited look. Anthony and Eva Barton live in a flat in one of the wings; they do occasionally use the big reception rooms for entertaining. A new orangerie is being contructed in the lovely park-like garden, with a parterre leading down to a swan-haunted lake, surrounded by fine mature deciduous trees, some I would imagine as old as the château.

Anthony Barton can be proud of what he has achieved in the few years since he has taken charge of the property: the fabric of the house, the wine-making equipment, the vineyards are all in prime condition, thanks to a prosperity not known to his uncle in all the fifty-five years he spent in Bordeaux. 'Now I have completed the first phase of the task—improved the quality of the wine. The next job is to get it better known, especially in France.' Anthony Barton's time is increasingly taken up with the myriad forms of that key preoccupation of the late twentieth century: public relations. The second day I spent at Château Langoa, a French television crew came and flooded the chai with a sulphurous glare inimical to its usual cool, semi-subterranean darkness. Anthony Barton is hospitable to journalists.

A glossy brochure showing the Barton family (including Brenda) at home on their beautiful estate has also been printed. Of Anthony and Eva Barton's two children, only one, their daughter Lillian, has decided to work for the family estate. Lillian's job is administration and public relations. She is married to a Frenchman from the Pas-de-Calais whose business, less romantic than château-owning but possibly more profitable, is selling sports shoes to supermarkets. They live in a house on the estate. Anthony's son Thomas is working as a journalist in Dublin—as far as wine is concerned, one of the alternate missing generations.

If Lillian takes over the running of the property in due course, as seems likely, she will be the first female Barton to have taken a serious interest in wine, but by no means the first female châtelaine in Bordeaux. Corinne Mentzelopoulos of Château Margaux and Mme de Lencquesaing of Pichon-Lalande are arguably the two most prominent proprietors in the entire region.

So the exceptional, somewhat improbable persistence of this Anglo-Irish dynasty in the Médoc, which has often appeared more interested in its other existence as an Irish landowning family, but which has maintained a deep attachment to its French home, now stronger than ever, looks set to continue for the next generation at least.

As for the current prosperity of the château-owners of the Médoc, to some observers it has an almost fairy-tale quality of unreality. Peter Allan Sichel, co-proprietor of Château Palmer and a leading négociant, appended to his authoritative annual vintage report in 1987 a cautionary tale. A trio of princes and princesses, easily recognisable as Michel Delon of Léoville-Las-Cases, Jean-Eugene Borie of Ducru-Beaucaillou and Mme de Lencquesaing of Pichon-Lalande, determined to attain regal status, pushed the prices of their wines too high. The market fell with a terrific crash. Wine, for a time, was sold for a song. Eventually sanity was restored: the prices of the wines returned to a level at which people could afford to drink them. Everyone lived happily ever after.

I pondered this tale as I returned to my quarters in a dreary town up the road. The hotel where I was staying was pompously named Hôtel France et Angleterre. It was not doing a very good job for relations between the two nations. It advertised a 'grillade au feu de bois'. All the smoke from the wood fire, and the grease from the grill, seemed to have been diverted away from the chimney and up the stairwell. From there, I soon discovered, it had seeped into the bedrooms.

I retreated back downstairs. The ancient patron and a couple of waitresses in black uniforms stood guard over an empty dining-room, looking like extras in a horror film. I fled. Outside there was a long broad street with a double avenue of plane trees leading nowhere, illuminated, for no apparent purpose, by a row of pompous globular lamps. On the far side of the street, a forlorn-looking pier led a little way into the broad brown river. Along this riverfront row was a line of the least inspiring eating-houses I have ever seen in France. I selected one at random and consumed a greasy omelette and a tired, yellowing salad. On the wine list were a few bottles of cru bourgeois claret at extortionate prices, very probably too old anyway. Almost certainly too old, in fact, because the bottles, coated in grease and grime, stood in a rack above the kitchen hatch. None of the few people eating in the restaurant was drinking bottled wine. The name of the town was Pauillac.

ESTATE BOTTLED   MISE AU, CHATEAU

CHATEAUNEUF-DU-PAPE
Tête de Cru
1986

PRODUCE OF FRANCE
CHATEAU-FORTIA
PROPRIÉTÉ DU BARON LE ROY DE BOISEAUMARIÉ

Alc 13.5% Vol   S. A. R. L.   75 cl ℮
CHATEAU FORTIA · 84 CHATEAUNEUF-DU-PAPE

Le Roy

of

Château Fortia

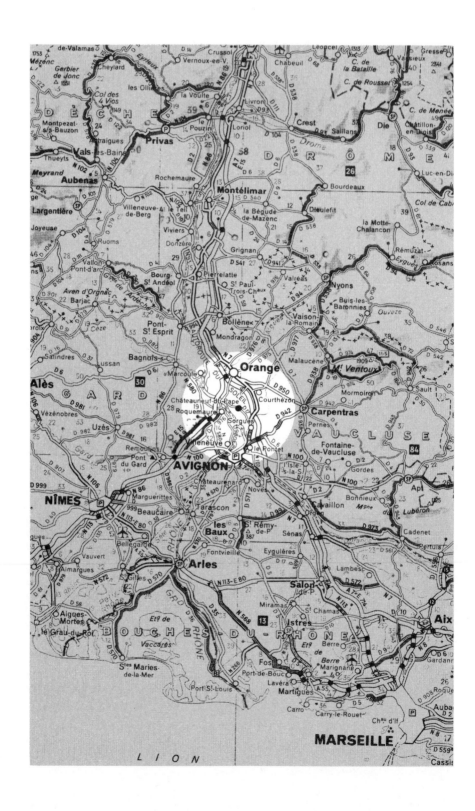

NORTH AND SOUTH ARE RELATIVE TERMS. In Spain, for instance, cities such as Barcelona or Pamplona are considered to belong to the far north, dour and cold, whereas from Britain they appear torrid and sunlit, symbols of southern zest. Paris, to the English, suggests boulevards and cafés on the pavements; the buildings do have shutters and balconies, allusions to the often absent sun, but to France south of the Loire Paris seems dank and chilly, distinctly lacking in *joie de vivre*.

There is one place in France, though, where the border between north and south is absolutely fixed and definite. It comes as you drive down the A6, the Autoroute du Soleil (a euphemism for most of its length), where it follows the narrow valley of the Rhône, south of Lyon, carved between the Massif Central and the Alps. Just south of the fruit-market town of Valence, one of the many helpful, not to say pedagogic, signs put up by the sides of French motorways tells you that you are crossing the 45th parallel of latitude—in other words that you are entering what the French call the Midi, the land of the midday sun. Actually, the south does not begin for another 30–40 kilometres. Valence is no man's land, neither one thing nor the other. But just south of Montélimar, capital of nougat if nothing else, the Rhône narrows into a dramatic gorge, the Défile de Donzère, with a sheer cliff on one side and needle-like rock spikes on the other. The natural beauty of Donzère may now have been upstaged by the combination of hydroelectric works, nuclear power stations and uranium factory which now squat below it, but it still marks the beginning of Provence. It also marks, in wine terms, the divide between northern and southern Rhône, a divide which may sound technical, but is as dramatic in its own way as the scenic one. The northern Rhône wines, such as Hermitage, Côte-Rôtie and Cornas, may be deep and powerful, but they are tannic wines which repay, and indeed require, keeping for several years. The sun of the southern Rhône loosens the structure, and makes its presence almost tangible in wines which actually taste warm. The greatest of these southern Rhône wines, the only one which is capable of ageing for twenty years or more, yet possesses that southern warmth in the highest degree, is Châteauneuf-du-Pape.

The vegetation changes; evergreen oak and the aromatic scrub known here as *garrigues* cover the hills, whose shapes seem suddenly sharper and more clearly defined. The light has changed: a Mediterranean clarity and intensity has taken over from the softer, more blended tones of central France. Around Orange you will see the first cypresses, planted in east/west lines to break the force of the Mistral which blows strongly one day in three, and the silver-grey of the olives. Orange deserves a stop: a modest town for the capital of a Principality (whose Dutch ruler became King William III of England), it possesses at least one extraordinary monument. The Roman theatre is, perhaps, misnamed: there is an auditorium, cut into the hillside, with impressive acoustics and mysterious passages behind, but the seats are all modern, which detracts from the aura of antiquity. What really does convey the power of Roman civilisation is the theatre's immense back wall, built of beautiful golden stone, the texture of Roka cheese biscuits or chocolate-coated Crunchy. For those who share Michelin's insatiable appetite for statistics, it is 338 ft long and 118 ft high. Louis XIV, having captured Orange from the Dutch in 1672, called it 'the finest wall in my kingdom'.

Beyond this wall, if you follow the road round, you will see a sign off to the right saying CHÂTEAUNEUF-DU-PAPE. It takes no time to get out of Orange; you find yourself in wide open country, the same golden colour as the stone of Orange, all planted with low, gnarled vines, not trained on wires but pruned into the shape of an ancient hand, with five arthritically bent fingers.

The road climbs on to a low plateau: huge views stretch out in three directions: south, over a flat land of silvery poplars, olives and cypresses to the low, jagged lines of blue hills called, with a certain irony, the Alpilles; west, to range after range of long, low ridges, the beginnings of the Cévennes; and east, most dramatically, to the great cone of Mont Ventoux, Provence's Fujiyama, snow-capped or at least dusted from December to April, with the broken teeth of the Dentelles de Montmirail at its feet. Further in the distance are the outposts of the Alps. After a few miles another broken tooth appears just over the near horizon. It is a man-made one this time, and built of golden stone—the solitary tower of the ruined summer palace of the Avignon popes.

As you get closer you discover that it is no puny watchtower but the ruins of an immense fortress. An L-shaped wall, with two storeys of soaring Gothic vaults abruptly truncated, are all that remains from its sacking during the wars of religion in 1562, and a not very successful attempt to polish it off completely by the retreating Germans in 1944. But the little village of Châteauneuf-du-Pape, which clusters round its skirts, turns out to be constructed mainly from the remains of its three circuits of fortifications. The village would suggest decline from greatness into obscurity, if it were not for the immaculate state of all the houses, with shutters painted in artful shades of deep red or, more usually, green, and the extraordinary number of restaurants. Châteauneuf-du-Pape is clearly a very prosperous little community, though with what seems a high proportion of elderly people, and not many between twenty and thirty. North African Arabs, some of them wearing bright-coloured robes, mingle with tough, weathered Frenchmen in caps.

It owes its prosperity quite largely to the efforts of one man, Baron Pierre Le Roy de Boiseaumarié of Château Fortia. When Baron Le Roy returned to his mother's estate after the First World War, the situation of the vignerons of Châteauneuf-du-Pape was, in his own word, 'la misère'. They had been reduced to penury by the rampant wine fraud which allowed grapes from almost anywhere to be passed off as the produce of Châteauneuf. This was in addition to the centuries-old fraud by which genuine Châteauneuf was shipped to Burgundy and added to famous names such as Corton and Pommard to make what some people call 'old-fashioned burgundy'.

Le Roy was approached by a delegation of local growers, petitioning him, as the best-educated man in the village, to do something about it. The rest is commonly quoted history: Le Roy formed an association with the local growers in order to establish a set of regulations to protect the authenticity and quality, in other words the good name, of Châteauneuf-du-Pape. After a long process, these regulations passed into law and became the basis for the whole, far-reaching system of Appellation d'Origine Contrôlée throughout France. Its influence quickly spread beyond France to the other wine-producing countries of Europe.

That much is generally known about Baron Pierre Le Roy, who was granted in his lifetime the title of 'premier vigneron du monde'. To find out more, I was to visit his son, Baron Henri Le Roy, the morning after my arrival, following a leisurely Sunday journey down the Rhône from Lyon.

The sign at the bottom of the drive, just outside the village, was not only rust-eaten but looked as if it had been used for shooting practice. The words Château Fortia were practically illegible. A few hundred metres up a rough track, with vines on either side, and I found myself at the working entrance of the château. Château in France can mean many things, often no more than an outbuilding. Here it denoted a solid turn-of-the-century villa adorned with two turrets, one low and round, the other octagonal and topped with a tall conical hat, the whole creeper-covered and set among beautiful mature pines. A name-plate by the bell in the smaller, round turret said simply HENRI LE ROY. I rang it and the Baron emerged, by no means the snobbish example of French aristocracy I had envisaged, but a small, spry, nervous man in his late sixties.

It transpired that I had not arrived at the most convenient time, nor, perhaps, on the most convenient business. 'I am sorry, things are not easy here at the moment. My mother, who is ninety-two, had a fall last week and broke her leg. She is in the hospital in Orange. She wants one of us to be with her all the time.' Sitting in the Baron's rather Spartan office in the corner tower, whose most obvious adornment was an exercise bicycle, while he hovered restlessly around, I attempted to express sympathy.

'As for my father, I really cannot tell you much about his career, for the simple reason that while he was travelling all round the world I was here looking after the estate. *Je faisais bouillir la marmite*, I don't know how that translates into English.' A literal English tanslation is, 'I kept the pot boiling.'

'My training was military—I was an officer between 1941 and 1946. When I came back here in 1948, the grass was higher than the vines. There had been only one woman and a horse to look after the vineyards during the war: my father, who had been a fighter pilot in the First World War, was remobilised. The first things we needed were scythes and pitchforks. Then we bought horses and began ploughing. To give you an idea what it was like, in 1948, the first year I was in charge here, we made 1200 litres of wine, from thirty hectares. In 1949 we made 4500 and in 1950 9000. Now we make 70,000 or 80,000 litres.

'It was a mission impossible, a labour of Hercules. We had to borrow a great deal from the banks, and it took twenty years to repay them. I could not afford to build a new *cuverie*, we had to make do with the old buildings. They are not very satisfactory, but what can we do? Now we have no reserves of money, though we do have good stocks of wine in the cellar. The inheritance taxes are so high in this country, that if anything were to happen, I do not know what we would do.'

The Baron looked despondent and worried, but not ready to give up. But he had not finished letting off steam.

'If I had known anything about agriculture when I arrived here, I would have sold up immediately. I had to learn. I read a good deal, and whenever I had a problem I went to the professors at the Institut Agronomique and they gave me the answer.

'I devised one or two things myself.' Here for the first time a wintry gleam of enthusiam came into the Baron's pale blue eyes. 'I invented this system of drying the grapes. We put them on long trays, six metres by one metre, made of wire mesh with perforated plastic on top. Then we leave them to dry in the loft. With the Mistral and good sunny weather we gain one degree of alcohol and lose ten per cent of liquid by evaporation in forty-eight hours. I once tried drying grapes for five days and gained nearly two degrees. With our drying system the grapes gain concentration—you get that sensation of eating the wine.

'You wanted to know about the history of the family and Fortia? Fortia is one of three oldest estates in Châteauneuf, with our neighbours Fines Roches and Château la Nerthe. It is named after the Marquis Fortia d'Urban, who was a notable character in the French Enlightenment, a philosopher and mathematician. He was also a grandee of Spain and descendant of the kings of Aragon. They made wine in those days, not very much, a few thousand litres: we still have the cellar books. This part of the building, the round tower and the tasting cellar, are what remains of the old structure. The Marquis had a vegetable garden, but that is now a vineyard.

'It was bought by my maternal grandfather, Hippolyte Bernard-le-Saint, in 1887, and he built a new house on the ruins of the old one. Unfortunately he employed a local architect from Avignon. My maternal grandfather was quite a character too. He was a naval officer and a trained engineer, and spoke fluent Arabic. When de Lesseps, the man who dug the Suez Canal, was looking for an assistant, he wanted someone who was not only an engineer but could also speak Arabic, so my grandfather got the job. He also became director of the King of Egypt's newspaper.

'I suppose my grandfather was looking for an estate to retire to, but he must have been interested in wine, because this had been one of the most famous estates in the area for a long time. My grandfather started winning medals for his wine in international competitions.' The Baron plucked two sets of framed medals from the wall. 'Here is one from 1905. These other medals have nothing to do with wine—they are for life-saving. My grandfather was a very fine swimmer, and saved many lives. And here are some military medals, from the war of 1871. He fought too: we have all been soldiers. I have some medals myself.

'The Le Roy family, my father's, came from Normandy. Boiseaumarié is a contraction of *le bois aux mariés*, a large wood near la Perthe, which used to belong to the family. It's an old crusader family; a great-, many greats-, uncle was abbot of Mont-Saint-Michel in the fourteenth century. I can find the family tree, if you want more details. Frankly, these things do not interest me, but my son knows all about it.' The Baron suddenly lost composure, as a frantic search for the family tree began. Every drawer of an old grey filing-cabinet was opened, to no avail. Then a large cupboard, which revealed at the bottom a collection of large-sized model cars. 'So many papers,' the Baron kept exclaiming, before he finally unearthed the tree, an impressively thick wodge of yellowed paper, inscribed in a careful genealogical hand.

'The Le Roys were all either soldiers or politicians. My father's father was a colonel, but resigned at the separation of church and state. My father would have followed a military career, but his father did not allow him to, because he did not approve of the new army. He studied to be a lawyer, then did his military service from 1911 to 1913, then the war came. He started the war as a plain soldier, then he switched to the air force. You will find out about all that from the people I put you in touch with. After the war he took the examinations for the Banque de France, but he did not like counting, and his mother-in-law asked him to come back here and look after the estate. You will learn all that story, how the vignerons came and asked him to help them, how he founded the syndicat, and drew up the regulations for the appellation. M. Pierre-feu, who worked with him at the Office International du Vin, and M. Joly, who has written articles about him, they both know far more than I do.

'Do you know Châteauneuf-du-Pape?'

I explained that it was my first visit.

'I suggest we visit the castle and the vineyards, to give you an idea of this region.'

The Baron led the way, stepping nimbly down the spiral staircase of the tower, out into the yard, looking over a rather melancholy formal pond, and into his car, small yet surprisingly quick, like its owner.

First stop was the castle, which I had seen but not visited the night before. We entered through a gate in a long, crumbling stone wall, which encloses the ancient papal vineyard. 'There was a castle here before the popes arrived in Avignon in 1309, which is why, when Pope John XXII had this castle built, between 1318 and 1333, it was called the "new castle". It is fifteen years older than the Palais des Papes in Avignon, which you can see quite clearly sixteen kilometres down the river.' The new castle of the popes certainly commands a magnificent view, south down the Rhône to Avignon and beyond to the Alpilles, and east to Mont Ventoux. Standing on its hill above the valley, it was also presumably cooler in summer than the vast white fortress in the heart of Avignon. There was also the attraction of its vineyard. The first mention of the wine of Châteauneuf comes in a document of 1157, in which the Emperor Frederick Barbarossa ceded the lands and vines to Gaufredus, Bishop of Avignon. But it was the coming of the papacy to

Avignon at the beginning of the fourteenth century, escaping the incessant wars of central Italy, which gave the wine a temporary glory, lasting less than a century, but leaving an indelible aura behind it.

The first Avignon pope was Clément V. He was a native of Bordeaux—where he founded what is now Château Pape-Clément in the Graves—but seems to have found no difficulty transferring his allegiance to a warmer, more southern wine. The Provençal poet Felix Gras wrote a charming testimonial both to his enthusiasm for wine and his humility:

> Pope Clément V, seated on his mule,
> Goes off to see his vines, up there at Châteauneuf;
> He carries in his bag, along with a good flask,
> A piece of ham, some bread and eggs!

Clément's pontificate was short, and it was under his successor John XXII that Châteauneuf became famous, both as the seat of the papal summer residence and as one of the chief suppliers of wine to the papal court. By 1345, a document in the Apostolic Chamber records the number of vines at Châteauneuf as no less than 3,300,000. Despite the higher density of planting then employed, that still represents a vineyard area of more than 600 hectares. What the wine of those distant times tasted like is impossible to determine, but it is pleasant to imagine it had at least some of the richness, warmth and high alcoholic degree which mark it out today. It was not made from the grape varieties which now dominate the vineyards, Grenache and Syrah, for these were hardly planted before Phylloxera. One of the thirteen grape varieties allowed at Châteauneuf, though, does have an authenticated history going back to the papacy. The Counoise, now planted in small quantities, but highly regarded by several leading growers, is named after the Spanish Vice-Legate Conejo, who presented some cuttings to Pope Urban V in 1362. The vine might equally well have been named Lapin, since Conejo is Spanish for rabbit.

The Baron led me down from the grassy hillock with the remains of the great keep to a doorway carved into the rock. 'Ah, the key,' remembered the Baron, and rushed round to the keep's main entrance. He returned in a fury: 'They will not let me have the key. The Président of the Châteauneuf syndicat has the key, but I am not allowed it.' The door, it turned out, however, was open. Inside was a vast stone hall, with narrow windows set high in the walls. 'This was the popes' cellar; they stacked the barrels along the side walls, with one row down the middle. There is a fair amount of space in here. Now it is used for official dinners for up to three hundred people, and receptions by the local wine committees. When the Germans blew up the castle they destroyed the ceiling, but the rest survived. Now let us go and look at the vineyards.'

We drove back out of the walled enclosure, still called the Clos des Papes, and along the road to Orange. A few kilometres on, we turned left where two hoardings advertised the Domaine des Cabrières and Château Mont-Redon. 'This is the Châteauneuf plateau, and the best terrain for vines. I wish my land were as good as this.'

Though flat, it is some of the most extraordinary vineyard land in the world. Between the widely spaced, black, gnarled, untrained vines you see no soil at all: just a mass of large, rounded, smooth, golden-pink stones like the petrified eggs of some vast prehistoric bird. These stones cover about three-quarters of the vineyard of Châteauneuf, but vary in size and in places give way to sandy soil. Here on the plateau they are at their largest and most impressive, stretching unbroken for kilometres. The advantage of the stones for viticulture is that they store heat and reflect it up at the bunches of grapes until long after dark. Their disadvantage is obvious: they are death to ploughshares.

'I will tell you the story of these stones,' said the Baron, full of enthusiasm, once more, for one of his pet subjects. 'When the glaciers melted at the end of the last ice age, these rocks were washed down from the Alps. They were milled into these rounded shapes by the torrents. After that deluge the sea stretched up as far as Lyon, and these stones were on the sea-bed. Then the level of the earth rose: the smaller stones were washed down, but the largest, heaviest ones remained on the higher and flatter ground. That is why the biggest and largest number of stones are here on the plateau, and there are fewer on the slopes.'

The Baron smiled at the conciseness with which his theory was demonstrated. Then his face clouded over once more. 'Now I am afraid you must excuse me; I have to be at the hospital to see my mother. You will be able to find out what you need to know about my father from M. Pierrefeu and M. Joly.' I was not sure if this was meant to be a definitive good-bye, before I had been able to inspect the workings of the Château Fortia estate or to taste its wine, but there was no detaining the Baron.

Next day I visited the two gentlemen in Avignon, to learn about the career of the legendary Baron Pierre Le Roy. 'It is very difficult to convey what a fabulous personality he was—the kind of person you encounter only once or twice in a lifetime,' said M. Pierrefeu, a solid red-faced man in his sixties and Président of the Comité Interprofessionel des Côtes du Rhône. 'He had enormous qualities, and defects too, on a grand scale—the defects of those qualities.' M. Pierrefeu seemed to be implying that the Baron was excessively authoritarian, but it was difficult to force him to be more specific.

One quality undoubtedly possessed by Pierre Le Roy was courage. As a fighter pilot he was part of the company of Guynemer, Nungessen and Pinsard, men of legendary dash. By the time he moved from the artillery to the air force, I learnt from M. Joly, an Avignon journalist engaged in researching a book on the Baron's life, that he had already been decorated with the Médaille Militaire, one of France's highest military honours, awarded only to simple soldiers and Field Marshals. As a pilot he chalked up seven official 'victories', but is generally credited with several more unofficial ones. His own Waterloo very nearly came on 14 September 1918 over Pagny-sur-Moselle, when he went in his single-engined plane to the aid of a comrade under attack from five German Fokkers. His comrade was able to fly back to safety, but Le Roy was not so lucky. His plane was shot down: Le Roy later recorded what went through his mind in what he expected to be his last seconds: 'I said to myself, "This time I have had it." I wanted to die, but I wished my face to be preserved, so just before I hit the ground I covered it in my arms.' He survived the complete wreck of his aeroplane with several broken limbs and recovered in a German military hospital.

It was in 1923 that Pierre Le Roy returned to Château Fortia, with a legal training, a brief experience as a banker, several medals, and, already, strong views about wine. When the famous delegation of local growers approached him to intercede on their behalf to put an end to the wine fraud which was ruining the community, Le Roy agreed on one condition. This was that the growers themselves would set the example of selling only wines which were honest and true to the best traditions of Châteauneuf-du-Pape. It was not the first time Le Roy had taken part in political action to defend the interests of wine-growers. As a student of seventeen, during the demonstrations by wine-growers in Languedoc in 1907, in protest against the bolstering of the alcoholic content of northern French wines by the addition of sugar during fermentation (chaptalisation), he had put the match to petrol poured at the gates of the Palais de Justice in Montpellier.

In October 1923 the Syndicat de Vignerons de Châteauneuf-du-Pape was formed; Le Roy and his colleagues set about defining exactly what should be implied by the appearance of the words Châteauneuf-du-Pape on a wine label.

It was not as simple as it might sound. Existing legislation, enacted in 1905 and 1919, was unsatisfactory, because despite good intentions it merely attempted to limit the areas where wine with a certain appellation should be made. Initially, the job of delimiting the areas was conducted from Paris. The Champagne riots of 1911, in which the growers went on the rampage in the small town of Aÿ and destroyed thousands of bottles belonging to the merchant houses, convinced the government that this was politically, and practically, impossible, and the responsibility was transferred to local courts. Interrupted by the war, they were very slow to act. In any case, delimiting of areas was only half the solution. As M. Capus, originator of the 1905 law, had realised, it was perfectly possible for growers within the properly defined boundaries of a region to use high-yielding vines to produce inferior wine, not worthy of its name.

The Syndicat des Propriétaires-Viticulteurs de Châteauneuf-du-Pape drew up a much more rigorous set of regulations. Its three most important principles were the following:

1 Delimitation of the area of production, based on the nature of the soil and traditional practice. Only land capable of bearing lavender and thyme, aromatics which can grow only in poor soil, was to be planted with vines.
2 Use only of the thirteen traditional noble grape varieties: Grenache, Syrah, Mourvèdre, Cinsault, Counoise, Vaccarèse, Terret Noir, Muscardin, Clairette, Bourbolenc, Roussanne, Picpoul and Picardan.
3 Strict control of method of cultivation (training on wire forbidden except in case of Syrah, irrigation forbidden except in certain specific cases).

In addition to these, the Syndicat stipulated that the minimum natural alcoholic degree should be 12.5 degrees (the highest in France), that an obligatory sorting of the grapes should take place at harvest, with 5 per cent being rejected, and that rosé wines should not be allowed the appellation.

The Châteauneuf regulations were, it is generally agreed, in advance of anything that had existed before. It was, as Pierre Le Roy himself said, with justifiable pride, 'a revolutionary initiative, adopted later by many others'. A prolonged legal battle lasting nine years, involving fifteen *avocats*, was necessary to get the proposals accepted by all the producers of Châteauneuf. At one stage, the wine produced by members of the Syndicat was boycotted by local merchants.

However, Châteauneuf had started a movement which quickly gathered momentum. It spread to the other Rhône appellations of Tavel, St Péray, Côtes du Rhône, and Hermitage, whose statutes of delimitation, supervised by Le Roy, were completed in 1927, 1929, 1930 and

1932, respectively. At the same time, the movement spread beyond the Rhône. Earlier, in the mid-1920s Le Roy, with M. Perrin from Champagne, M. Checq from the Aube, the Marquis d'Angerville from Burgundy and M. Laligand from Chablis, formed the Association des Grands Crus within the French Federation of Viticultural Associations. Le Roy was elected as chairman.

Their pressure, and the pioneering example of the Châteauneuf syndicat, bore fruit in the Capus-Bender wine law of 1927, which prescribed that no wine had a right to appellation if it did not come from an area of production and grape varieties consecrated by *usages locaux, loyaux et constants*—local, faithful and constant traditions of practice. A law with no teeth is a useless law: Le Roy saw to it that frauds were zealously prosecuted by the Service de la Repression des Fraudes, set up in 1905. Two hundred charges of fraud, in Châteauneuf alone, were brought between 1927 and 1932.

Despite this, Le Roy saw the need for a national organisation to co-ordinate and protect the system of appellations of origin. The problem was how to finance it.

In the course of a viticultural congress held in Cognac, the members of the Association des Grands Crus found themselves visiting the oyster centre of La Tremblade. They noticed that each oyster carried a green label. One oyster-salesman said that this was a health control. No oyster could carry the appellation Marennes without a green label. And the labels did not come free of charge: each one cost forty sous. This gave Le Roy and the others the idea of a tax of two francs per hundred litres to finance the organisation of the appellation system.

So it was, with due acknowledgements to the oysters of Marennes, that the National Committee of Appellations of Origin was created by law on 30 July 1935. The first candidate for Appellation d'Origine Contrôlée under the new law, presented by the Committee to the Minister of Agriculture in 1936, was Châteauneuf-du-Pape. All that the minister had to do was inscribe in law the proposals originally put forward by Le Roy and the Châteauneuf syndicat in 1923. It is thus that Pierre Le Roy and Châteauneuf-du-Pape can claim to being the instigators of the French system of Appellation d'Origine Contrôlée.

Certainly the cardinal importance of Le Roy's work was acknowledged in his lifetime. In 1945 he became Président of the National Institute of Appellations of Origin, and in 1949 he was elected unanimously by the representatives of the twenty-two participating nations as Président of the Office International du Vin, wine's highest international authority. Despite a clause in the OIV's charter stating that the Presidency should rotate, Le Roy remained in office until his death in 1967. In his frequent travels around the world, advising other nations and regions on the drawing-up of wine legislation, Le Roy was granted the equivalent of ambassadorial status. As far as wine was concerned, he was more than an ambassador: he was a de Gaulle. Perhaps the most distinctive testimonial to his contribution to wine came in 1954, when he was invited to unveil his own bust, erected in the Côtes-du-Rhône village of Ste Cécile-les-Vignes. Only the poet Mistral, in recent Provençal history, had been accorded a similar honour. According to M. Pierrefeu, who was present at the ceremony, Le Roy gave his speech in the form of an interrogation of his statue. He imagined his stone replica looking at him and saying, 'Well, mon brave Le Roy, you have got out of a number of scrapes in your time, but this one beats them all.'

Here is evidence of the humour of a man, the bare record of whose achievements does not convey much about his exceptional character. M. Pierrefeu had another anecdote which is worth repeating. Le Roy, who loved shooting duck in the Camargue, was in his element one day, when he leant too far out of his hide and pitched into the marshy water of the Rhône delta. Unperturbed, he stripped off and continued shooting for the rest of the day stark naked.

My favourite story about Pierre Le Roy, though, is told by Alexis Lichine in his *Guide to the Wines and Vineyards of France* (1979): 'One of my last memories of the Baron is of a special occasion when we opened the oldest bottle of wine either of us had ever drunk. It was an amphora retrieved by Jacques Cousteau from the floor of the Mediterranean, and presented to the Baron with the seal still intact after what M. Cousteau judged to be close to two thousand years. Having removed the top of the vessel with some difficulty, we poured a sample of the ancient liquid into our small glasses. It had no colour, bouquet or taste; all of the tannins, tartrates, pectins, and other elements of flavour and aroma had long since precipitated to the bottom of the amphora. The wine had returned to the water and minerals from which it had had its genesis. After eyeing it thoughtfully for a minute and giving it an occasional swirl in the glass, the Baron pronounced his verdict: "Some bad Burgundian shipper, no doubt." '

A great man, then, but not the easiest man to have had as a father. And how much time could this towering figure in the history of wine politics and legislation have had for the running of his own estate? I recalled another anecdote of M. Pierrefeu: when news came that a statue in honour of Pierre Le Roy was to be erected, his son commented, 'What we need is a tractor, not a statue.'

M. Joly had stressed Le Roy's legendary rectitude and honesty, and the principle of altruism on which his life's work was founded. A price had to be paid: 'There is no doubt that the family suffered.'

With a greater understanding of the reasons why Henri Le Roy might be reluctant to speak about his father, then, but with considerable uncertainty about how I would be received, I returned to Château Fortia the following afternoon. I need not have worried. I found a charming note from the Baron, apologising for the inadequacy of my reception two days before and promising that he would be returning soon from Orange to give me a proper tour of the estate, and a tasting of some older wines.

It was a day of fine April sunshine, with the Mistral blowing, and the clouds seemed to have cleared from the Baron's mind too. In the bright southern sun, the creeper-covered château had a less forbidding air; the purple blossom of the Judas trees rang out against the dark green of the splendid Egyptian pines. Even the mirky Louis XIV pond looked ornamental rather than dejected.

The Baron took me round the back of the house into a large copse of mixed deciduous and evergreen oak, and handsome umbrella pine. 'These trees were planted by my grandfather,' the Baron told me. 'You can see, even with the Mistral, it is quite still here. It is also shady—it is good to come here for picnics in summer. Other people in the area have cut down their trees and planted vines. It is a grave mistake, in my view. Without the trees, the soil does not retain moisture so well. They also act as wind-brakes, and prevent the soil from being blown away. If I cut down these woods, I might have an extra hectare of vineyard, but what is the point?'

We moved out of the wood and into a vineyard—Grenache vines, pruned low in the five-fingered hand-like system called Gobelet, each with a tall blue wooden stake by it. They are needed because of the fierce wind. 'My stakes are twenty centimetres longer than standard ones—but it means I can reuse them for young vines when the old ones are uprooted.' At the bottom of the vineyard was a small overgrown field surrounded by low trees, holm-oak, olive. Along one side was a great heap of Châteauneuf's famous, honey-pink quartzite rounded stones. 'They used to pile up the stones to mark the edges of the fields. Now, of course, the stones are generally redistributed in the vineyards. This little field is a typical old Châteauneuf corn-field.' Kept as a kind of archaeological curiosity, perhaps, it now grows only the wild thyme and euphorbia which are as common as grass in Provence.

Next, the Baron took me round the back of the château again to inspect some agricultural equipment of which he was clearly proud. Two tall tractors, designed to straddle a row of vines, one used for spraying, the other for ploughing, contrasted with a much smaller one, which looked as if it could fit between their wheels. 'That small one goes between a row of vines; it still works, and I use it when one of the others breaks down.' The Baron was even prouder of his crusher/ destemmer, fitted with adjustable rollers. 'It is very important that the rollers should be set quite far apart, so that the grapes are burst but not crushed too severely. Otherwise too much harsh tannin is extracted. In lighter years, though, you can set them a little closer.'

Not a Turnip Townsend at heart, I was glad to move round to the cellars, which contain things I understand better than agricultural machinery: bottles and barrels. Château Fortia has extensive, vaulted cellars, the oldest of which go back to the time of the Marquis Fortia d'Urban. The barrel cellar, where the red wine stays for two years (less in light vintages) in large oak *foudres* containing 5000 litres apiece, was extended by the present Baron Le Roy's grandfather, and the bottle cellar, where unusually large stocks of older vintages, going back to 1979, are kept in tall bins, was added on by Baron Pierre le Roy.

'I have some '79, which I was drinking with my family for lunch, for you to taste. I will get down a bottle of '85 as well.' One half-empty bin was found to contain '83. The one next to it was full to the ceiling with '85. The Baron found a rickety table and clambered on to it. Stretching perilously on tiptoe, he could not quite reach the top row of bottles. Scanning the cellar, his eye lit on a three-barred metal apparatus like a heavy clothes rail. He dragged it over and alongside the table, clambered back on to the table, then stretched out one leg on to the topmost, smooth metal bar. I held my breath. Balancing on the bar like a tightrope walker, and clutching the next-to-top row of bottles for sup- port, the Baron grabbed a bottle of '85 and handed it down. As he jumped back off the table, he smiled almost mischievously. 'I do not drink these days because of my back, but I have not tasted the '85 for some time. I want to see how it is developing.'

The tasting-room at Château Fortia is part of the original eight- eenth-century structure: it has a wooden-beamed ceiling and contains a fine Renaissance tallboy and some copies of fifteenth-century paintings done on wood by Baron Le Roy's paternal grandfather, a talented amateur artist. The Baron is particular about glasses; he uses only the large Burgundian type of red wine glass, with a bulbous bottom and tall tapering sides. He says these glasses are best for capturing the wine's scent.

The '79, poured from an almost empty bottle, had a gorgeous, deep, virile, blood-red hue, shading to red-brown at the rim. The bouquet was magnificently full-blown, suggesting many different scents—deep berry fruit, game, spices—all held together in harmony. 'It is the nose of mature Syrah,' said the Baron appreciatively. 'This '79 had ten to twelve per cent Syrah, a little Mourvèdre, but not too much— too much Mourvèdre is a mistake, a little Counoise, which gives a peppery aroma, the rest Grenache of course.' To taste, the wine was warm, rich and generous, yet refined. Whereas some Châteauneufs almost knock you out with their alcoholic potency and raisiny ripeness, this introduced itself with suave elegance, masking its considerable power. A true aristocrat.

We moved on to the '85. The colour was surprisingly similar, but there the resemblance ended. The nose this time was pungent and peppery, tarry—full of youthful vigour but not yet harmonious. The first taste in the mouth was smooth and round, but then the peppery pungency of the nose repeated itself in a finish still tannic and firm. A young wine of considerable promise, not yet ready to drink.

'That is exactly the point!' cried the Baron. 'I make wines which need to be kept at least seven or eight years. I tell my customers that they must wait—I will show you the leaflet I send them.' A frantic search through various drawers ('So many papers!') produced a mauve-printed sheet entitled 'Château Fortia—Some Remarks and Advice'. In this characteristic document the Baron explains to his customers that, apart from a small percentage of white (a soft, rounded wine with a scent of pears), Château Fortia produces only *vins rouges de garde*, red wines for keeping. They are made in a traditional manner, which involves controlled crushing of the grapes, prolonged maceration on the skins and some stalks lasting two weeks, and two years' ageing in oak casks. The result is very different from the type of wine made from uncrushed grapes, by the method known as partial or complete carbonic maceration. The latter produces attractive, fruity wines which are agreeable to drink when young. Wines made by the traditional method acquire greater depth and complexity, and express the character of the soil, not just the grape variety—but only if they are given time to mature.

Herein lies the rub. The red wine of Château Fortia is released when it is three and a half years old, and is thus subject to what the Baron calls 'taxation de la plus-value fictive engendrée par l'érosion monetaire'. The Baron explained the full iniquity of this punitive tax. 'I have a wine which costs ten francs. I keep it for ten years and sell it for twenty francs. If inflation is running at ten per cent, twenty francs is less than the original value plus inflation. But that is not how the government sees it. They decide that I have made ten francs profit—yes, profit!—by keeping that wine ten years, and so they take half of those ten francs in tax. I tell you, this country is governed by idiots.'

A look of gloom replaced his excited indignation. 'It is no use. I will have to follow the example of my colleagues and produce wines using carbonic maceration.'

'That would be a great shame,' I ventured.

'Of course! You have seen with the '79 that, using the traditional method, we produce wines which are a match for the best crus of Bordeaux and Burgundy. But we cannot afford to go on doing so. That is how they are destroying an appellation.'

Taking my leave of the Baron, a singular, if not a contented man, I reflected on several ironies. The first was that the very fact which was causing the Baron to despair, namely that he was making wines which required long maturation, and was then punitively taxed for his pains, was one which the château-owners of Bordeaux had turned to their very great advantage and profit. The legendary keeping qualities of the great Bordeaux had made them into 'cast-iron' investment commodities. Not only had the prices of the top Bordeaux wines become inflated beyond any level at which they might be drunk by ordinary people, but the demand had become so intense that the Bordelais were able to sell them when they were only a few months older than Beaujolais Nouveau. The Baron's three-and-a-half year-old Château Fortia 1985 was selling at the cellar door for fifty-five francs, roughly half the price of a six-month-old Bordeaux or Burgundy of comparable class of the 1988 vintage. Despite the efforts of the Barons Le Roy, father and son, Châteauneuf-du-Pape was perhaps the most undervalued of the great wines of France.

Understandably, Baron Henri Le Roy wishes to have nothing to do with associations of wine-growers, syndicates, politics, legislation. Reluctantly or not, he has remained at Château Fortia and concentrated on producing one of the very best, most refined and elegant wines of the appellation which his father helped to establish sixty odd years ago. He is helped by his one surviving sister and her husband, who live, surrounded by nine cats, in a modern addition to the château.

The succession is fraught with uncertainties. Baron Henri Le Roy has three children: a daughter and two sons. His daughter is married and lives in Paris. His elder son is slightly handicapped. His younger son works for a pharmaceutical company in Avignon. An impressive thesis on the history, viticulture, geology and especially wine-making traditions and innovations of the Châteauneuf appellation, written while he was a student at Montpellier University, attests to considerable interest in, and knowledge of, the subject. His father is obviously proud of this piece of work. But the signs are that this younger son will not be prepared to leave his job and take over the running of the estate. In that case the work of Baron Pierre Le Roy, remembered with gratitude by historians of wine and wine-growers throughout the Rhône valley and beyond, will lose its dynastic link.

PRODUCE OF FRANCE
*Grand Vin
de Bourgogne*

Récolté - Elevé
*et mis en bouteille
à la Propriété*

Clos-de-Vougeot

GRAND CRU
APPELLATION CONTROLEE

S.C. JEAN GRIVOT
VITICULTEUR A VOSNE-ROMANÉE (COTE-D'OR) FRANCE   750 ml

*Grivot
of
Vosne-Romanée*

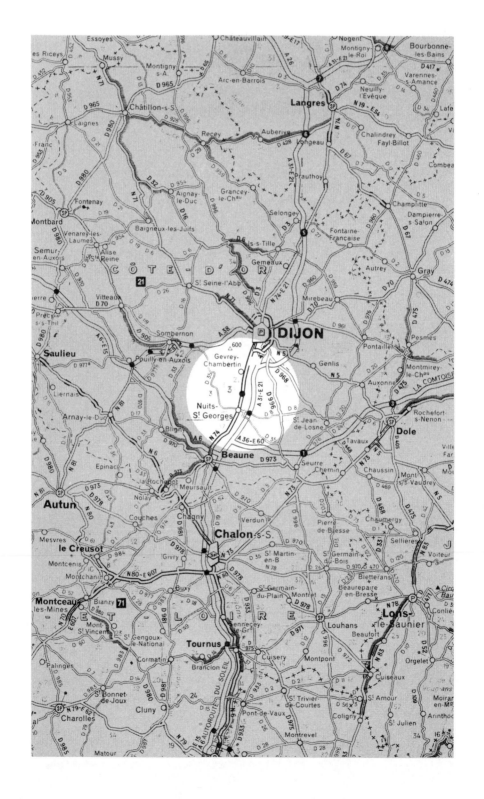

Burgundy: the very word conveys richness and fertility. One can hear the burgeoning of crops and the gurgle of delightful streams. The streams turn deep red and gurgle down the throat—they consist of velvety, sumptuous, perfumed wine. But just as burgundy's reputation as a full-bodied, deep-coloured red wine can be deceptive, so Burgundy can disappoint those who expect a smiling pastoral paradise. Burgundy has its riches but does not wear them on its sleeve.

Certainly the Côte d'Or, the golden slope where the greatest burgundies, some would say the greatest wines in the world, are produced, has a dour and unsmiling look for much of the year. South from Dijon, a long, lowish wall of hillside, crested with thick scrub, and broken periodically by rocky defiles, stretches on indefinitely. To the east, a featureless flat plain extends for many miles. The vineyards cover a narrow band from the middle slopes of the hillside to the beginning of the plain. In winter, and in spring, when the vines are no more than blackened stumps, and the vineyards are patches of dark-brown earth, the Côte can look dismal. Its villages are hardly eye-catching either, the houses built of pale limestone and roofed with small tiles the same dark-brown colour as the fields. From a distance these roofs have a look of worn brown corduroy.

One of the quietest and dullest of these villages is Vosne-Romanée, 'la perle de la Côte', as the locals like to call it. There is one moribund café by the plain church; not a single shop, restaurant or hotel. A short walk along the path leading from the back of the church takes you out of the village and to a low stone wall with a cross by it. The name carved in stone by the gate is Romanée-Conti. This, the greatest of all the Burgundian grands crus, is probably the most precious vineyard in the world; possibly the most expensive piece of agricultural real estate on the planet. Knowing this, you may look at it with respect, but it will continue to give nothing away, just brownish-red, quite stony earth, densely planted with low-pruned, gnarled, damp-looking vines in rows with wires along them.

Above, ahead of you, is an even smaller grand cru vineyard called La Romanée; to the left, the other side of the path, is a narrow vineyard which for some reason is only a premier cru, La Grande Rue;

the reason is obscure (some say the owners wished to undervalue their property for tax reasons) because just the other side is another very famous grand cru, La Tâche. Over to the right are two more grands crus, Grands-Echézeaux and the larger Echézeaux. Above, below and in some cases in between the grands crus, which lie on the middle-to-lower slopes of the Côte, are the premier cru vineyards of Vosne (first growths come below great growths); above and below the premiers crus, the vineyards producing wine called simply Vosne-Romanée. But there are, by local consent, no common wines in Vosne. A non-local may dispute that, but one thing cannot be disputed: there are no inexpensive wines in Vosne.

It is time to walk back along the path, past the church and left along the village street. A few yards along there is a rusty iron gate on the right leading into a small courtyard. This is the entrance to the Domaine Grivot, though there is no name-plate to tell you.

Facing you as you enter the courtyard is the roughly mortared limestone wall of a sizeable house which has obviously been added to at different periods. In the corner, by some stone steps leading down to a cellar, is a low wooden door. When you go in, you find two offices side by side. The first is dark and painted deep red; an ormolu clock hangs from one wall, a carved eighteenth-century dresser covers another. The refectory table which does duty as a desk is stacked high with papers arranged in no discernible order. Leading off it is its antithesis, a cool, grey and beige, immaculately tidy machine for working, dominated by a large Tandon computer. You could be in a bank, an insurance company, anywhere in the world.

The offices belong to Jean and Etienne Grivot, *père et fils*, who jointly manage every aspect of the 15-hectare Domaine Grivot, the work in the vineyards, the work in the cellar, sales, public relations, marketing.... Well, perhaps not marketing. It is a concept which is not fully understood in Burgundy, and long may it not be. Public relations, on the other hand, are becoming increasingly important. Why else would these Burgundians be prepared to explain the secrets of their *métier*, passed on from parent to child for centuries and traditionally not revealed even to other vignerons in the same village, to a passing English journalist?

It is Etienne who receives me, a handsome, serious man in his early thirties. When Etienne's photograph appeared on the front cover of an American magazine, as a leading representative of Burgundy's dynamic new generation of wine-makers, he received more than twenty proposals of marriage by post.

'As you can see, each of us has his office and his part of the work, but it's a team activity. We talk about everything, consult each other. I regard it as fundamental for a successful passing on of the domaine's activity that there should be a good understanding between father and son. It is very important to avoid rivalry and make sure that the succession is natural. As it is, I have been working here for several years, and all our customers know that there is an Etienne Grivot at the domaine. As I gradually take over the reins from my father, there will not be a violent shock. I am in charge of wine-making and supervising the work in the vineyards: my father does a lot of the selling and talking to customers.'

Was it inevitable that Etienne would follow his father in the domaine?

'I had a general education up to the age of sixteen, then went to the Lycée in Beaune to study general agriculture. It was a very wide-ranging course, and dealt with cereals and livestock as well as vines. I found that very useful in terms of understanding the soil, and how to implement a plan of fertilisation.

'Up to the age of eighteen, I had no special interest in viticulture or wine. But then I started a two-year specialisation in viticulture and oenology, in the course of which I did two *stages*, in Bordeaux and California, which I think were the turning-points.'

A Burgundian vigneron in Bordeaux sounds strange enough, let alone one in California.

'Yes, I think it was very unusual for someone from these parts to go to Bordeaux. I chose a small family domaine of two châteaux in the Libournais, in Fronsac, Château Croix de la Borde and Château Jean Denon, not at all famous, but good wine-makers. I wanted to open my mind a little and find out about Bordelais methods of vinification. It proved absolutely decisive for my technique of vinification. I now use long fermentation periods of eighteen to twenty-one days, not the eight to twelve days usual here.

'The following year I spent six months at St Helena in the Napa valley working for the Jaeger family of Freemark Abbey and Rutherford Hill. I did everything: the first day I cleaned the fermentation tanks, then I helped with the reception of the harvest. I was lucky enough to win the confidence of the wine-maker and helped with the *assemblage* of different *cuvées*. I did not learn so much about techniques of vinification there as about the organisation of work. Californians are very open to everything which is happening elsewhere, whereas our education in Burgundy is perhaps too individualistic and restricted. I have been back three times since then, to Oregon twice and once to California.'

I could not resist asking Etienne what he thought of California and Oregon's attempts with the red grape of Burgundy, Pinot Noir. I imagined his father's reply might be dismissive. Etienne was much more circumspect. 'It is a huge question. I think it is a good idea for people in different regions to make Pinot Noir, because everyone agrees that it is one of the most interesting, one of the most delicate, of grape varieties. As for Pinot Noir from California, I am sure in the next few years they will find the best sites and microclimates. In general, up to now, I find the wines come from vineyards which are too hot and where the vegetative cycle is too short. In terms of aroma, they do not have much in common with what we produce here. You can tell it is Pinot Noir, but not much more than that. The aromas are more cooked and heavy: they lack spirituality and grace.

'In Oregon they are making some remarkable wines, but they do not resemble burgundy. And I find that encouraging, because a grape variety is not simply a grape variety, it varies according to the surroundings where it is grown. Here in Burgundy we have had centuries of experience to find the sites best suited to the vine: we vinify with a spirit of *terroir*, of the particular land and locality. They are trying to do that in California and Oregon: they have not fully succeeded yet, but given time, I am sure they will.

'Some people round here say that it is dangerous to start planting Pinot Noir in Oregon. I am completely against that view. In the last ten or twelve years wine-drinking has taken off in the States. People start with the local wine and then move up to French wines. There is a big potential of fine-wine-drinking in the world.'

The New World has tended to stress the importance of the wine-maker rather than the grape-grower, technology and know-how rather than soil. Etienne Grivot remains a true Burgundian on this point. 'I find it pretentious and ridiculous to think that a wine-maker alone can make a great wine. Top-quality wine can be made only from top-quality grapes. When you are making good everyday wine, it is true, the esprit du terroir is not necessarily the determining point. But when you are talking about exceptional wine, the terroir is fundamental.

'Speaking of New World wine-makers, though, there is something I admire, and that is that most of them come from outside the world of wine. Often these people are more effective as wine-makers because they have had contact with something else. I think it is immensely important not to become too enclosed within the circle of wine-growing and wine-making. You can end up not understanding anything. Although I have a lot of friends who are wine-makers, the majority of my friends are not in wine.

'Here in Burgundy we are lucky to have a marvellous terroir and the possibility of making great wines. But we will do that only if we have the necessary competence. We must deserve our terroir, we must be creative and search for perfection. What we must not do is wear a laurel wreath on our heads and say "We are the greatest." It is quite possible for us to make very ordinary wines too.'

There is implied criticism here of what the Grivots themselves acknowledge to have been a bad period in Burgundy's recent history, the decade of the 1970s, when a great many of the region's red wines grew visibly feebler, more pallid, less capable of ageing, while their price continued to soar skywards. This is the period which inspired one of the most admirable of London wine merchants, Anthony Hanson, to write his critical and perceptive book, *Burgundy*.

Hanson's two most celebrated comments will be remembered for as long as burgundy is drunk: the first, an unlikely tribute, is that 'great burgundy smells of shit'. The second is that 'most burgundy is…a rip-off'.

The generation of Etienne Grivot has been credited with restoring a good deal of Burgundy's lustre. 'I am not happy about all this talk of the new generation in Burgundy,' he says modestly, while acknowledging that he is widely considered one of its leading lights. 'Each generation reacts against the previous one. My parents' generation had many difficulties. To start with, their parents' generation had enormous difficulties in making a living from wine-growing. In those days it was the négociants who made money, and the growers were pulling the Devil by the tail. Then my parents' generation arrived with a very considerable professional education. My father is a trained oenologist, and so are several of his friends here in Vosne. They were the first generation who had really studied. They had a lot of success—the American market took off, estate-bottling took off. I think there was a kind of euphoria and everything became too easy. Another factor was the growth of office work, which they did not always find easy to manage.' I remembered the piles of papers on Jean Grivot's desk. 'They tended to get distracted from the work in the vineyards and the cellar.

'On a more technical point, the advice they had from the consultant oenologists of the region was in my view very bad. There were fundamental errors in the planning of fertilisation. They used too much nitrogen, which gave the vines excessive vigour and made them overproduce. The wines were too light and lacked colour. They also used too much potassium, which leads to a lack of acidity.

'So the point with my generation is not that we are a formidable bunch of people, simply that we recognise the errors that were made in the 1970s—not by everybody, I should add. In the great years, they made great wines. But there were too many small years. Our approach is twofold. First, you must know how to organise yourself so that you can remain close to the vines and the cellar, and not too close to the office. Hire a secretary and buy a computer.' For the first time in our conversation, Etienne Grivot allows himself a slight smile.

'The second thing is to restore the equilibrium of the soil. Great wines have to be made from properly constituted grapes. You cannot expect a man to run a marathon unless he has been eating properly for a month beforehand. Our soils had become too rich. We needed to bring back the necessary elements to them. People overstress the importance of the wine-maker. Before being a good wine-maker you need to be a good cultivator of the vine. But then you also need to be good at bringing wines up in the cellar. And then you need to be a good businessman, and a good salesman, because if the money is not coming in, you will not be able to buy the equipment you need, the sprays, the new barrels. You need to be a real all-rounder to be a good wine-maker in Burgundy.

'Another aspect of the job is communication—the theatrical element. You have to know how to talk about your wines. This is not something egotistic, but a matter of communicating your pleasure in wine to other people. It is not simply salesmanship, either. When I have people in the cellar, I am not simply selling them wine. I am doing that, of course, but it goes beyond selling. Wine, like literature or music, is part of culture and civilisation.'

It was time to go down to the cellar ourselves and have a sniff and a swill of something more than air. Before we got among the barrels, Etienne showed me the cuverie on the ground floor to the left of the courtyard. The Grivots recently bought the house which adjoins theirs and gutted it to create a spacious two-level store for bottles and equipment. The cuverie itself, the area where the grapes are received, crushed and fermented, was quiet, as it remains for all except the few weeks of the harvest. 'It is a very intense period of work, which lasts about six weeks. It's a round-the-clock job during that period. Every year I lose about eight pounds.' The main piece of equipment here was a grape mill, or *fouloir-égrappoir*. 'There is a choice to be made every year about how many of the stalks to keep. I taste the stalks and pips to determine the level of tannin in the grapes. In lighter years I use more stalks.' The fermentation *cuves*, made of steel lined with glass, are in an odd assortment of different sizes. 'We have eighteen different types of wine, Vosne-Romanée village, Vosne-Romanée les Suchots, Richebourg and so on, in all sorts of quantities, so we need all these sizes of tank. As for the material, wood looks prettier, but it is very bad, very difficult to keep clean.'

After fermentation, though, like all fine red burgundy, the Grivot wines go into the 225-litre oak barrels which in Burgundy are called *pièces*. Their home is the barrel cellar, built into the limestone directly beneath the house. We went down the stone steps to the right of the front door. Inside, the temperature, 12°C all year round, was a good deal warmer than the bitter April air outside, though on my first visit I had noted that it was exceptionally cold. The first section of the cellar is more like a tool-shed; here Etienne picked up the angled glass instrument, known colloquially as a 'thief', for drawing off samples from the barrels, and a small crowbar for knocking out the bungs.

In this low-arched cellar the barrels stand in rows two high. They are of different ages, some the pale creamy colour of new oak, others stained a deep grey-purple. All of them are ribbed with strips of chestnut, rather than metal hoops. According to Burgundian folklore, chestnut keeps away the spiders which can be a pest in the cellar. Etienne uses a mixture of new and older barrels for his premiers crus and grands crus, only older barrels for the simple village wines. He also uses oak from different forests, and with different degrees of toasting. He explained: 'I went to a conference in Oregon on different kinds of oak organised by the Tonnelerie de Bourgogne. Of the various kinds I preferred Allier, but I liked the assemblage of all the different kinds even better. As for new oak, it is like salt in a sauce—it should add something but not stand out. There are people here whom I admire greatly, Henri Jayer in this village for instance, who use entirely new oak, but that is not to my taste.'

The first sample came from an older, grey-purple barrel. The Vosne-Romanée village 1988 had a deep purple colour and a splendid nose full of rich, rooty, perhaps beetrooty aromas, with a whiff of deep flower scent too. It was much harder to taste than to smell, high in acidity, raw, tannic. 'The acidity is a good sign—it means it will keep. The '88s are big, powerful wines.' We moved on to premier cru, Les Beaux Monts, this time from a newer-looking barrel. The colour was darker; the nose much less developed, though I detected the sweet toasty savour of the oak. This was a denser and more concentrated wine, big and meaty. It would take years, five to seven at least, to reach maturity. No sign of feebleness here. Premier cru Les Suchots was perfumed with the scents of violet and raspberries; a lighter, softer wine to taste. Nuits-St-Georges Les Boudots was in a quite different style, tight, compact, meaty, almost forbidding.

Finally we tasted the two grands crus. Clos de Vougeot was

rich, velvety, gamy: a big, complex wine, needing time for all its components to be knit together. I remembered tasting the 1986 Clos de Vougeot on a previous visit to the Domaine Grivot: Etienne pronounced it 'anarchique'. Last of all came Richebourg, as deep as the Clos de Vougeot but both smoother and more powerful.

We moved back a year to 1987, an underrated vintage. The Vosne-Romanée Les Beaux Monts was a lovely rich toasty wine. The Echézeaux, a grand cru belonging to Etienne's aunt Jacqueline Jayer but made and sold by the Grivots, was finer, more elegant, with a nose of raspberries and flowers: 'beaucoup de spiritualité', said Etienne.

Clos de Vougeot was big, frank, hearty, warming, velvety. Best of all, though, was the Richebourg, which combined the raspberry, floral elegance of the Echézeaux with the power of the Clos de Vougeot. A beautifully composed wine.

Conclusions? The premiers crus really do have an extra dimension compared to the simple village wines, and the grands crus compared to the premiers crus. Partly it is a matter of power, indeed of alcohol. The grands crus have half a degree more than the premiers crus, the premiers crus half a degree more than the village wines. But it is more than that. Echézeaux, year in, year out, makes a lighter, more delicate, more 'spiritual' wine than Clos de Vougeot a few hundred yards away.

It was time to take a look at those terroirs whose subtle spirit is captured by the wine-maker's art. 'We have time to see a few vineyards before lunch,' said Etienne, motioning me to his solid Volkswagen estate. We drove back along the track by the church and past the vineyards of Romanée St Vivant and Romanée-Conti. The Grivots do not own land here. After turning right at the upper limit of La Romanée, France's smallest appellation at less than a hectare, and going a little way along the hillside, we did stop. Beneath us were the vines of Richebourg. It was in 1984 that the Grivots bought just under an acre, which is to say a twentieth, of this priceless vineyard. How much they paid for it, I did not feel it was quite polite to ask, yet.

We proceeded along the rough track for a short way, then stopped again. Below us this time was Vosne-Romanée, premier cru, Les Suchots and in front of us Les Beaux Monts. Why should these be premiers crus and their neighbours grands crus? Part of Les Suchots faces slightly northwards, rather than east, like most of the great Côte d'Or vineyards. Les Beaux Monts is situated high up, on the side of a gully. One might expect it to produce somehat lighter wines than vineyards lower down—but I found the wine of Les Beaux Monts to be richer than that of Les Suchots.

Etienne turned off along a very rough track leading up into the woods above the vineyards. We passed a few small vineyards cleared out among the trees. 'It is too cold up here to make very good wine— these vineyards only have the appellation Hautes Côtes de Nuits.' It is rough, rocky, backwoods country up here—terrain more suitable for wild boar and deer than man. We wound round the side of a gully and descended once more on to the Côte d'Or. Below us was a great walled vineyard, in one corner of which stood a sober, square stone building, with mansard windows and two modest turrets. More impressive than the Château du Clos de Vougeot itself are its medieval outbuildings behind with their immensely tall and steep-pitched roofs. We drove down to the track by the high stone wall which the Cistercian monks built to surround all 51 hectares of this single grand cru, now owned by eighty different co-proprietors. With nearly two hectares, the Grivots own one of the largest holdings in the Clos. Keeping the wall of Vougeot on our left, with Grands Echézeaux, then part of Echézeaux, then Les Suchots on our right, we returned to Vosne. At the Domaine Grivot, we were met by Etienne's mother, a handsome, vigorous woman in her fifties, looking ten years younger, and his father Jean, a lean ascetic man with a pointed grey beard, giving him an ecclesiastical look. Also on the doorstep were Etienne's wife Marielle, the tall, pretty daughter of the well-known vigneron Simon Bize from Savigny on the Côte de Beaune, and their small daughter Matilde. 'You are very welcome to stay for lunch, if you like. It is very simple, nothing special at all.' Madame Grivot sounded apologetic. I felt honoured. The Burgundians, for all their reputation for expansive jollity, are private people, wary of outsiders, slow to open up. Here was further evidence of Burgundian *glasnost*.

I followed Mme Grivot through the kitchen with its splendid, massive stone Burgundian fireplace. 'That must be very old—fifteenth or sixteenth century?'

'Yes, probably.' Madame Grivot was not particularly impressed by such antiquity. 'This is certainly the oldest part of the house.' The attractive, tiled dining-room is a couple of steps down from the kitchen: the house is built on different levels, revealing the ancient contours of the village street. The dining-room looks out on to a walled garden where peaches, plums and cherries grow.

The first course was a salad of tuna and hard-boiled egg, accompanied by a sharp, gooseberry-like Aligoté. The white Aligoté grape is traditional in Burgundy, but its green, thin wine is much less highly prized than the richer, rounder and more complex wine of Chardonnay. This Aligoté is made by the Grivots for home consumption only, on land where the Pinot Noir does not flourish. Gazing somewhat ruefully over her garden, now gripped by unseasonal April cold, Mme Grivot commented that only last week the thermometer reached 28°C. Today it was barely three degrees.

'Spring weather is always fickle,' replied her husband.'But as the buds have broken very early this year, frost could be extremely dangerous. It was around zero on Saturday morning: that is not dangerous, but if it got down to minus two, it would do a lot of damage.'

Over the main course—thick, rich *boeuf bourguignon*, what else?—conversation turned to that age-old Burgundian theme, the war of the growers and the négociants. The last fifteen years have seen a dramatic, and perhaps permanent shift in the balance of power in favour of the growers. They discovered that they could make more money selling their wine in bottle, rather than in barrel to the big houses in Beaune. In 1970, 95 per cent of Côte d'Or wine was handled by négociants; by 1984 that figure had dropped to less than 50 per cent. 'I regret that there is not a better accord between growers and négociants,'said Jean Grivot. 'Neither side has been perfect.'

'But excuse me,' his son butted in heatedly. 'It is the négociants who have been stupid. They have not been prepared to pay a fair price for the wine, and that is why the production of great wine escapes them.

'Also from my experience I would say it is impossible to make fine wines in large quantities. Of course the négociants are capable of making fine wines, but in too many cases their wines lack personality. Take a Corton, a Chambertin and a Richebourg from a négociant: in each case you can say, it's an impressive wine, but you cannot recognise the specific qualities of the vineyard.

'We have a relatively large domaine here, just under fifteen hectares, but during the racking and bottling I am there all the time. I taste everything. I believe it is very important to work with the lees. They nourish the wine. When one is racking there comes a moment when the wine is more and more turbid, before the true thick lees appear. With a négociant it will be a workman who is doing this job. When will he stop? He will stop as soon as the wine becomes slightly turbid. Whereas I will stop only after opening the tap and tasting the wine and deciding that the taste of the lees is no longer good. That is the difference between making an average quality wine and a really fine wine.

'A négociant, logically, will succeed in making average quality wine, year in, year out. But he will never reach the perfection which a small vigneron can achieve. There is more risk with a small vigneron:

you know that in some years the wine will be great and in others, like 1984, it will be less good. But wine is an individual, a character. When you even out the vintages and the appellations you lose character and achieve a commercial product. The wines of this domaine are not commercial products. I don't sell a bottle of Vosne-Romanée like a pair of socks.'

The Vosne-Romanée Les Beaux Monts 1978 which we had been drinking with the boeuf bourguignon bore little resemblance to socks — to new ones, at any rate. In its splendid rooty, gamy nose there was hint of decay, as there is with all great mature red wines, but it was a noble, complex decay which would continue for many years. On the palate the wine combined fire and velvet as only the great red burgundies can.

I complimented Mme Grivot on her fine boeuf bourguignon. She smiled, 'Ah, that's a little secret. That's a frozen bit which I made a couple of weeks ago. I didn't know you would be having lunch with us, so when I heard, I took it out of the deep freeze and popped it in the microwave. It works quite well, I think.' It all goes to show that tradition and technology can co-exist, in the right hands.

After lunch both Grivots were busy with customers: I was directed down the street to a shuttered, detached house at the other end of the village. It belongs to Jacqueline Jayer, sister of Mme Grivot, aunt of Etienne, whose fine dowry of vineyards is managed by the Grivots, though the wines carry the Jacqueline Jayer label. Mademoiselle Jayer is a delightful, petite lady in her late fifties, who could easily, like her sister, be ten years younger. She was dressed in practical, working trousers, and there was a spring in her step and a girlish sparkle in her eyes which testified that a life spent among the vines had not been an unhappy one. She told me about it as we sat in the parlour of her neat, sparsely decorated house.

'I began working in the vineyards for my father in 1942, when I was fourteen, and I am still working in the vineyards now. My compulsory schooling finished then, when I was fourteen: I would have liked to continue my studies, but it was the German occupation and my father didn't consider it safe for me to go to school in Beaune. If I had been a boy, it might have been different: my brother, who is three years older than me, did continue studying. But I don't resent it: the same thing happened to many others here.

'Four Jayer brothers came here from the Saône valley, thirty or forty kilometres away, at the end of the last century. My grandfather Jean-François got a job with the négociants and growers, Maison Faiveley, in Nuits-St-Georges. He did not do any viticultural or oenological studies, but he had a fine palate. He learnt how to look after the wines in barrel and Faiveley gave him complete responsibility in the cellars. Eventually he was able to buy four hectares of his own vines. Incidentally Henri Jayer is the son of the youngest brother of Jean-François, so even though he is only a few years older than me he is my first cousin once removed.

'My grandfather had no employees, just his wife, and his son when he was old enough. My father Louis Jayer was the only child, and so he inherited the domaine. Four hectares is enough for a family to live on—in fact, it is possible to live honourably here with two. The 1930s were a bad decade: there were natural catastrophes, frost and hail, and on top of that business was depressed. But around here families generally stay put. Part of it is love, but most of it is the necessity of living.

'It was only in my father's time that the horse-drawn plough arrived. Before that all the work was done by hand. There used to be many more small domaines, two, three, four hectares, in Vosne-Romanée. The tractor changed that.

'The work on the vines, traditionally done by women, has not changed that much. Pruning, staking, planting: it must all be done by hand. Hard work? Yes, you must be tough, you must be able to resist the bad weather, frost, rain. But there is also the taste for work well done. I think it's a pity that the younger generation will not work in the vines. Etienne's wife, who is the daughter of a vigneron, as you know, and a splendid girl, does not work in the vines: she works in the office with that computer. One discovers little anomalies, little things going wrong in domaines when the boss's eye is not on them the whole time.

'The intellectual formation is obviously a good thing, but you also need an enormous amount of practical knowledge. After all, our ancestors had only their palates, and they made Burgundy famous. But speaking of palates, you must taste some wine.'

Mademoiselle Jayer led me through the kitchen to the small cellar at the back of the house. But in the kitchen there was an introduction to be made. 'Meet my mother. She is eighty-nine years old, and she is still with us. Elle est toujours là.' A very old lady was sitting by the kitchen window looking out on to the village street, in a patch of fleeting, pale April sun which felt warmer through the glass. She got up when she saw me, and repeated her daughter's words in a tone which combined a rueful irony with strength and pride. 'Oui, toujours là. Comme vous voyez.' She was still there in every sense.

At the back of Jacqueline Jayer's house there is a decent-sized walled garden, all inside Appellation Vosne-Romanée Contrôlée, and therefore rather a valuable little piece of land, and a small yard where the grapes used to be brought in. Underneath it is the cellar. 'As you can see, it is too small to be practical. Apart from a small private stock of bottles, all my wine is at the Grivots now.

'My sister married Jean Grivot in 1952 and my father gave her one hectare of vines—he had five and a half hectares by then. I continued working with my father on the domaine until he retired in 1968, when he was seventy-one. At that point he completed the sharing out of the domaine. He gave us different parcels rather than dividing everything up in two—everything would just have become too small. I decided with the Grivots that we would manage the two domaines together.'

The prize portion of Louis Jayer's domaine was about an acre and a half of the grand cru Les Echézeaux, which he gave to his elder daughter Jacqueline. It was a bottle of Echézeaux from the great 1971 vintage which Mlle Jayer, most generously, brought back from the cellar to the parlour. The colour was deep blood-red at the core, shading to brick-brown at the rim. The nose combined the rich gamy, rooty scents of controlled decay which I noted on the Vosne-Romanée Les Beaux Monts 1978 with something more ethereal, the fragrance of flowers. The wine tasted sweet, velvety, harmonious—not particularly big or powerful, but beautifully complete. It is obvious that Mlle Jayer has a special love of the wine of this vineyard. She is widely respected in the region for her tasting ability, and when barrel samples are to be tasted prior to racking and bottling at the Domaine Grivot, she joins her brother-in-law and her nephew to taste the wines blind. 'Etienne's palate is much closer to mine than to his father's. I think he has inherited it from my side.'

'Can we go and have a look at your Echézeaux?' I asked.

'Mais bien sûr. I would have taken you there before but I didn't think you would be especially interested.' We then got into Mlle Jayer's Opel and set off up on the D109 with grand cru Romanée-St Vivant on our left and Vosne-Romanée premier cru Les Suchots on our right. Jacqueline Jayer's piece of Echézeaux is in the parcel called Les Cruots in the southernmost corner of the cru, on the same level as Richebourg and La Romanée, just below Vosne-Romanée premier cru Les Beaux Monts. We got out of the car and paced out the twenty-five rows of vines, between thirty-seven and forty years old, planted in the heavy, red-brown, stony soil. They were not much to look at, just beginning to push tiny furled leaves from their shredded, ivy-like stems, but in three or four years out of ten, they produce 3600 bottles of one of the world's most sophisticated, perfumed, sensuous wines. There are worse ways of spending £30 than on a bottle of Jacqueline Jayer's Echézeaux.

We returned to the Domaine Grivot for the last stage of my visit, a talk with Jean Grivot about Burgundy's, and the domaine's, recent past, and its prospects for the future. I sat in a wooden chair at an angle to M. Grivot's work-table. He was shuffling papers into what looked like an immensely complicated game of patience. 'I know it looks disorganised,' says M. Grivot, 'but I have my system. I know where everything is, in the end. You wished to know about our origins. I do not have much information about the origins of our family, for the simple reason that our ancestors were more concerned with cultivating their vines than making family trees. They were vignerons: they gathered the grapes and made the wine. But we have documents showing that my great-grandparents bought the house next to this one—the house we have turned into the new cuverie—in 1830. They already owned this house. They had a smaller area of vines than we do today: each generation, as the tradition is in Burgundy, has added a certain number of vines. We found some old cooper's tools in the house next door, which indicate that they were coopers, and also made some wine.

'In those days there was a big difference between vintages. There were acceptable years and bad years. In bad years they might sell no wine at all, but the loss was not so great because they had no wages to pay or other expenses. Now it is different. A year without a harvest for us would be a very serious loss. We must continue to pay wages, taxes, social charges, the upkeep of the tractors and so on.

'My grandfather and my father had a horse. But the horse cost very little because we had a field for pasture as well as the vines. They cultivated oats, hay and straw, and that fed the horse. They also kept a cow, or a couple of cows, rabbits, chickens, so they were almost self-sufficient.

'The domaine has increased with marriages. My mother was the daughter of a vigneron who had vines in Vosne-Romanée and also in Nuits-St-Georges. She was also a Grivot, indeed both her parents were born with the name Grivot, which means that three of my four grandparents were born Grivot, but all from different families. My maternal grandfather, Emile Grivot, was a far-sighted man: he was a member of a group of proprietors who started bottling their own wines rather than selling them to négociants. The group was called the Consortium des Propriétaires des Grands Crus. It didn't last very long, because each domaine was able to make a name for itself independently, but it was an important first step. The father of Emile Grivot, Etienne Grivot, was mayor of Vosne-Romanée after the Revolution. There were many more small proprietors in Vosne then, and the vineyards looked different. Among the vines there grew grass and convolvulus, which they fed to the cows. And there were fruit trees, cherry-trees, peach-trees, peartrees, in the vineyards. Now they get in the way of the tractors, and there are very few left.

'These ancestors built up the domaine by buying not very well-situated vineyards and then selling them to buy better ones. My father, Gaston Grivot, for instance, had vineyards at Meuilley in the Hautes-Côtes, then sold them to buy vineyards in Vosne. He bought our share—nearly two hectares—of the Clos de Vougeot in 1926.'

'Was it expensive?'

'Yes, but not as expensive as it is now. There was not such a price differential between the grands crus and the premiers crus as there is now. And my father also bought something which was on the market. The Richebourg, for instance, which we bought in 1984, that was very expensive. But it was the first parcel of Richebourg to come on the market for seventy years.'

'How expensive is very expensive?'

Jean Grivot looked canny for a moment, then his expression softened. 'I do not see why I should not tell you. That parcel, just under a third of a hectare, cost us three and a half million francs, which is about three hundred and thirty thousand pounds.' One thing which has helped us build up this domaine is that my father and I were both only children. At least my father had a brother, but he was killed in the First World War. My father was gassed in 1918 and suffered from emphysema for the rest of his life.

'My father was one of the first oenologists in Burgundy. He studied oenology at the faculty in Dijon after the war. I also gained a Certificate of Oenology at Dijon, but it was not so rare then. And now Etienne has his degree in Oenology, which is quite normal these days.

'My father had three workers in the vineyards on a domaine of seven or eight hectares: we now have five or six on a domaine of just under fifteen hectares. He spent more time working on the vineyards than I do, because he had less office work to do. In those days they used to do the accounts on a corner of the kitchen table.

'My father bottled about fifteen per cent at the domaine: the rest was sold in barrel to the négociants, houses such as Faiveley, Jadot and Latour, or in small barrels to private customers. When I took over from my father after the Second World War—in which he was mobilised again, incidentally—I gradually increased the proportion of estate bottling. But it was difficult to finance it. If you sell in barrel you receive money a few months after the vintage. But if you sell in bottle you have to finance all the time—two years or more—in which the wine is maturing in barrel. So I increased the proportion of estate-bottling little by little, year by year. I think 1959 was the first year in which the majority of the wine was bottled here.

'Domaine-bottling is more satisfying for the spirit. Just selling the grapes or the new-made wine you cannot follow the wine's progress. It is possible to make a living like that, but it is less satisfying. If you bottle at the domaine you can taste older bottles with customers and follow the whole cycle of the wine.

'In some years, like 1988, you do not make any more money selling the wine in bottle, because the négociants pay well for wine in barrel. In the lesser vintages you certainly make more money selling in bottle. But the extra satisfaction is important. I try to keep a little wine back, to age it here in bottle and keep a record of older vintages. But I have more and more friends, and I am weak. When a friend says, couldn't you let me a have a dozen bottles of this for my son's wedding, or of that for my daughter's communion, I always say yes.'

It occurred to me that the whole question of selling the wine had hardly been discussed. But the Grivots do not regard wine as something which you go about trying to sell. 'There is an element of selling, of course, but it works by word of mouth. One customer talks to another, and it snowballs. We have never been travelling salesmen, if that is what you mean. My ancestors would not have had time, they were too busy working in the vineyards and the cellar. Now we export about fifty-five per cent of our wine, mainly to the United States, Switzerland, Britain and Belgium, and sell the remaining forty-five per cent within France, especially to the best restaurants, like Pic in Valence, and in Paris.' I mentioned the fact that there was no name outside the gate. 'We are not interested in people who pass through here on their holidays in August. They are not usually good connoisseurs.'

Has the style of wine changed appreciably since the time of Jean Grivot's father and grandfather? 'The technique was the same, in principle, though the equipment was more primitive. They did not have electric presses or electric pumps. They fermented the wine in wooden cuves, rather than steel, and there was no control of temperature.'

What about chaptalisation—the bolstering of the wine's alcohol content by means of sugar added during fermentation, which is perfectly legal—up to two degrees alcohol, at least—in most French wine regions, but has become somewhat controversial in the wider world of wine? Californians and Australians, at least, make much of this use of 'the sun in sacks', which has never been permitted in the New World. Or in Italy, come to that, or even in Germany for the higher échelons, *Qualitatsweine mit Pradikat*. This was clearly a question Jean Grivot had had to answer many times.

'One does not chaptalise for pleasure. It is a correction of nature, and it is done to increase quality. The sugar is quite expensive, you know—it costs nearly a franc a kilo. And there is tax to pay also. But there are two points here: fermentation must be active in the cuves, so the grapes must have sufficient sugar. And secondly alcohol is an essential support for flavour and especially for aroma. They have tried to make non-alcoholic wines, but, of course, they do not taste of wine. And a good crème de cassis must have eighteen or twenty degrees alcohol, not sixteen.

'But to go back to the wines of the past, I think that the style has not changed so much, at least in the good vintages. They had fewer technical resources for dealing with problems in bad years, especially grey rot, a fungus activated by moisture to which the thin-skinned Pinot Noir is particularly prone. So we make good wine more consistently now. But there is a danger now, in that more and more people study wine as if it were a science. Science is necessary, but wine is more than science. It is also the constantly changing moment, it involves experience and flair.'

I remembered Etienne Grivot saying that he considered his father had a remarkable artistic sensibility for wine, which might have been expressed through other media.

Jean Grivot smiled self-deprecatingly. 'I do like talking about wine with clients. And I am invited to speak at conferences. I have recently been to London to speak at a conference on Burgundy. Later this year I will be going to Belgium and Switzerland.

'My maternal grandfather Emile was one of the first members of the Confrérie du Tastevin—the organisation for the promotion of Burgundy wine which is based at the Château du Clos de Vougeot. My father was a Chevalier du Tastevin'—the word must be pronounced as if it had no 's', incidentally—'and I am now a Commandeur. I go to soirées at Clos de Vougeot and receive guests. I enjoy it, because I meet people who love wine. It is a kind of public relations organisation for Burgundy, I suppose.'

Does Burgundy need to open itself up more to the outside world?

'Burgundy is small. It should remain intimate. We are not the kind of people who wish to put everything out in the public square. We are also a conservative region. We must not refuse progress, but we are not here to overturn tradition. I am not in favour of revolutions.'

Another position which Jean Grivot holds is President of the Propriétaires of Clos de Vougeot. It is not a public relations position. They meet to discuss the control of quality, the quantity of the harvest, the surveillance of the vineyard. Occasionally, however, something different crops up. In 1987 they were approached by the producers of the Danish film *Babette's Feast* with an unusual request. In the climactic sequence of the film, based on a short story by Karen Blixen, a sumptuous French dinner is served to a group of people in a remote village of northern Jutland. It is a celebration of the centenary of the founder of the strict, self-denying religious sect to which they all belong. They view all kinds of luxury with mistrust, and wine as the work of the Devil. As the meal proceeds, however, they overcome their scruples and begin to enjoy the marvellous dishes set before them. In fact the magic of the culinary art (the meal is prepared by Babette, an émigrée Parisienne chef) and the fine wines serve to heal the rifts and bitternesses which have sprung up between them. The wine served with the main course of *caille en sarcophage* is a Clos de Vougeot 1915. The producers, showing a commendable spirit of fidelity to the text, insisted that the wine in the bottles captured on celluloid should be the genuine article. I asked Jean Grivot if he had enjoyed the film, which I consider one of the finest to have been made in Europe in the 1980s. 'It was a very beautiful, very pure film,' he agreed.

'And the vintage of Vougeot?'

'Ah, that I could not tell you.'

The film, I reflected, was a kind of post-Christian parable, showing the miraculous power of wine to transform people's lives, to touch the humdrum with glory. A parable apposite to Burgundy as well as to Jutland.

CHAMPAGNE

EXTRA CUVÉE   DE RÉSERVE

Pol Roger & Cᵒ

▲ EPERNAY   FRANCE

BRUT 1982

12 % vol. NM-276-001   ÉLABORÉ PAR POL ROGER & Cᵒ, EPERNAY, FRANCE   e 75 cl

Pol Roger

of

Epernay

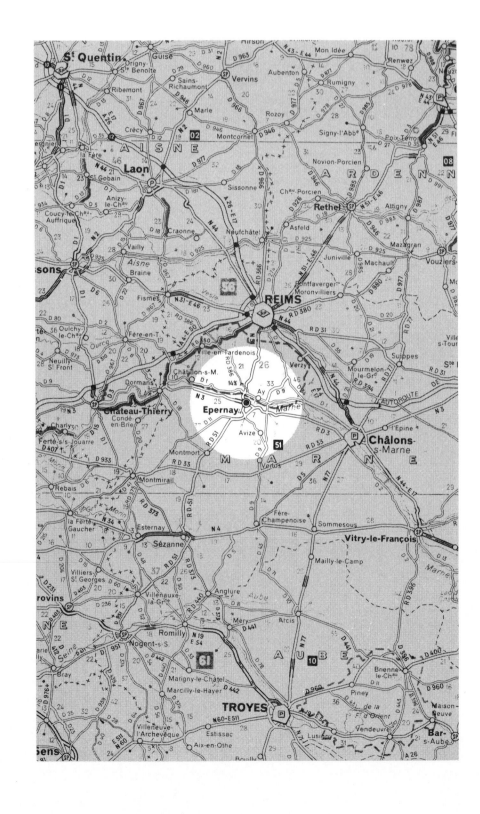

IT MAY SOUND ARROGANT to say so, but there is only one reason to visit Epernay, a small country town 30 kilometres south of Reims, 150 kilometres east of Paris: as Victor Hugo remarked, 'C'est la ville du Champagne. Rien de plus, rien de moins.' The grandest street is called—what else?—the avenue de Champagne: it is almost an architectural theme park, which has a good deal to tell the visitor about a wine which has always been more than simply wine. As you proceed down it from the town's central round-about, you come first, on the left, upon a Renaissance château, which would not look out of place in the Loire valley; further on, on the same side, is what looks like the orangerie of Versailles; and down by the river Marne is a campanile not so much from an Italian hill-town as from a Turner painting of an Italian hill-town. The Renaissance château is the Château Perrier, formerly headquarters of Perrier-Jouet, now the town library and museum of champagne (inexplicably run-down). The orangerie is a copy, built for Moët et Chandon by the Napoleonic miniaturist Isabey; and the campanile towers over a grimy brick ware-house belonging to de Castellane.

The message of this weird architectural display is that cham-pagne is the first wine of the age of advertising. Champagne names are brands, not vineyards, châteaux or grapes. The Bordeaux brand, Mouton Cadet, caused a scandal when Baron Philippe de Rothschild brought it out in the 1930s. By that time the great champagne firms had been selling brands for a hundred years and more. At least Baron Philippe didn't call his mass-produced wine Rothschild: presumably it would have been thought to cheapen the name of the great banking dynasty. Ironically enough, Alfred de Rothschild is a brand of cham-pagne, owned by the enormous and far from aristocatic Marne et Cham-pagne group. The champagne makers never had any qualms about giving their product their family name. And when Brian Croser, one of the most gifted wine-makers in Australia, came to produce a high-quality Australian sparkling wine in the champagne mould he proudly dubbed it Croser. 'Sounds better than Brian, I suppose,' was the com-ment of one wine-writing wit.

Champagne's affinity for advertising, and its associations of somewhat decadent high living (epitomised by the Bollinger Club of

Evelyn Waugh's *Decline and Fall*), have made it suspect to some purists and puritans. 'You're only paying for the bubbles and advertising; the wine itself is ordinary, indeed unpleasant.' How many times have I heard that said, usually by wine producers who are understandably envious of champagne's astonishing success and profitability. Whereas the majority of the world's wine-growers struggle to break even, or experience wild swings between popularity and neglect, the champagne families have grown rich—very, very rich—on the world's ever-growing thirst for champagne, and preparedness to pay for it two or three times the price of any other mass-produced wine.

I suspect, though, that most of the critics of *le champagne*, the wine, have not visited *la Champagne*, the region. For the idea—a tempting one, certainly—that champagne's success has more to do with skilful promotion of image than with true substance does not stand up to close examination of the way the wine is made.

You might expect the chairman of a great champagne house to resemble the head of any other large, prestigious corporation: smooth, dignified, a little self-satisfied, even pompous. That was what I was expecting, anyway. So when I stepped off the train at Epernay station at 9.30 on a late-September evening and found a short man in a blazer with thick glasses waiting to meet me I thought Pol Roger had sent a chauffeur. It was in fact Christian de Billy, a delightfully bubbly man with bright eyes and cox's orange pippin cheeks who is chairman and managing director of one of the last important family-owned firms in Champagne. He ushered me swiftly up the stairs and out of the station, passing a group of poorly dressed young people.

'Vous avez du boulot?' one of them asked as we went past.

'There are these funny-looking people around,' said Christian. 'We do not know if they are looking for work as pickers or what. But with unemployment so high, what can you expect?'

After dropping me off at the Hôtel des Berceaux, and not before we had shared half a bottle of Pol Roger White Foil (of which more later), Christian arranged to pick me up at 9 next morning. We would be visiting various grape-pressings. He himself had his first, literally pressing, appointment at 6.30 a.m. So much for the idea that chairmen of champagne houses sit at Louis XVI desks twiddling their thumbs.

A man of meticulous punctuality, Christian appeared shortly before the agreed time and we set off, bearing south-east, down the avenue de Champagne. Christian pointed out the Pol Roger headquarters as we drove past: characteristically understated (perhaps this is the quality which has always given Pol Roger its cachet in England, and made it the favourite wine of Winston Churchill), these are probably the least flashy on the avenue: a forecourt flanked by severe, yellow brick walls. Views opened up: to the north, wooded hills rose steeply from the far bank of the Marne. Eastwards the valley broadened: miles of dark-green fields growing maize and sunflowers, punctuated with the pale silver-green of poplars.

Just outside the town, some gypsy caravans had parked by the side of the road. I saw a small boy practising hand-stands. 'About 15,000 people come down from the north of France every year for the harvest, including a few gypsies,' Christian told me. 'The gypsies are very popular because you don't need to provide them with food and accommodation.' Here too a new housing estate was going up: the excavations had sent up masses of chalk dust, covering the verge and dusting several fields. This chalk is the greatest secret of champagne. The isolated range of hills called les Falaises de Champagne, on which nearly all the grapes used to make champagne are grown, is part of the same great system of chalk downs, formed of marine deposits, which runs across northern France, and across the Channel to include the South Downs. The Falaises, though, are made of a special kind of chalk called *Belimnita quadrata*, uniquely favourable to the cultivation of the vine. So all the experts say, at least: one of the proofs is that at certain points in the Falaises, *Belimnita* gives way to microcaster chalk, and there no vines grow. Even if a Champenois knows no other word of Latin, he will almost certainly be able to rattle off the name of the compacted mass of ancient sea organisms which gives him his livelihood.

Not only is *Belimnita quadrata* wonderful subsoil for vines, it is also perfectly suited to the construction of vast underground cellars, almost equally essential for the making of champagne. Some of those cellars, in Reims, are made out of old Gallo-Roman quarries, for, improbable though it may seem when you pick some up and can almost crumble it in your hand, this soft chalk makes an adequate building material.

The village of Oiry, where we attended our first pressing, is made entirely out of chalk, which gives it a slightly plastic, if not edible feel. Oiry is the easternmost village of the Côte des Blancs, a long hill running from Epernay about 20 kilometres south-south-east. Like several other villages on the Côte, and only seventeen villages in the whole of Champagne, it is a grand cru, the highest grade of appellation in the region. The way the CIVC, the powerful organising body of Champagne which classifies all the vineyards, puts it is that Oiry grapes are 100 per cent échelle: top price grapes, the touchstone for the others. The lowest-priced grapes (from outlying vineyards in the Aube, 130 kilometres from Epernay) are 80 per cent échelle: in other words they cost eight-tenths the price of grand cru grapes. These differentials have been greatly reduced in recent years.

The mainly east-facing slopes of the Côte des Blancs are planted with the white Chardonnay grape, which gives the most fragrant, delicate and, these days, the most highly prized wines of Champagne. Oiry stands in the plain a little way off from the hills; its flatter vineyards are planted with the black Pinot Noir and Pinot Meunier grapes.

We passed through a gateway into a sloping, cobbled courtyard, where plastic hampers of grapes were being unloaded from a tractor trailer. A strong-looking middle-aged man with a weather-lined, intelligent face was directing operations; he came over to greet us. 'This is Serge Martin, brother of our vineyard manager,' said Christian de Billy. 'One of the very best growers we buy from.'

Serge Martin is an example of the backbone of Champagne, the 15,000 or so small wine-growers who own the bulk of the land. The number of wine growers in Champagne, contrary to the trend in almost all other wine areas, has grown in the last twenty years. Champagne may seem like a place of big wealthy firms and families, but while they dominate the export markets, they own less than 20 per cent of the vineyards. Serge Martin, with 7-8 hectares, is an important grower. It is possible to make a living with two hectares. His whole operation gave out an air of efficiency and stout independence, also of continuity: some growers in Champagne have been tending their vineyards since the Middle Ages.

Serge Martin has been selling grapes, or rather grape-must, to Pol Roger for over twenty years. At one time, Christian de Billy would have been able to control the quality of the grapes by rejecting unsound bunches. The boot is now on the other foot. The big firms cannot afford to reject anything from growers such as M. Martin. It is a seller's market, particularly for Chardonnay grapes, which pay a special premium. At 23 fr/kg in 1988, these are among the most expensive grapes in the world. Christian's presence is, in a sense, unnecessary. But he still likes to attend as many pressings of the grapes he is buying as possible. 'We try to make sure that one of us is present at all the important pressings. This kind of public relations is immensely important.'

Serge Martin, a quiet, almost taciturn man, led us down the courtyard to the small, immaculately clean, covered press-house, next to the farm-house at the end. A circular press, like a section of a very wide barrel, was full of bunches of black Pinot grapes. Coming down very slowly on the bunches was a circular lid, fitting exactly over the press-basket, formerly operated by a screw, now by hydraulics. This type of pressing, peculiar to champagne, is about the most natural in use anywhere, except for the treading in the lagars of the Douro: it is also attractive to watch, because the grapes are not destemmed or crushed and turned into a muddy mash, as they are in most other forms of wine production. The reason for the persistence of this distinctly low-tech method is simple: three-quarters of champagne is made from black grapes (Pinot Noir and Pinot Meunier), which need to be pressed gently, and whose juice needs to be separated from the skins rapidly, to avoid extracting colour from the skins. The juice running off from the press, as the lid pressed further—almost imperceptibly slowly—was a pale pink colour; however, all the pink disappears during fermentation.

I tasted both grapes and juice: the grapes, contrary to what many people say about wine grapes, were good to eat, quite sweet yet well balanced with acidity. The must was full of flavour. I would have predicted a fine, well-balanced vintage. This, it turned out, was not as fanciful as it sounds. 'You can tell a lot about the quality of the wine from tasting the grapes,' Christian de Billy confirmed. Hopes for the 1988 vintage were quite high, though a light rain which began to fall as we stood in M. Martin's courtyard was not welcome. Despite the grapes' sweet taste, their sugar content and therefore potential alcohol were not particularly high: around 9 per cent. This is perfectly normal for champagne grapes. The eventual 12 per cent alcohol of champagne is achieved by chaptalisation, the addition of sugar to the fermenting must, and the additions of *liqueur de tirage* and *liqueur d'expédition*. The important thing, above all, with sparkling wines is to start the process from grapes which have a good level of acidity. That is what *Belimnita quadrata*, and the northerly position of Champagne, combine to achieve.

It was time to say goodbye to M. Martin and his two stout sons. As we left Christian asked one of them how the hunting had been. Hunting is the greatest love of the Champenois, apart from champagne, and a very effective social bond between different parts of the Champagne world. The son's eyes lit up: 'Three rabbits, two partridges and a hare—just round here in the vineyards.'

'Pas mal, pas mal du tout,' said Christian non-committally. 'A few years ago that would have been considered nothing at all,' he confided to me. 'The game has suffered a lot. Soon there won't be any left at all.' Was this the reflection of ecological disaster, the result of excessive use of pesticide and fertiliser, or the golden-age syndrome prevalent among hunters, fishermen, poets and others? Almost certainly both.

We drove back towards Epernay and then turned left. The long line of the Côte des Blancs, not very high (perhaps 600 ft above the plain) but imposing, rose up on the right. Christian took a side-road off to the right, leading steeply up to Cramant, the tiny village perched half-way up the hillside, between the woods and the vines, which produces the most super-fine, delicate Chardonnays in Champagne. The next, somewhat larger village, Avize, which also produces Chardonnay of the highest class, is, Christian told me, the richest village in France. You would not guess it, because like all the Champagne villages, Avize is solid, grey and dour, not in the least pretty. On the other hand the great view eastwards over the Marne valley, a vast flat plain stretching as far as the eye can see, makes prettiness redundant. There is something special about the light in Champagne, a slightly hazy yet intense whiteness: the Champenois say it comes from particles of *Belimnita quadrata* suspended in the atmosphere. On this September morning pickers were moving among the vines, bright-coloured blobs like flowers in an Impressionist painting.

We continued through two more grand cru villages, Oger (where Pol Roger buy grapes) and Le Mesnil-sur-Oger, before arriving at our destination of Vertus, near the southern end of the Côte des Blancs. Vertus is a premier cru, rather than a grand cru: its grapes are rated at 95 per cent, which still sounds pretty good. But the Co-operative La Goutte d'Or in Vertus is different from Serge Martin's family set-up in Oiry. The co-operative movement in Champagne is important, but, as usual with wine co-operatives, goes largely unnoticed outside the region. Only a small proportion of the wine grown by co-operative members, and pressed using co-operative facilities, is sold by the co-operatives themselves. Their main function is to provide pressing facilities for their members, who sell on to the big firms.

Quite a lot of champagne, on the other hand, is sold by individual co-operative members (who sound like a contradiction in terms) called *récoltants-manipulants*: they have over 40 per cent of the French market.

'Co-operatives vary a lot,' Christian de Billy told me. 'If the President is strong, doesn't drink too much, controls his troops well, it is fine.'

La Goutte d'Or is a streamlined modern operation: four large horizontal Vaslin presses, each holding 8000 kg, twice as much as a standard vertical champagne press, stand under a barn-like structure. All were fully loaded and revolving away when Christian and I arrived. We were greeted by a tall, grey-haired man in his sixties, with something of the look, and the authoritarian manner, of General de Gaulle. 'Bonjour M. le Président,' said Christian de Billy. Another typically strong-featured Champenois, perhaps in his early seventies, was introduced: 'Ah, M. l'ex-Président.'

We were invited in to the functional dining-room for *un verre* of the co-operative's own champagne. 'There are so many presidents,' Christian murmured. 'But we must drink some of their champagne. They'd be offended if we refused.' Predictably, a second and third verre followed the first: the co-operative champagne, 60 per cent Chardonnay, 40 per cent Pinots, was pleasant but rather light and short. The conversation, on the other hand, was prolonged and vigorous, illustrated, by both presidents, with emphatic gestures, and so fast and idiomatic that I caught only about half of it. The general problem, everyone agreed, was the greed of the growers: they all wanted to be paid 100 per cent prices wherever their grapes came from. In terms of indignant patronage of the workers, the Co-operative presidents had nothing to learn from old-style capitalism. 'When you go to the butcher,' the ex-President remarked, 'you don't pay the same price for a pig's trotter as for a fillet steak.' The current President, reminded of food by this pithy carnivorous analogy, and also by the rich odour of stewing meat coming through from the kitchen, went off at a tangent: 'You eat much better during the *vendange*, because they cook bigger bits of meat, with more flavour.'

The ex-President, not to be side-tracked, continued button-holing the Président-Directeur-General of Pol Roger: 'But you can't do anything about it, can you, M. de Billy? If you rely on growers for sixty per cent of your needs, you're at their mercy.'

'He's right, of course,' Christian told me when we had finally extricated ourselves, warding off the threat of another bottle; the current President had to go somewhere himself, and departed at high speed in a space-age Renault Alpine. 'But that's why this kind of public relations is so important: it shows that we are serious and care about quality.'

Pol Roger own 73 hectares of vineyards, concentrated largely in the Marne valley area around Epernay, with small holdings on the Côte des Blancs. These supply 40 per cent of the company's needs, a highish proportion by Champagne standards. The biggest champagne house, Moët et Chandon, for instance, own 459 hectares of vineyards; but these supply only 20 per cent of the grapes needed to fill the 25 million bottles Moët sell every year.

Pol Roger started to buy vineyards only in 1955, following scarce vintages in 1950 and 1953 which meant that demand suddenly started to outrun supply. This was by no means unusual: Krug, the most prestigious champagne house of all, owned no vineyards until 1970. 'My grandfather always said that we did not know much about growing grapes, but we knew how to buy the best grapes. Our real skill was in making and blending the wine.' Christian de Billy was referring to Maurice Pol Roger, one of the great characters in the history of champagne, of whom more later.

It was Maurice's father who founded the firm. Pol (this was his Christian name, a version of Paul more commonly found in Brittany) Roger was the son of a notary from the small town of Aÿ, famous as the headquarters of several great champagne houses: Bollinger, Deutz, Ayala, Gosset. Pol decided very young that he did not want to follow his father in the legal profession, and before he was twenty he had started a small private trade in champagne. He would have been using ready-made wine, blending and bottling it himself. His friends told him, or so legend has it, that he had a talent for champagne-making: Pol took their advice and set up Pol Roger et Cie in 1849 on the same premises, on the corner of the rue de Commerce and the rue Henri Lelarge, where the rather grander offices are today.

These were heady boom-time days in Champagne. Many of the great houses were founded around this time: Bollinger in 1829, Piper-Heidsieck in 1835, Pommery et Greno in 1836, Krug in 1843, Charles Heidsieck ('Champagne Charlie') in 1851, Mercier in 1858. Champagne had been a famous wine for at least a century and half: indeed, it was the favourite wine of Louis XIV, and its popularity was transferred to Restoration London through the agency of the Marquis de St Evremond. A few of the current champagne houses were established in the eighteenth century, Ruinart in 1729 and Moët in 1743, but it was the end of the Napoleonic Wars, and the establishment of peaceful relations between France, Britain and Russia, which laid the foundations for an export boom.

Pol Roger saw the possibilities for exporting his brand, especially to Great Britain, the country with which Pol Roger has been closely associated ever since, quite early on. The very first bottle Pol Roger ever exported went to Britain. In 1865 Pol Roger started an agency in England, run by a Mr Reuss. Pol Roger's agents in England are still Dent & Reuss, now part of the Bulmer's cider group.

Pol Roger does not seem to have been the kind of man who attracts stories or legends. On the other hand he must have been a businessman of great energy and ability, who built up in the space of his own lifetime a firm with an enviable reputation for quality and reliability, which it has never subsequently lost. He also made a good deal of money: apart from the imposing mansion in the rue Henri Lelarge built by him as a private house in 1889 in a rather pompous

Louis XIV style, there are three ample residences on the avenue de Champagne, all belonging to members of the Pol Roger family and all dating from the last years of the nineteenth century. Pol Roger died in 1899: his widow—one of the great line of champagne widows starting with Veuve Clicquot and including Mme Jacques Bollinger—ran the firm for a short time after his death, before handing it over to the elder of Pol's two sons, Maurice. Realising that the founder's Christian name had become an inseparable part of the champagne brand (and thinking perhaps that Roger on its own was somewhat unmemorable) the family changed its name by decree (not nearly such an easy business as the English deed-poll system) to Pol-Roger. Maurice Pol-Roger was apparently the more outgoing of the two brothers, better equipped as a salesman: he was a tall, imposing man, an excellent shot and dedicated *chasseur*. His younger brother George was more the technician: a respected taster, he was always on the premises to deal with production matters. Maurice himself was far from always on the premises: he was celebrated for a routine which, from October to March at least, went as follows: 7.30: arrive in the office, already dressed in hunting clothes; deal with paper work until 9.00; 9.00, arrival of chauffeur to take Maurice shooting; from 9.30 to 4.30, shooting, in the woods around Epernay and the Montagne de Reims; 5.00: return to the office to sign papers; between 6 and 6.30, on to the British Club to play bridge before dining at 7.45. People in Champagne found it difficult to understand how Maurice managed to combine this *modus operandi* with the very successful running of a champagne house, the reputation of which went from strength to strength in the early years of this century, despite a disastrous collapse of the cellars in 1900, in which 500 casks and over a million bottles were destroyed. As for Maurice's own skill as a shot, a painting on the brown suede-lined wall of Christian de Billy's office records the shooting of his 500th wild boar, on 16 January 1947, in his seventy-eighth year. He shot four boar on that January day, and went on to shoot another twenty before becoming bed-ridden for his last ten years.

There was one period of Maurice's life dominated by more serious matters than business or even boar-shooting. At the outbreak of the First World War in August 1914 Maurice Pol-Roger was Mayor of Epernay. The short period of German occupation from 4 to 11 September was to be both Maurice's finest hour and the source of a grievance which remained with him until he died. Fortunately, M. Pol-Roger wrote a detailed account of those days, which is not only a fascinating historical document but also a narrative of considerable literary merit.

The real drama began on 3 September. The Mayor discovered

that the Municipal Receiver of Monies had gone off with his till, leaving the municipality with no funds to pay urgently needed war allowances, hospital expenses and so on. He called an immediate council meeting, which resulted in two measures: an official protest to the Sous-Préfet about the abandonment of the town by the administration and the premature closing of the public till, and the decision that the town would issue 100,000 francs of its own notes to cover emergencies. After the war Maurice Pol-Roger always liked to say that even the Rothschilds never financed an entire town.

On the following day the Germans arrived in Epernay. Such was their confidence, wrote Pol-Roger, that General von Plattenberg drew up in the main square in an armoured car with only two soldiers in attendance. His greeting to the mayor was peremptory: 'You will answer, Mayor, for the maintenance of law and order in the town.'

'What with, General?' inquired the Mayor. 'My police commissioner has left, taking all his policemen with him.'

'Well, Mayor, if your police commissioner has left, so much the worse for you. You will answer for the maintenance of order on your own head.'

Pol-Roger never forgave police commissioner Boineau for, as he saw it, deserting his post. He dismissed him in his absence, an action technically outside his remit which had momentous consequences. Meanwhile, Pol-Roger had to bear the brunt of a series of measures which showed the Germans at their least likeable. An hour after General von Plattenberg's arrival, a huge requisition order was drawn up, demanding 120,000 kg of oats, 21,000 kg of bread, 500 kg of coffee and other commodities by the same evening. By a minor miracle, Pol-Roger and a team of bakers, butchers and others managed to assemble everything bar 10,000 kg of salted lard. The Germans slapped on a massive fine of 176,000 francs. Immediately afterwards, a furious German guard commandant threatened to hang the mayor on the spot for switching off the water and gas supplies. He had broken into a boarded-up house and found the water and gas meters switched off, as a precaution. Pol-Roger was able to reassure him that the town supplies were still in operation, and saved his neck.

That same evening, following a dinner at the town hall, the Mayor, his deputy and two councillors were taken hostage. Released for a short time next day (in order to arrange for the electricity supply to be reconnected) Pol-Roger managed to get hold of a tin of tuna and another of crab. The dinner that night in the town hall was a melancholy affair.

A couple of days later, a German soldier was taken to hospital with a bullet wound in his leg, claiming he had been shot by a Frenchman. Once again the Mayor was threatened with death if the culprit were not found. Preserving sang-froid, the very British quality for which he was later publicly praised, Pol-Roger found witnesses and established that the wound had been self-inflicted. Neck saved again.

Not for long, though. At 6 p.m. on 8 September, the Mayor was brought before two officers who accused him of having replaced the German flag at the station with a French one. Almost lost for an argument, the Mayor came up with an ingenious line: French railways were private companies and not directly dependent on the State. The flags they hung at their stations were their own affair. All the same, the German officers threatened to raze Epernay to the ground if a German flag were not hung by 6.30 next morning. Madame Debone, the town hall concierge, came to the rescue with an old black apron: her daughter sewed it into the semblance of a flag, and the Mayor, 'death in his soul', as he wrote, went up to the first floor and hung it from the flagpole. 'I personally nailed the window so that nobody could touch it,' he recalls in his war memoir. 'That is certainly the most disturbing and painful memory I have of that terrible war; and it will remain, until my dying day, a melancholy obsession.'

That was the nadir of the grim days of Occupation. Elsewhere, on the Marne, the fortunes of war were turning. On 9 September the requisition fine, assembled from private donations, was returned; on 11 September the French, unopposed, retook Epernay.

On 16 September, the town council met for the first time after the liberation. The Mayor paid tribute to his loyal colleagues. The members of the council returned the compliment with a public expression of praise for the immense services rendered to the town by the 'courage, intelligent firmness and sang-froid' of Maurice Pol-Roger. The next day an even more distinctive tribute was organised: a Livre d'Or, which was to be signed by every citizen present in Epernay during the Occupation and presented to the Mayor. The signatures were gathered with great speed: on 20 September the presentation ceremony took place. Maurice Pol-Roger was, he writes, 'overcome by profound emotion. A mayor could not hope for a finer or higher recompense. This is for me a magnificent testimony of recognition which I can bequeath with the most legitimate pride to my family and descendants.' In the event the Livre d'Or, a unique honour, apparently, in French municipal annals, had to make up for a lack of recognition from other, official quarters.

In the meantime, though, the Mayor's thoughts turned towards the vintage. With so many men mobilised, and severe shortages of food and money, it posed great problems. Maurice Pol-Roger solved them by advancing his suppliers a loan of 25 francs per barrel delivered (remember that at this stage Pol Roger owned no vineyards) to cover living expenses. In the end 4000 barrels of made wine were delivered to the Pol-Roger cellars. It is known that twenty children died during the 1914 harvest; the number of adults killed is not recorded. The Director of the Champagne research laboratory stated in his report: 'I should add that the grapes of 1914, ripened and gathered to the sound of cannon, will give an excellent wine.' He was proved right: the fine wine of 1914 is still served at very special occasions throughout Champagne. In late autumn 1914, British champagne drinkers celebrated the victory of the Marne with a veritable cannonade of champagne corks: exports to Great Britain more than doubled from 48,885 gallons in 1913 to 100,881 gallons in 1914.

At the beginning of 1915, though, the row between the Mayor and the Préfet of the Marne, which had been dormant since the start of the war, erupted. On 23 January Maurice Pol-Roger received a letter from the Sous-Préfet demanding the reinstatement of police commissioner Boineau, whom he had dismissed illegally, and the repayment of 300 francs of allowances to two headmasters, which the Mayor had docked on the grounds that they had deserted their schools at the start of hostilities. Pol-Roger called a council meeting: he reiterated his view that, since he had been left on his own in Epernay with no legal or administrative assistance, he had been forced to take exceptional measures; he also gave a list of functionaries who displayed enough of the 'sang-froid et zèle patriotique' required of them by the government not to desert their posts. This, not surprisingly, did not go down well with the Préfet of the Marne, who had left his headquarters at Chalons on 3 September. The Préfet wrote to the Mayor on 3 March suggesting that their dispute should become a private matter; he added that in leaving his post he had simply been obeying military orders. Pol-Roger, in his reply of 11 March, vigorously refuted this: the dispute was not between M. Pol-Roger and M. Chapron but between the Mayor of Epernay and the Préfet of the Marne. He accused the Préfet of 'systematic disorganisation of his department's services' and of 'causing panic among the town functionaries'. He also said that as far as he knew no orders had been given by military authorities for functionaries to leave their posts.

Accused of cowardice and of lying, M. Chapron demanded immediate retraction of the letter. Pol-Roger stuck by his guns. So it was that on the morning of 17 March, in the park of the Château de Saran, the Mayor and the Préfet fought a duel 'unique in the annals of the Great War', according to the historian Louis le Page. The meticulous detail of the minute of proceedings, drawn up while infantrymen were dying 20 kilometres away, has a surreal quality: 'Combat swords with town gloves without gauntlets; unstarched shirts; omission of braces; footwear as desired.' Fortunately the duel was not a particularly sanguinary affair: it ended during the second reprise when the Mayor received a wound in the right wrist.

It did not really settle the matter, however. Three years later Pol-Roger resigned as Mayor when his proposal to pay a bonus to functionaries who had stayed at their posts was deferred by the town council. Thus it was that he did not receive the Légion d'honneur, which was awarded at the end of the war to his assistant Jacquet. The town of Epernay also suffered as a result of the rift betwen Mayor and Préfet: unlike the two neighbouring towns of Châlons-sur-Marne and Château-Thierry, it was not nominated for the Order of the Army. Only some sixteen months after the end of the war was redress made when Epernay was awarded the Croix de Guerre.

In fact, Epernay's greatest trial took place in July 1918, when the town found itself caught up in Ludendorff's offensive, the last great spasm of the war. It suffered heavy bombardment for the best part of two months. Most of the war-toll of nearly 300 killed, 400 injured and 1800 houses destroyed was incurred at that time. On the night of 20 July, Maurice Pol-Roger was very nearly killed in his house on the rue de Commerce when a shell exploded a few yards away, in the courtyard. He suffered severe shock, and it was four months before he had fully recovered. Later, he planted a fruit-tree in the crater left by the shell, one of the last to fall on Epernay.

The word Churchillian does not seem inappropriate for Maurice Pol-Roger. On a provincial rather than a world stage, he was the man for the moment, who focused the resolve and courage of his fellow citizens. His character, described as 'perhaps too authoritarian for peace-time', was of just the mettle for a crisis.

There is another Churchillian connection of a different kind. From his early days, Churchill, whose favourite wine was champagne, had a favourite brand, Pol Roger. On 13 November 1944, invited to lunch at the British Embassy in Paris by Lady Diana Cooper, Churchill found himself sitting next to a beautiful woman in her early thirties. She was Odette Pol-Roger, one of the much-admired Wallace sisters who was married to Maurice's son Jacques. They formed a friendship which lasted until Churchill's death in 1965.

Odette Pol-Roger is now in her late seventies, still a handsome, graceful woman who combines great style with ease of manner. When I visited her in her home on the avenue de Champagne, which shares many of her own qualities ('I like the informality of English houses—a comfortable old sofa next to a Chippendale bookcase'), she was happy to talk about Churchill but regretted not having made a record of her conversations with him.

'All I remember are silly, personal things, stories, anecdotes. What struck me about him was his immense goodness and great sensitivity—and a marvellous sense of humour, of course. I remember having dinner at the French Embassy in London, and sitting next to Winston, with León Blum, the French socialist leader, sitting opposite—this was after Winston had lost the election in '45. Winston took a second helping and said to Blum, who was a very intelligent man, "I'm getting thinner, because since the Socialists won the election there's nothing to eat in Britain." He was pulling Blum's leg, of course.

'Whenever I was London I saw Winston. Once I was staying at the Ritz, and the receptionist called me and said, "There's a call for you." I was a little surprised, but even more surprised when he said, "The Prime Minister wants to speak to you." It was after the '51 election. And Winston said, "Do you want to come and see your horse run at Brighton?" He had named a horse after me, Odette Pol-Roger. So I went to Downing Street, we had a bottle of Pol Roger '34 (not my favourite vintage), and drove in his official car to the station. On the way people waved and said "Good luck, Winnie!" I was very intimidated. I had a lovely time in Brighton but the horse didn't win. It came fifth. It didn't win very often.

'Another time I was having lunch with him at Hyde Park Gate, and he said, "What are you doing this afternoon?" I said I was going shopping. So he lent me his car. And you can imagine, this Rolls-Royce with Lord of the Cinque Ports written all over—c'etait une voiture terrible. I remember we dropped him off at the little entrance of the House of Commons—it was winter, he was wearing an overcoat, and he stood there at the door with his hat in his hand until the car was out of sight. He had such wonderful manners. I got the chauffeur to drop me at Lillywhites and then said, "Allez-vous-en."

'The last time I saw him was in December 1964. Anthony Montague Brown, his private secretary, showed me in and said, "It's Odette Pol-Roger, you remember, the champagne you like so much." He just muttered. When I left I heard him say to Anthony Montague Brown, "You must remind me about the champagne." I was so sad to see him in that state that when I left the house I stood on the pavement and cried. There was a policeman on the door who said, "What's the matter with you?"

'Unfortunately he never came to see us in Epernay. He used to say, "Invite me during the vintage, and I'll press the grapes with my feet. I have lovely feet." We should have given him a specific date.'

A black-framed photograph of Winston Churchill, signed and dated 1946, stands on a side-table in Odette Pol-Roger's drawing-room. She also has a complete set of the *War Memoirs*, in French, inscribed to his dear friend Odette Pol-Roger. After Churchill's death, a black border appeared on the label of every bottle of Pol Roger destined for the British market. The Churchill link is assiduously maintained: when Pol Roger came to bring out a cuvée de prestige champagne, equivalent to Moët's Dom Perignon or Roederer's Cristal, they called it Cuvée Sir Winston Churchill. A firm, full wine, not released until it is nearly 10 years old, it is, they say, the kind of wine Churchill would have liked. It is certainly, in the opinion of most experts and this writer, one of the relatively few cuvées de prestige which is worth its price. After the terrible storm of 17 October 1987, Christian de Billy went over to Chartwell, the Churchill home in Kent, to present a cheque to help pay for the replanting of trees.

Odette Pol-Roger also makes the connection between her father-in-law, Maurice, and Churchill. 'Maurice was very good as a father-in-law, but too authoritarian as a father, rather like Winston with Randolph. They both crushed their sons a little. And my husband, who was very intelligent, had too little chance to show his initiative.'

When the Second World War broke out, Maurice Pol-Roger showed the same fighting spirit as before. He was the first person to offer himself as a hostage to the German occupation forces. At the same time, he managed to donate 400,000 francs to the Résistance. When the war was over, the head of the Maquis gave him a Sten gun. 'My father-in-law was delighted,' Odette recalls. 'He hung it against a magnificent seventeenth-century tapestry.'

Maurice Pol-Roger died in 1959 aged ninety. His son Jacques died young; he and Odette had no children. The firm was run for a time by Guy and Jean Pol-Roger, the two sons of Georges, Maurice's younger brother. Guy, however, a man of great ability, died of cancer in 1956. Jean became chairman; but he was a man in the mould of his father Georges, a dedicated technician, not a salesman or communicator by nature.

Christian de Billy, the current chairman and managing director, is the son of Maurice's daughter Antoinette, who married Alfonse de Billy, an officer in the air force who was a member of the famous Cicogne squadron in the First World War. 'From quite a young age I knew I would be working for the company. If Odette and Jacques had had children, things might have turned out differently—unless their children had decided to do something else. I always liked Champagne, and champagne, anyway: although I was educated in Paris, I always spent part of the holidays here. Quite honestly, I never thought of doing anything else.

'I started pretty young, in 1950 when I was twenty, working in the office, doing everything and nothing. Then after business school I went to England to learn English—I worked for our agents Ben and Tony Reuss. English is very important for us—our two biggest markets are Great Britain and the United States. We speak English on the telephone every day here—a day without English would be a day without sun!

'After England I went to Madrid, to learn Spanish. My grand-father Maurice thought it would be a good idea: he had high hopes for the South American market, Argentina, Venezuela.

'When I returned from Spain, I worked here in the cellars for a year. I did everything, *remuage* (riddling), disgorging and so on. It might have been interesting to do that as a *stage* in another house, but my grandfather said, 'Do it at Pol Roger.' I travelled a good deal after that—five months in the States in '53, a big trip to Brazil, Venezuela and the States again just before I got married in '55.'

Christian de Billy married into another champagne dynasty: his wife Chantal is the daughter of Louis Budin, former chairman of Per-rier-Jouet, which was subsequently run by her brother Michel. The de Billys are warm and hospitable people; despite its size and rather gloomy architecture (gingerbread Gothic), their house on the avenue de Champagne manages to be a comfortable and welcoming place. Chantal collects porcelain and silver tastevins, and Christian has a formidable array of hunting trophies, vast stags' antlers and eighty wild boar figurines. 'My wife and I love entertaining,' says Christian de Billy, and visitors are assured of excellent, but not over-elaborate food at their table. The wine will most probably be Pol Roger White Foil, the stand-ard, but fresh and reliable non-vintage house champagne. The de Billys are essentially modest, unpretentious people.

The atmosphere at the house just along the road belonging to Christian Pol-Roger (son of Guy, second cousin of Christian de Billy) and his wife Danielle is rather different. The drawing-room walls have a striking Bargello tapestry covering: the dining-room walls are lined with turquoise cloth. Christian and Danielle aim for a certain style, more chic than the English comfortableness of the de Billys, and they bring it off with panache and without affectation. The champagne before lunch was the rare, and magnificently full-flavoured PR Réserve Spéciale '82; the red wine was Château Lafite, the 1969, ethereal and a little consumptive, followed by the 1962, firm and surprisingly power-ful. Christian Pol-Roger collects vintage cars: a Pol Roger promotional video features the younger Christian driving round the vineyards of the Côte des Blancs in a 1940s Citroën.

The two Christians remind one of a comedy double-act: Chris-tian de Billy small, bubbly, with a twinkle in his eye belying the essential seriousness of a man dedicated to the métier of champagne; Christian Pol-Roger taller, debonair, with an infectious charm and a wit that can be mocking and irreverent, occasionally at his cousin's expense.

It is a double-act which works, and which both Christians work deceptively hard to sustain. Of all the champagne houses, Pol Roger seems the most quietly sure of itself. The line laid down by the founder has been pursued without deviation. Scale - annual sales of round 1.3 million bottles—remains human, not too large, not too small. There are no plans for expansion. In terms of reputation, Pol Roger may not have quite the brilliance of Roederer or the chic of Taittinger, but no house has a more firmly established identity. It is seldom that one hears a complaint about a bottle of Pol Roger.

Pol Roger's identity is based on tight family control. The com-pany is entirely family-owned, apart from an insignificant 2 per cent on the Nancy stock exchange; and Christian de Billy, in this case *primus inter Christianos*, together with his wife and four children, owns 57 per cent of the shares. As he says, family control is assured for at least another generation. Such stability is a rarity in Champagne these days. The last few years have seen a succession of mergers, swallowings and disgorgings among the champagne houses: there is now a monster group consisting of Moët et Chandon (by far the largest champagne house by itself), Mercier, Ruinart, Veuve Clicquot and Henriot. Sea-grams, the Canadian liquor company, own three houses: Mumm, Per-rier-Jouet and Heidsieck Monopole. Even Krug, the most prestigious of all the houses, is owned by the Rémy Martin cognac company.

'We are asked two or three times a year to sell the company,' says de Billy. 'But what would I do with all that money?' He makes a gesture of a substantial pile, which his share must certainly represent. 'Buy a Rolls-Royce or a yacht, live in the south of France? But I enjoy this work.'

This is not something one could doubt after spending more than a few minutes in his company.

'We are quite small—I am not ashamed to say we are small—compared to Moët et Chandon or Seagrams. My feeling is that if we stick to quality, and if we work on the image of a family firm, and on personal contact with customers, we can survive. It's not that easy, because we work mainly with our own money; we use banks, of course, to pay growers during the vintage, but not too much. You must not put yourself in the hands of banks.

'The personal touch is the most important thing. You must always be free to see people. We have over a thousand visitors a year—in my grandfather's time it was probably only a tenth of that number. It means a lot of work: I would like to do more shooting—and not only shooting, travelling also. To give you an example, this year we will be taking a stand at Vinexpo in Bordeaux (the world's biggest wine fair). We will be there from the first day to the last, 9 a.m. to 6.30 p.m., and it will not be possible for anyone to come to the Pol Roger stand and not see either Christian or myself. You could put a nice young man, or a pretty girl, or a girl who is very nice also, on the stand, but it is not the same thing. We do not employ people to do our public relations for us, we do it ourselves.'

Christian de Billy combines his busy, but rewarding life at Pol Roger with the important job of Président d'Information et d'Acceuil for champagne's governing body, perhaps the most powerful and effective in wine, the CIVC. 'I have been doing this job for nine years, for too long frankly. I would like to leave, but they will not let me. There are two qualifications for the job: you must be liked, first, and you must be sure not to use the position to promote your own company. Whenever I give a speech for the CIVC, especially in front of wine-growers, I always squeeze quality into it, pour enforcer le clou.'

Quality comes first from the vineyards, and we have seen how Christian de Billy does his best to ensure that quality is maintained by attending pressings and talking to the growers. On the other hand, it is the work in the cellars which transforms the raw material of a rather thin and acid wine into the magical product with its bubbles and its foil and that most important, but least definable, of qualities, the house style.

Pol Roger's cellars are situated on the avenue de Champagne. From the forecourt, you enter a long hall, used for tastings: in front of you, up a few steps, is a large double door, with a gleaming brass plaque above it saying 'Cellier Sir Winston Churchill'. Through the door is a series of halls which resemble the engine room of a beautifully maintained old-fashioned steam-ship. They are filled with line upon line of yellow-painted fermentation tanks. 'The unfermented grape-must is brought here by tanker, and fermentation takes place at a controlled temperature, about 20°C. Of course, it is not as romantic as the old barrels, but it works well.'

Just a few houses, notably Bollinger and Krug, still use barrels for fermentation. It gives a distinctively full-bodied richness to the wine.

'Our style has certainly become lighter over the years. It is not just a question of temperature-controlled fermentation in tank, but also of a higher percentage of Chardonnay. Now that people travel more, and drive a lot, their taste has altered slightly; we could see that was the way things were going, and we adapted our style—it was not exactly a case of following fashion,' Christian de Billy maintains.

After the first fermentation, Pol Roger, like most houses—Lanson and Piper-Heidsieck are notable exceptions—make sure that the wine goes through the malo-lactic fermentation, which makes it softer and rounder.

If the ground floor resembles a ship's engine-room, below ground the atmosphere changes to that of a vast set of catacombs, with black-gleaming bottles instead of skulls lining the walls. Pol Roger's cellars, dug deep into the tractable *Belimnita* chalk, are some of the deepest and coolest in Champagne. There are two levels: the lower, consisting of nine linked galleries, is 34 metres below ground level, where the temperature is about 9.8°C, more than 2 degrees cooler than many champagne cellars, all year round. Here nearly 6 million bottles, representing more than four years' stock, sit, quietly undergoing the second fermentation or *prise de mousse* (taking on of the bubble is the literal translation), which is induced by a dose of wine, sugar and yeast, called the liqueur de tirage, added at bottling. The more slowly this process goes, the finer and more constant are the eventual bubbles. Pol Roger has always been known for the finesse and persistence of its mousse.

These endless, echoing corridors are immensely eerie. Hanging electric wires, coated in a fur of fungus, cast weird shadows like cave-paintings on the damply glistening walls. Sometimes, when the level of the Marne rises, a few inches of water cover the floors and the cellar-workers must wear gumboots.

The job of *remueur*, or riddler—the person who has to twist the bottles on their wooden stands (called *pupitres*), so that the sediment formed by the second fermentation is shifted into the neck of the bottle—is not one I have ever fancied. In fact I have always considered it a job unfit for human beings. 'Do not worry about our remueurs, they earn good money, you know—12,000 francs a month. I will introduce you to them,' said Christian de Billy.

Bernard Gay, one of Pol Roger's four full-time remueurs (the company will not have anything to do with the automatic systems now becoming more popular), confounded my preconceptions. 'I do like the peace and quiet down here. Sometimes I listen to the radio, and occasionally my mind wanders.' Bernard gave a demonstration of his art, twisting the bottles in pairs, separated by a couple of rows, with delicate, gliding dexterity. A practised remueur can turn 50,000 bottles a day. I was reminded of Bruno Hoffman, virtuoso of that strange instrument, the glass harmonica. When I mentioned this to Monsieur Gay, he revealed that he was a musician himself. 'I used to play trumpet in a variety band—we did gigs every weekend. I don't play so much these days.' Bernard Gay, who looks no more than thirty-five himself, has been working in the Pol Roger cellars for thirty-four years. 'I started at fourteen, and I am now forty-five. In another six years I will be able to retire.'

Guy Baudouin is in his fifties, a powerful-looking man with a black beard. He was more reserved than M. Gay, serious and unsmiling. Christian de Billy greeted him with respect. After we had moved on, he told me, 'Monsieur Baudouin is the union leader. A very good man, very strong, but he sometimes fights with Monsieur Coffinet and can be a bit naughty.'

Monsieur James Coffinet—despite the English Christian name he is a Champenois born and bred—is in many ways the most important man at Pol Roger. He is the *chef de cave*, who makes all the important wine-making decisions. Monsieur Coffinet, red-haired with a goatee beard, has the air of a research chemist—fastidious, meticulous, not a man to suffer fools gladly. When I visited him in his laboratory, he was busy taking in and recording the samples of must being delivered from growers to the cellars. According to myth, the laboratories of the new scientific wine-makers of Champagne are clinically clean. I was reassured to see a half-eaten baguette and a hunk of *saucisson* sitting on one of the benches. 'Yes, our customers like fresher wines,' M. Coffinet confirmed, 'so fermentation in cask is not a good idea. And the malo-lactic is greatly preferable to de-acidification afterwards.' If I had no more questions, the look in M. Coffinet's eyes said, he would appreciate being allowed to get on with his work.

There is one decision though, which M. Coffinet does not take, and that is perhaps the most important one of all. The assemblage or making up of the blend is done only by members of the family: at present, by Jean Pol-Roger, the two Christians and Christian de Billy's son Hubert. The Pol Roger assemblage has been called an 'assemblage de coeur'. More practically, it is done in one morning, from 9 a.m. until 1 p.m.

The assemblage is the ultimate secret in champagne. One

would not expect the head of a champagne house to give everything, or indeed very much, away. But on two controversial points Christian de Billy is surprisingly, refreshingly open. 'There are two non-U subjects in Champagne: Pinot Meunier and the *tailles*. Pinot Meunier (literally floury Pinot, a relation of Pinot Noir, and also a black grape) is the unfashionable grape in Champagne—everyone wants Chardonnay, and to a lesser extent Pinot Noir. Certainly Pinot Meunier on its own makes undistinguished wine, wine which lacks finesse. But Pinot Meunier contributes a lot, especially to younger wines—it brings the flavour forward in the mouth. We are not ashamed to say we use it, always in the non-vintage champagne, seldom in the vintage; we also own Pinot Meunier vineyards. And if anyone tells you they don't use Pinot Meunier, you have my permission to laugh. After all, Pinot Meunier covers 42 per cent of the champagne vineyard. If they don't use it, where does it go?

'As for the tailles [the second and third pressings, which contribute just over 600 of the 2666 litres allowed to be obtained from 4000 kg of grapes], the premiere taille of Chardonnay is, if not better, just as good as the cuvée [first pressing]. We use the first and, sometimes, the second taille of Chardonnay. We do not use the second taille of Pinot, which tastes harsh.'

The assemblages made by the Pol Roger family result in a range of champagnes with different qualities but a family trait of unexaggerated elegance. They are not as full bodied and powerful as Krug or Bollinger, not as light and super-fine as Taittinger's Blanc de Blancs or Moët et Chandon's Dom Perignon, but at their best, as in the '82 vintage, the '79 Chardonnay (buttery and mature) and Cuvée Sir Winston Churchill and above all the '82 PR Special Reserve, they achieve a perfect balance of power and finesse.

The only complaint one could make about these wines, and it seems a churlish one, is that they are rather expensive—though not by champagne standards. Do rising prices worry Christian de Billy, and his son Hubert, now working on the export side, when they look forward to the future?

'At the moment the future of champagne is a bright one. Sales are rising, by 9 per cent last year, and you British are setting the pace.' Exports to Britain, once again firmly established as the leading export market for champagne, reached 20 million bottles in 1988, 6 million more than our nearest rivals, the United States. The success story of champagne seems almost miraculous.

'No, I don't find it surprising,' comments Hubert, a well-built young man in his twenties who already radiates certainty and confidence. 'The price of champagne has been going down in real terms, and quality and image remain high. If Hermès ties suddenly halved in price, everyone would buy them.'

'All over the world there is a big demand for sparkling wine,' his father points out, from Spain, from California, from Australia, even from Russia. As people have more money, and their standard of living increases, they will start on sparkling wine, because the bubbles are always an attraction, and do good to the health and the spirit. And as they have more money, they will go up from ordinary bubbles to champagne bubbles. Then from cheaper champagne bubbles to *grande marque* bubbles.

'Champagne is unquestionably number one among sparkling wines. In order to stay number one, quality must be maintained. If we stick to quality, I think we will remain on top. The word champagne has so much magic. But in order to stay magic we must work. It must not be a magic image alone, there must be substance behind the image.'

SCHLOSS VOLLRADS

Rheingau · Riesling
1988er Kabinett
blausilber
Qualitätswein mit Prädikat

Weingut
Schloss Vollrads
D-6227
Oestrich-Winkel
Rheingau
9,5% vol

Erzeugerabfüllung
Graf Matuschka-
Greiffenclau
A. P. Nr.
27074 020 89
e 750 ml

Matuschka-Greiffenclau
of
Schloss Vollrads

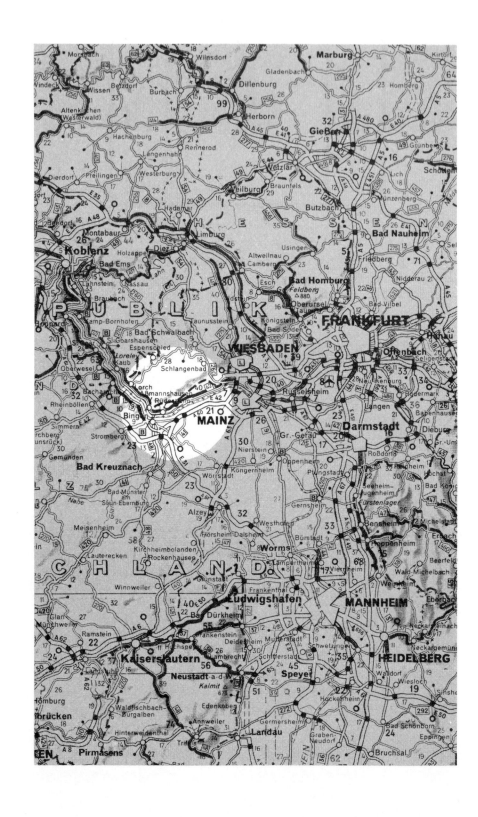

THE REPUTATION OF GERMAN WINE outside Germany is probably at its lowest for five hundred years. Ask a wine drinker, especially one who wishes to appear sophisticated, what he or she thinks of German wine and you are likely to receive a dusty answer. 'You mean that sugary Liebfraumilch rubbish?' Of course, Liebfraumilch (mass-produced German blended wine) has its followers, millions of them in the UK alone, where it remains the best-selling type of wine, but it is thought of as a beginner's wine: fruity, light, slightly sweet, quite refreshing, lowish in alcohol, but without the challenging, individual character which marks out fine wine, and not least fine German wine.

The success of Liebfraumilch has more or less blinded people in the UK and the other traditional markets for fine German wine to the existence of the great German tradition of quality wine: meticulously made vintages from single vineyard sites (often many different levels of quality from a single site), recognised by authorities from Hugh Johnson to Jancis Robinson as some of the world's finest and most delicately satisfying wines. They are largely ignored by the new wave of wine drinkers who prefer Australian Chardonnay to Riesling from the Mosel-Saar-Ruwer.

This disastrous decline in reputation is a post-war phenomenon, and has as much to do with new technology and marketing decisions as with Hitler and the Third Reich. After the First World War, when anti-German feeling was particularly virulent, the reputation and prices of German wines remained strong. They were, after all, firmly established as the world's greatest white wines—the white equivalent of the great red Bordeaux—as they had been for a hundred years and more. In the late seventeenth and early eighteenth centuries the Rhine and Mosel wine-growers, together with those of Bordeaux, were at the forefront of the new movement towards high-quality, specialised, bottled-wine production. In the London auction catalogues and wine lists of the nineteenth century, the top hocks (Rhine wines) such as Marcobrunner and Johannisberger concede little or nothing to the top growths of Bordeaux, Lafite, Margaux and the rest. At a Christie's auction in May 1877, for instance, Steinberger 1857 (from one of the greatest vineyards of the Rhine—and twenty years old) sold for the same price, 90s a dozen, as the celebrated 1865 vintage of Château Lafite. Schloss Johannisberger 1862 was 40s a dozen dearer. On the lists of Hedges & Butler and Berry Bros & Rudd, two leading London merchants, from 1893 to 1896, the best Rhine wines are, on average, 20 per cent more expensive and two to three years older than the top red Bordeauxs.

After the Second World War, however, drinking habits in Germany changed: wine was drunk increasingly on its own, either at the beginning or end of a meal, rather than with food. Taste changed also: some say that the sweet bottled and canned drinks, such as Coca-Cola, favoured by American GIs, created a taste for sweet wines. Sophisticated technology (stopping the fermentation before the conversion of all the sugar, and the use of unfermented grape juice, called Sussreserve) made it possible to produce clean, stable wine with a considerable degree of sweetness in every year. Previously, most German wine would not have been sweet at all, but fermented out to dryness, or semi-dryness; only in exceptional years, when the grapes were harvested so ripe that not all the sugar could be converted to alcohol, would significant amounts of sweet wine (*Auslese*) be produced. A market was found for the new, rather bland, clean, fresh, slightly sweet wine, and the name Liebfraumilch filched from a small vineyard around the Liebfrauenstiftskirche in the cathedral city of Worms. Walter Sichel of Mainz invented the bizarre symbol of the blue nun and what was to become the world's most successful branded wine was born. Vineyards were planted in flatter parts of the Rheinhessen, Rheinpfalz and Nahe where previously potatoes had grown. New grape varieties were crossed, able to ripen earlier and to produce higher yields, all at the expense of quality.

No doubt Liebfraumilch had its uses in the rebuilding of the shattered German economy after the Second World War: the restoration of the quality estates would be a slow process; something speedier was required, to provide a cash return for the thousands of small wine growers in the Rheinhessen and Rheinpfalz, the two most heavily planted German wine regions between Bingen and Mannheim. Now, however, the German wine industry is paying for concentrating on mass-produced blended wine sold at the lowest possible price. The base price of wine, as low as 75 pfennigs per litre in the Nahe and Rheinpfalz, is hardly economic in many areas: growers are going out of business or turning to other forms of agriculture, or to industry. Liebfraumilch has brought down the reputation of quality German wine, and cut its own throat in the process. The diethylene glycol scandal of 1985, when quantities of the chemical used as antifreeze in car radiators were found in a number of German wines, was another heavy blow for the already damaged reputation of fine German wine. Almost overnight, the American market, the most important one for quality German wine, collapsed.

For the last ten years, one man has been conducting a campaign to restore the reputation of the country's great wine estates, taking arms in the fight for quality and individuality (or some would say aristocratic élitism) against a sea of mediocrity. Not everybody likes Erwein, Graf Matuschka-Greiffenclau, 27th in the line of the Knights of Greiffenclau of Schloss Vollrads; some, in a more consciously democratic country than Britain, regard him as arrogant and high-handed in his dealings with other sectors of the German wine industry; but nobody can ignore him. He is an imposing physical presence; tall (6 ft 4 in.), black-haired, with an aquiline nose suggestive of aristocracy and Prussian authority. More important still, he is tirelessly energetic and persistent; a man of firm will and determination; always prepared to argue his case with well-marshalled evidence and not without humour, never prepared to admit defeat.

Graf Matuschka could hardly be better placed to conduct his campaign. He has the great advantage not only of personal gifts but also of possessing one of the most perfect wine estates in the world. Schloss Vollrads is one of only two *Ortsteile*, that is estates of such high and long repute that their wine need carry only the estate name, without further geographical appellation, in the whole of Germany. The other is Schloss Johannisberg, a couple of miles due west.

Schloss Vollrads, residence of the Greiffenclau family since 1330, is situated in the middle of the Rheingau, one of the smallest but without doubt the most prestigious of Germany's wine-growing regions. The distinctive geographical feature of the Rheingau is the sharp bend of the Rhine by Wiesbaden and Mainz which sends it, from its northerly course, due west for 30 kilometres. The reason for this is the meeting of the river with the solid barrier of the Taunus Hills; the consequence is a line of south-facing slopes leading down to the broad river, circumstances ideally suited to the vine in such a northerly latitude. The Rheingau, slap on the fiftieth parallel (marked by a stone in the garden of Schloss Johannisberg), is very near the northern limit for the cultivation of the vine; its climate is comparable with that of southern England. The vineyards were planted in Roman times, but it was only, as Edward Hyams remarks in *Dionysus* (1965), 'the loving care and Teutonic thoroughness with which the Rhineland vinearoons turned their disadvantages into advantages' which made this into an economically viable area for wine production. The Rheingau was also favoured by having several important monasteries, especially the Cistercian Kloster Eberbach and the Benedictine Johannisberg, which had the resources and the will to improve the quality of their vineyards.

As it flows westwards, the Rhine broadens to over half a mile in width; its course is broken up by willow-covered islands, and red and black buoys mark the constantly changing channel for the barges which ply this most industrial of European rivers. The Rheingau is a busy route which links the centres of Koblenz and Mainz-Wiesbaden, and a popular tourist destination: major roads and railways line both sides of the river here, but the bridge linking Bingen and Rüdesheim, blown up during the Second World War, has not been rebuilt. The northern, Rheingau bank is heavily populated with largish villages or small towns every mile or so. Winkel is a typical smallish old Rheingau village: a couple of streets of shuttered, plastered houses with high tiled roofs, and an old stone church; pleasure boats are tied up to a pier on the river the far side of the fast road; Näglers Hotel sports parasols on its veranda.

From Winkel signs point to Schloss Vollrads, two kilometres away. The road leads uphill, away from the river, towards the wooded crest of the Taunus through vineyards which stretch for miles to the right and left. Through copper beeches appears a massive yellow-ochre building, three storeys to the beginning of the high, fish-scale-tiled roof, then a further three in the roof itself, with a little onion-domed turret tacked on to each corner. To its right a great square tower with a high, onion-turreted roof stands aloof and isolated, protected by an oblong moat. Jackdaws infest the tower, flapping and cawing around the baroque roof; in the moat, great grey shadows loom, monumental carp with letter-box mouths. The garden, surrounded by a blind-arched stone wall and dotted with squat little yew pyramids, has a half-neglected air.

Vollrads seems suspended not only in time but also in place, half-way between the busy Rhine front and the wild, wooded hills. Behind, forest stretches for miles into an empty hinterland, where only a few isolated farms make inroads into the wilderness. The Rheingau still has a higher proportion of forest than any other district even in well-wooded Germany.

I am lucky to arrive on an April day of cloudless sunshine; there is cherry blossom and a tall magnolia just coming into bud. Going through the pink granite porch, though, I find myself in a gloomy baronial hall, dark-panelled and hung with sombre ancestral portraits. The suite of rooms on the second floor where my interview with Graf Matuschka takes place are very different: they are decorated in a light nineteenth-century neo-rococo, with gilded arabesques on pale green panels, murals of periwigged courtiers and damsels in the rustic mode.

The Graf himself is hardly a rococo man: he would have made a formidable figure in heavy armour with a two-handed broadsword. The family history goes back beyond the Middle Ages, and Graf Matuschka, speaking fluent but idiosyncratic English, has it all well rehearsed. 'Our family originally lived in the Graues Haus near the river in Winkel, which we still own and which is now a gourmet restaurant. We have two theories about the Graues Haus: one is that it was built in the ninth century—there are columns, doors and window frames from that time. The other theory puts it in the eleventh century. We had the age of the wood which was used for the roof checked and carbon dating showed that the trees were cut between 1035 and 1070. Every normal person would say that the house was built in the ninth century and got a new roof in the eleventh. But one professor said that the older material was stolen from the castle of Charlemagne across the river at Ingelheim. I think that is a misunderstanding of the name Greiffenclau—Greiffen means to catch and Klauen means to steal.

'They started to clear the woods back from Winkel to here in the twelfth and thirteenth centuries, then the tower was built in 1330. In those times if you wanted to have one hectare of vines you needed four hectares of general agriculture: you had to solve the problem of your own housekeeping, and you paid your employees with natural produce. You needed room to pasture animals, for fertilising and for ploughing. On the other hand, wine growing was three times as profitable as normal farming.

'My family lived for 350 years in that tower, and another one next to it. It cannot have been very comfortable. Then an ancestor at the end of the seventeenth century had three wives—all at different times, of course—and twenty-six children, so he had to build the palace. The out-buildings around the courtyard were built by his son from 1700 to 1720. He did two clever things also: he built cellars under all the out-buildings so that he could store larger quantities of wine, and he bought a farm in the Taunus a few miles from here. That enabled him to farm out all the general agriculture and use Vollrads entirely for wine.'

But the Greiffenclau had other interests besides wine.

'My family was very closely associated with the Catholic church, which was not only a religious but also a political power. Seven members of our family were administrators of this region. There have also been a number of archbishops. For example, when the big discussion between Luther, the Emperor Charles V and the Catholic church took place at the Reichstag of Worms in 1521, the chairman was my ancestor.' The Graf does not mention that four years later, during the peasant uprising in the Rheingau, Friedrich von Greiffenclau was asked by the peasants to be their leader. In the words of the official family history, 'He thought it wiser to take command than to fight against it.' The habit of command is still evident in his descendant.

'They lived from the jobs they had and reinvested the money Vollrads made back into the property.' Several centuries later, the 27th Knight of Greiffenclau was to pursue exactly the same policy. 'Apparently they got very well paid. But this was the position of all the aristocratic German families at that time. For instance the Schönborn, another great Rheingau wine-growing family, built the Residenz at Wurzburg. Then a member of my family invited Tiepolo from Italy to paint the frescos.'

The Graf considers the late seventeenth and eighteenth centuries to have been the family's heyday. That period marks the beginning of what might be considered a modern, specialised approach to making quality wine—not only in the Rheingau but anywhere in the world.

'You know, the Rheingau was always the leading area in Germany for quality. The monks at Kloster Eberbach and Johannisberg had done a good deal. The most important thing was finding the best grape, which is Riesling. Riesling appeared five hundred years ago, but in those days there were a lot of different grape varieties planted in the same vineyard, red and white. The Rheingau was the first place where they had only white and only red. They made Riesling successful. Johannisberg played the leading role in this story.' It was in 1803 that the Benedictine priest and cellar master of the Abbey of Fulda, Otto Staab, wrote: 'The Riesling is now the only variety which may be planted in the whole of the Rheingau.' Riesling is a white grape which produces wines of refined fruity aroma, sometimes grapey but often suggestive of green apples, and invigorating acidity. Riesling ripens late, not before mid-October, which in poor, wet, autumns makes the harvest a miserable, angst-ridden affair. But its long growing season gives Riesling the subtle zest which the best late-picked English apples also possess. And Riesling grapes, slow to ripen, produce wines with an almost unlimited ability to age in the bottle, where they acquire tones of apricot, honey and even, as the Alsatians insist, petrol. I have tasted fifty-year-old Rhine Riesling wines as fresh and invigorating as if they were only a tenth of that age.

Another highly significant factor in the development of quality was the bottle. 'We learned to manufacture bottles on an industrial scale in the late eighteenth century. Johannisberg started to bottle in 1775 and we followed a year later. Schloss Vollrads had the oldest cabinet cellar, where people stored the better wines. There is a long history of quality here.'

Was the wine business profitable in those days, I wondered?

'There was a big difference between the vintages. They were not trained to protect the vineyard in the way we do today. In very good vintages, they made a lot of money—far more than we can today. In a really good vintage they could make as much as 600 per cent profit. But in bad vintages there were tremendous losses. In the seventeenth and eighteenth centuries I think they made a lot of money. It was certainly more than just a hobby—otherwise they would never have made the decisions they did at the end of the century.'

The nineteenth century was not such a happy time.

'There were a lot of problems, economic crises, wars: people did not have enough to eat. It was a hard time. The Greiffenclau also failed to produce a male heir for the first time in their history. In the past they had tended to produce rather a lot of children. Otto von Greiffenclau died in 1860 without an heir. His niece had married a Graf Matuschka from Silesia in what is now East Germany, and in 1862 the King of Prussia allowed the two families' arms to be united. Then their son, my grandfather, married Clara von Oppenheim, a lady from a banking family in Cologne. My grandmother invested a lot of money in Schloss Vollrads around the turn of the century, and she restored the castle and the cellars. She was a very active person, and took a greater interest in the property than my grandfather, who was President of the Police in Wiesbaden.

'My father was born in 1893, which was, incidentally, a wonderful vintage. He fought in the First World War, in which his brother died, then came back to Vollrads in 1924 when my grandfather died. He studied viticulture and oenology at the Geisenheim Institute, the top wine school in Germany, five miles from here—unlike me, he was a trained technical expert. My father was one of the people most actively involved in fighting Phylloxera.'

That was a successful struggle. As in the other European wine regions, Phylloxera was defeated in Germany by the grafting of European vines on to American rootstocks. Another campaign, against an even more deadly plague, was less successful.

'My father was in a horrible situation during the time of Hitler and the Third Reich. He was a member of the Christian Democrat party in the Weimar republic, and my family was always in opposition to Hitler. One of the Matuschkas was involved in the attempt to assassinate Hitler on 22 July 1944, with Adam von Trott and others. He was killed a few hours after the attack. Then they went looking for other members of the family. My father had to hide out in the woods behind Vollrads for a time.

'We were lucky here in the war. Vollrads, as you can see, is in a side valley: it is very difficult to find, except from the river. Johannisberg, only two miles away, was completely destroyed by the Americans: it stands up on a knoll and is very visible. We had one plane—a fighter—which hit the roof where the out-buildings join the palace, and then crashed into the vineyards. Near the end of the war the SS parked their tanks in the courtyard and fired at the Americans on the other side of the Rhine. The Americans were polite enough not to fire back. For the last two weeks of the war we slept in the cellars: it was nice to sleep down there among the bottles with all the other people— remember I was only six years old.

'My father was very clever to be able to keep Schloss Vollrads. He had always to look on both sides of the coin, never talk too much, never do too much. He had to be very careful with money during all that time—which included the economic crisis of 1929. If a water pipe burst in one place, he would renew it just in that one place, he would not replace the whole pipe.

'A lot of things were destroyed in the Second World War in Germany by bombing. But I think the Thirty Years' War was much more horrible: their technique was to set fire to all the fields so that people died of starvation. Once again, we don't know exactly how, but the family was able to keep Schloss Vollrads going at that time. Later in the seventeenth century Louis XIV was on the other side of the Rhine; he came across and destroyed much of the Rheingau, but the Greiffenclau family hung on here. I consider the strength of my family was that they were always very clever in bad situations.

'The big job my father did was to keep the estate going during the time of the world crash, of Hitler and the Second World War. After the war he became active in politics, which was always his first love. He was founder of the Christian Democratic party in the *Land* of Hessen. The Youth Organisation of the Christian Democratic party was founded here at Schloss Vollrads. My father was also very active in the lobby of the German Winegrowers' Association, of which he was president for sixteen years. Then he became president of the Association of Winegrowers of the EEC.'

Did all this political activity take its toll on the running of the estate?

'Perhaps yes, but there was no possibility of investing money in the estate immediately after the war. By the time that Germany returned to good economic health, and money was available, my father was an old man, and interested mainly in politics. I understand my father very well. You cannot tell a man of seventy, please stop your interest in politics and work very hard so that your son has a better time. I think my father did a fine job in holding on to Schloss Vollrads.'

The next job, that of restoring the estate and the palace to prime condition, and making Schloss Vollrads into a profitable concern, was for his son to accomplish. Before hearing this latest chapter in the long Greiffenclau saga, though, it is time to inspect the working parts of Vollrads, and to taste its celebrated products.

Outside, the sun is shining as brightly as ever. A gardener is weeding the flowerbeds while his small daughter plays football. In the centre of the courtyard a tall lime tree is just coming into leaf. There is a Vergilian sense of the arts of peace returning after years, or centuries, of conflict—all something of an illusion, I suppose; two kilometres away, BMWs tear up the road by the Rhine, more representative symbols of the new Germany of the *Wirkschaftswunder*, which can still so often seem driven and haunted, driven to success, haunted by past guilt.

Within the confines of Vollrads, though, the peace is not all illusion. Dedication to a culture of wine-growing which has persisted through all the wars can bring a genuine fulfilment. Herr Senft, the Vollrads cellar-master and chief wine-maker, in whose charge I am left while his employer goes off to meet some customers, certainly seems a fulfilled man. With his ascetic features, penetrating eyes and goatee beard, he has the look of an El Greco priest—a man seeking perfection, if only on the earthly plane.

The working out-buildings cover three sides of the big court-yard. Their yellow-ochre walls, pink stone archways and tall, steeply raked roofs blend harmoniously with the architecture of the palace. Herr Senft leads me through one of the big arched doorways into what was once a great barn, with animals housed on the ground floor and corn and hay up above. Now a second aluminium door, like an inner skin, leads into a modern, temperature-controlled bottle store, on two floors. The conversion work was done in the 1970s, carefully keeping the external structure unaltered.

Beneath the three ranges are seven separate (and quite unmodernised) cellars, low, vaulted and extremely moist, thanks to a number of underground springs. The cellars house an assortment of the traditional 1200-litre oak casks, called *Stucke* in the Rheingau, and stain-less-steel tanks. The wine-making philosophy at Vollrads leans towards the pure, fine, clean fruity style which is achieved by maturation in neutral, anaerobic stainless steel, rather than the rounder character, with just a touch of oxidation, which wooden barrels bring.

'You want to taste the individuality of the year, the soil, the grape, the particular part of the vineyard, and that comes better with steel,' says Herr Senft; 'wood hides differences, averages everything out.' He is no dogmatist, however. 'I could speak to you for one hour on the advantages of steel over oak, and another hour on the advantages of oak over steel,' he remarks gnomically. 'But the most important thing of all is the selection at harvest: 2000 litres of *Kabinett* (superior) quality for the pneumatic press here, 10,000 litres of QbA (the lowest grade of quality wine) there. And fermentation must be done slowly.'

My personal view is that barrel maturation helps tone down the harsh acidity of young German Rieslings: I find some of the Vollrads wines dangerously lean, at least in their youth.

As we climb out of the dank, gloomy cellar into the almost blinding spring sunshine, I notice neatly kept window boxes on the sills of the windows in the roof-floors of the out-buildings. 'Do some of the people who work on the estate live here also?' I ask.

Herr Senft smiles in a Confucian manner. 'I would say that we who live here also work on the estate. But to answer your question, there are ten families living here, the Graf and his wife and daughter, my wife and myself, the vineyards manager and his wife and seven others.' The implication is clear: a community with the Graf as *primus inter pares* rather than autocratic boss. It is a picture, belying his some-times autocratic appearance, which Graf Matuschka confirmed later.

'Here we do not have the situation of "I'm the boss, you are the employees." I need a very well-qualified wine-maker who makes the decisions as if for his own company. He is totally free to do what he thinks is best for the wine. I talk to him and I am in charge of the success afterwards. Everyone is totally free in their own sphere, so long as they do a good job. That way everyone has more fun.

'It is the same with children. The position of the father is completely different from what it was before the Second World War. I don't tell my daughter, "That's the way you must sit at table." We are friends; we help our children to have fun and to grow in the right way. If they don't want to, we can't force them.'

Back once again from the bright sunshine into the baronial gloom: a tasting has been set up for a group of restaurateurs, in the ground-floor dining-room with its sixteenth-century Spanish leather wall-panelling, long refectory table and seventeenth-century heavy chairs.

First on the list come a group of wines from the latest (1987) vintage—an unusual one which seemed to be heading for disaster throughout a dismal summer until fine weather in October restored at least respectable quality. The must-weight, the measurement of sugar and therefore of ripeness in the grapes at harvest, by which all German wines are graded, was high enough for QbA, but not for the higher grades of quality called *Kabinett, Spätlese, Auslese* and so on up to the dizzy height of *Trockenbeerenauslese*. Nevertheless, ripeness is not all. The best QbAs are the most versatile of German wines, sufficiently full-bodied to be drunk with food and capable of long ageing.

There are ten different samples from the 50-hectare Vollrads estate, which covers the slopes behind the palace and some of the flatter land in front of it, and thus produces wines of different characters. A couple of hundred feet can make a crucial difference in this marginal climate for vines. The first noticeable difference is in sweetness: the samples range from a gum-puckering bone-dryness to medium sweetness. This is partly a matter of natural selection: some tanks stop fermenting with a certain amount of sugar left unconverted, others carry on through to complete dryness. But it is also a matter of choice and technology—and the market. Fermentation can be stopped at any point by removing and filtering the fermenting must. Graf Matuschka has made Vollrads known for dry and medium dry wines, which in his view go better with food; few wines in the sweeter style, the one generally associated with German wines in the UK, are made at this estate.

Whatever their grade of sweetness, all the 1987 Vollrads samples are notable for their high degree of fruity acidity: the tasting terms which come to mind are lean, steely, bony, austere. There are considerable differences in character between the different tanks: some show the green, herbaceous, faintly grapey aroma of Riesling: others give very little away.

'Vollrads wines are always difficult to taste when young,' says Graf Matuschka. 'Do not worry, they will develop.'

On the other side of the table are a group of nine samples from the neighbouring estate of Fürst Löwenstein in the village of Hallgarten, which Graf Matuschka has leased since 1979. These immediately show more in the way of fruity aroma and rounded, plump body. Frankly, they are considerably more appealing, especially the samples from the vineyard called Hallgartener Schönhell, with their rich, earthy intensity. 'Yes, these often show better at this stage,' Matuschka agrees. 'But the Vollrads wines always come through in the end.'

His argument is supported by two special bottles at the end. The first is the 1983 Schloss Vollrads Kabinett Blausilber Halb-Trocken.

(Vollrads makes up for the simplicity of the single Ortsteil appellation with an insanely complicated system of grading in terms of sweetness and quality according to different coloured capsules: green capsules are used for QbA wines, blue for Kabinett, pink for Spätlese, white for Auslese and gold for Beeren and Trockenbeerenauslese. As if this were not enough, a solid capsule indicates a 'mild, mellow' wine, a capsule with a silver band a dry or semi-dry wine and a capsule with a gold band a rich, sweet wine.) The ripe, honeyed aroma characteristic of mature Riesling is just beginning to show itself; the acidity remains bracingly fresh but not too sharp; to taste, the wine is on the dry side of medium, the style favoured by Graf Matuschka. In a different world altogether is the 1976 Schloss Vollrads Beerenauslese—a wine made from selected bunches of over-ripe grapes affected by *botrytis cinerea*, the noble rot. The colour is an extraordinary orange-gold, and the bouquet suggests oranges again—marmalade oranges this time. On the palate this is an intensely rich, sweet dessert wine, of astonishing length and complexity of flavour, its opulence balanced (just) by the fine acidity which Vollrads wines preserve even in the ripest of vintages. No such wines as this have been made at the estate since the drought year of 1976. Some say Graf Matuschka does not like sweet wines, but he protests: 'That is nonsense. We simply have not had the sun and those levels of ripeness in any year since 1976. Of course I would make a wine like this every year if I could.'

The tasting over, it is time for lunch. Across the drive from the palace is a garage in which there sit a Porsche and a relatively harmless-looking silver BMW. Very deceptive, as I already know. The first time I met Graf Matuschka he kindly drove an ailing friend and myself from Winkel to Frankfurt airport. Once we had turned on to the main road, the acceleration sent my back thudding into the hardish seat. 'This has a 320 hp engine,' the Graf mentioned, 'they only ever made three of them.' We got on the Autobahn and I watched mesmerised as the speedometer climbed past the 200 km/h mark to reach 250. At regular intervals, I should add, an ominous knocking came from the off-side rear wheel. 'That isn't good,' the Graf said, looking over his shoulder. 'She has just been in the garage and they have done something wrong.' He did not slow down.

As we walk towards the car I remind him of the incident. 'What was the matter with the car in the end?'

'The brakes.'

We are heading for the Graues Haus, not normally open for lunch. The grey stone building with its steeply gabled roof stands somewhat isolated from the village, only a few yards from the riverbank. Along the first floor, breaking up the building's barn-like plainness, runs a row of Carolingian-columned windows with pink and white granite striped arches, architecture poised betwen Roman and Gothic.

Inside, the ninth century gives way to the twentieth, or even the twenty-first. The interior, gutted by fire in 1964, has been redecorated in the most extreme of modern functional styles. The chairs are made of black metal grilles, not unlike those you would find protecting the engine of a BMW. They are no more comfortable than a BMW's seats.

The cuisine at the Graues Haus is conscientiously based on local Rheingau products: game from the Taunus, river fish, local vegetables. The wine list contains only Rheingau wines, though by no means only wines from Vollrads and Löwenstein. Of the generous selection of more than three hundred wines, only a handful come from Matuschka's twin estates. Matuschka is proud that his restaurant has achieved a Michelin rosette—'the only restaurant specialising in German food which has a rosette'—but he darkly suspects the perfidious French of ulterior motives. 'They have given me one rosette to keep me quiet. Whatever I do they will never give me a second.'

I must admit to a reservation about the food at the Graues Haus. Individual components of dishes—a poached mousse of grayling, a delicate dill sauce—are exquisite, but the net effect can be bland. On both occasions that I have eaten there I have secretly yearned for something traditionally German, hearty and solid, yes, Wurst and Sauerkraut. I would not dare tell Graf Matuschka. As for the wines, the 1985 Vollrads Blausilber Kabinett is piercingly dry—too lean and steely by half, at least for the moment. The wine I enjoy most, drunk with a delicious raspberry parfait, is a distinctly old-fashioned Hattenheimer Nussbrunnen Auslese 1976, from the small estate of Siegfried Gerhardt, peachy rich yet well balanced. Meanwhile, the conversation has focused on Graf Matuschka's personal progress.

'I was in a special position. My elder brother studied viticulture at Geisenheim, but when he was ready to take over Vollrads, my father didn't want to give it to him. As President of the Association of Winegrowers of the EEC, you see, he felt he needed to have his own estate, and so my brother lost his chance to work here. He went into radio journalism, and then decided he didn't want to return to Vollrads.

'I studied law and had totally different interests. Then my father asked me very hard'—Matuschka emits a wry chuckle—'to come home. I came home. It was 1965: half a day I studied wine in Geisenheim, and the other half of the day I did the book-keeping at Vollrads. It didn't work really. My father was very intelligent but he hated one thing: for the family to know how he conducted business. So my father never really gave me a chance to understand what was happening at Schloss Vollrads. So I said to him, let us do the following: we have a beautiful relationship. Let me go and please employ a book-keeper. I assure you that when you want to retire, I will come home. My father didn't like the idea but he had no choice.'

Matuschka took a job in the German sparkling wine, or *Sekt*, industry, through which he not only gained experience in selling wine but also met his future wife, the daughter of a customer in north Germany. After two years he was offered a more lucrative job.

'I had just signed a three-year contract as sales manager with Olivetti when my father died. He never retired: he said to me twenty times that he was going to retire, and even gave me dates when he was going to stop work. And always ten or fourteen days before he forgot all about it. He died in January 1975. It was not possible for me to leave Olivetti then. Fortunately my younger brother was able to step in for two years; I took over at Vollrads on 1 April 1977. The estate was not in good condition. Nothing had been restored for fifty years. The cellars were in a bad state. And on the sales side, 96 per cent of Vollrads wine was sold overseas. It had a good reputation in Germany but was hardly available.

'So I decided to work double time: I got jobs as a consultant to various computer companies, and lived off that money. All the money we made at Schloss Vollrads I reinvested. It was very hard work—a fifteen- or sixteen-hour day. But if you're the twenty-seventh generation, you don't like to lose a property.'

The restoration of Vollrads under Graf Matuschka sounds curiously similar to the restoration of Germany itself thirty years earlier. 'Very quickly we got Vollrads back into better condition. I made an analysis of what needed to be done and above all the priorities: what needed to be done first. One important thing was to increase the vine area: in my father's time there were only thirty-three hectares under vines, not enough to make it profitable. In 1979 I leased the estate of my neighbour Fürst Löwenstein in Hallgarten, which brought the total to seventy hectares.

'I also changed a lot of the personnel. I looked for the most highly qualified people. I wanted to have real quality in the wine, and you can achieve that only with the best people. All the people we had were nearly at retirement age, and so it was possible to replace everybody in the leading positions without sacking anybody. I think we have a very strong team now: two wine-makers and a vineyard manager with university degrees, and seven qualified wine-growers. No other estate in Germany has such a highly qualified team.'

The next stage was marketing—the Matuschka speciality. He wanted to maintain the position of Vollrads abroad, but also to rebuild the home market. 'Today the market is all-important. I studied what France was doing and I found that wines sell best with food. In all countries where people drink wine with food, consumption is high, and vice versa. So I decided to check whether Schloss Vollrads wine goes well with food.' This was the start of a campaign which has become central to Graf Matuschka's activity.

He and Vollrads have been at the forefront of the move towards making drier wines in Germany. It seems no coincidence to Graf Matuschka and other estate-owners in the Rheingau that the reputation of German wines has declined since they have become sweeter. When the great hocks were fetching prices similar to, or even higher than, first-growth Bordeaux, they were dry or dryish wines, and they were normally drunk with food.

The characteristic style of Vollrads wines today is technically known as Halb-Trocken: in true German fashion, the exact amount of residual sugar, not more than 18 g per litre and not less than 9 g, is laid down in the law; the result is, to the British taste, on the dry side of medium. Vollrads wine made in the Trocken style, with less than 9 g per litre residual sugar—immensely fashionable in Germany's gourmet restaurants—is almost always too lean and bony for my taste.

Graf Matuschka claims not to be a Trocken fanatic. 'For me dry wines were never a question of religion, as they were, and indeed are, with some wine and food writers in Germany. I like harmony: that is the important point. In hot countries the grapes have more sugar and less acidity. The sugar converts to alcohol, and glycerine is also produced during fermentation. Glycerine tastes slightly sweet. Non-fermented grape juice and glycerine are both sweet: we have a little bit more unconverted grape-juice, the southern countries have a higher degree of glycerine, but in taste the sweetness can be the same.

'We studied how wine and food go together because we wanted to formulate some simple rules which everybody could understand. We discovered that the rule of always drinking red wine with red meat and white wine with white meat was nonsense. Also, red wine and cheese do not always go well together.'

Here I agree with Graf Matuschka. I have always found that soft, white-rinded cheeses such as Brie and Camembert completely alter the flavour of red wines, especially claret, making them taste sweet and soapy. Graf Matuschka explains why.

'I learned that cheese in its ripening process goes through up to five different fermentations. In any fermentation different acids are produced. We discovered how the cheese acids go with the wine acids and discovered some completely new solutions.'

Graf Matuschka's campaign to promote the drinking of drier Riesling wines with food takes various forms, of which the most notable is the Graues Haus. For some years he has also been holding so-called Lucullan wine tastings in Vollrads' vast first-floor dining-room, like a magnificent College Hall, with a monumental baroque carved stone fireplace dated 1684. The format is typically precise and unchanging: eleven wines accompany a five-course meal, prepared by the Graues Haus chef, Egbert Engelhardt. Graf Matuschka introduces each wine and serious gastronomic conversation is the order of the evening. A place at one of these tastings has to be booked well ahead.

A broader campaign within the whole Rheingau region has been the formation of the group of Chartered Estates, called Charta for short. The aim of Matuschka and his co-founders Bernhard Breuer, owner of both Weingut G. Breuer and shipper Scholl und Hillebrand, both based in Rüdesheim, Hans Ambrosi, of the State Wine Domaine in Eltville and Professor Becker of the Geisenheim Institute, is to promote the Halb-Trocken style of Rheingau Riesling wine, specifically designed to partner food. Charta has grown rapidly to number over thirty estates, including some of the most famous in the region. Charta wines, presented in the old-fashioned tall, elegant Rhine bottle, embossed with a striking logo of a romanesque double-arch, taken from one of the windows of the Graues Haus, must pass a stiff set of quality controls. The minimum must-weights for the various quality levels are several degrees higher than those required by the law: there is also a minimum degree of acidity, essential to ensure long life.

For the last three years, Charta has laid on a lavish dinner at the Intercontinental Hotel in London to try to prove that its wines are not only good in themselves, but can partner a wider range of dishes than the sceptical British, who have become used to drinking German wines on their own, would imagine. Responses have been mixed: at the first dinner there was a notable success with a wild duck dish, perfectly complemented by an '83 Charta wine from Rüdesheim. When roast beef was served at the second dinner, however, the British wine trade and press collectively sighed for some decent claret. At the third dinner, I felt dissatisfied on two counts: first, the nine Charta wines were not sufficiently dissimilar; secondly, almost all of them (mainly from the 1985 vintage) seemed too young, high in acidity, not yet formed in character. That may well change when Charta has a few more vintages under its belt, but I feel that the Charta members would do well to remember that even when the reputation of hock was at its height, the British did not drink it throughout the meal. Right through the meal, after all, was the slogan of Blue Nun, not the kind of wine Charta are aiming to produce.

The case of Charta, and of drier German wines as a whole, is far from being won, at least in Britain. We have all the world's wines to choose from, and at the moment the current of fashion is flowing strongly in the direction of more full-bodied dry white wines, especially made from the Chardonnay grape. If one thought in terms of a wine world cup, the score at the time of writing would be Australian Chardonnay 5, dry German Riesling 0. It may be that the tide will change, and the world will respond once more to the keenly appetising acidity and lightness of German Riesling. Perhaps the alcohol-restriction lobby will have an influence, to the advantage of German wines, which, as is strangely little known, are considerably lower in alcohol than those of France, Australia or Spain.

I have a feeling that excessive emphasis on dryness has been a mistake. The real question, as Graf Matuschka is prepared to admit, is about quality. 'I am working very hard at the moment, as President of the VDP, the German Association of top-quality estates, and of the Rheingau Winegrowers' Association, to try to change the German Wine Law. The problem is to change people's minds away from quantity towards higher quality. The political people are not interested in quality, because the strongest lobby is that of the Co-operatives and blenders who represent the most jobs. When we enter the free market in 1992, the quality standards in Germany will need to be equivalent to those in France, Italy, Spain and so on.' At the moment the apparently rigorous German Wine Law allows 99 per cent of the country's production to pass as 'quality wine'. Nearly all of it is clean, and decently made, but the facts of viticulture in such a northerly climate mean that a high proportion of such 'quality wine' is very ordinary, made from grapes simply not ripe or concentrated enough to produce wine of character. The second gross anomaly of the current (1971) German Wine Law is that it is impossible to tell from the label whether a German wine is the individual product of a specific vineyard or a blend from a sub-region. Only the most dedicated specialist could be expected to know that a wine labelled Rüdesheimer Kirchenpfad, for instance, comes from a smallish, single vineyard, whereas one labelled Rüdesheimer Burgweg could come from anywhere in the twin parishes of Rüdesheim and Geisenheim. The final decision, as always, has been made by the market, which has relegated Germany to the position of stockist of the bargain basement.

'We have to fight to change these things,' says Matuschka. 'Everybody here wants Germany to have a beautiful reputation, but nobody wants to do what is necessary to achieve that. Should Liebfraumilch, a 'quality wine' which at the moment need only contain 51 per cent of 'traditional' varieties, which include the high-yielding, rather neutral Müller-Thurgau, and the Kerner, which lacks staying-power, be down-graded?

'I would not say that, but suggest instead, that we should increase quality. We must increase the proportion of Riesling, and do away with many of the plantings of inferior grape varieties which were designed to increase yields at the expense of quality. We must have better quality controls. You should not be allowed to buy grapes and juice from other growers, because you can only control your own production. The glycol scandal showed that people with good reputations bought from other people and did not know what they were buying.

'What German wine needs above all is a clear line. Chablis is a wine of good but not exceptional quality, but it has an extremely high price and a good reputation, because a child of three knows that Chablis is dry and goes well with fish. If you try to supply all styles of wine, dry, sweet, heavy, light, to different sets of customers, you never get a reputation.'

Graf Matuschka is a man with a public mission: to act as ambassador and spokesman for high-quality, single-estate German wines at a time when they are languishing in the doldrums of international esteem. He performs this role with style and effectiveness. It helps that he is a natural salesman: even official ambassadors have to be salesmen these days, and they have not always received such a useful training as Graf Matuschka, selling calculating machines for Olivetti. Sometimes one feels it is difficult for him to shake off his public mantle: you tend to hear the same jokes and stories—always well told—more than once.

The private man is hard to reach. Over coffee and a glass of Asbach Uralt (the Rheingau's answer to Cognac) at the end of our lunch, however, he becomes more expansive.

'The other day the magazine *Bunte* said they were running a feature on aristocrats who were doing a good job keeping their estates. They sent down a lady to interview me who turned out to be a sort of ex-aristocrat with a chip on her shoulder. I have never been the decadent type of aristocrat—my wife and I are simply not interested in that type of socialising. In the old days people got titles for doing a good job.

And the title was passed on to the next generation so that they should remember that. It was not a social position first, only secondarily. Today many people are interested only in the social position, not in the work. And that is the reason why so many aristocratic families come to grief. I am not saying you need to be a businessman: you can be a pianist, you can even be a politician.'Matuschka's scornful chuckle betrays a lowish opinion of the latter métier.

'When I went to university in Munich to study Law, my father gave me an allowance of 200 Deutschmarks a month. My rent cost 120. He also gave me a black tie and a dinner jacket. So I would go to smart parties in smart hotels, but I would never know how I was going to get home. It was difficult keeping both sides going, but it was good training.'

Another thing which Graf Matuschka regards as good training is his private passion, motor-racing. 'My first car was a BMC Mini-Cooper, which I got in 1964. I drove it in the German Championship in 1965 and came third. I stopped racing for a few years, then I switched to BMW. I raced in '69, '70 and '71 in the German and European Championships. In '71 I had a bad accident when a wheel came off. BMW claimed it was my fault, though it clearly was not. I injured my back quite badly, and have not been able to play some sports since.' Graf Matuschka used to play hand-ball in the top national league, ice-hockey in the second league and, something of which he seems especially proud, football for the Winkel village team.

'Motor-racing is an extraordinary self-discipline. You need to be completely alert, to stretch yourself to the limit. I learned in the Netherlands on a circuit greased with oil and soap how to handle a car in a skid. It saved my life twice, once when a wooden support became detached and got jammed under the accelerator, and a second time when the brake fluid drained.'

At the end of our lunch, Graf Matuschka hinted that the time might be approaching for him to take on a new challenge. After all, he has fulfilled his primary obligation as 27th of the Knights of Greiffenclau. The palace and the estate are probably in better order than they have been for centuries. Recently, the job of restoring the moated tower was completed: it had cost 900,000 Deutschmarks, almost all out of Matuschka's pocket. The succession is assured. Following the family tradition, Matuschka married quite late, at forty-four: 'My father married at forty-three and my grandfather at forty-eight. We know, as wine-growers, that the very best vintages need to be matured for a long time.' Now he and his wife Sabine, a former model, have a daughter, Francesca, aged five.

Back in England, a few months later, I learned that Graf Matuschka's new challenge had already presented itself. The Suntory company of Japan, spirit manufacturers, owners of Château Lagrange in St Julien, and distributors of Schloss Vollrads, had decided to buy a number of top German wine estates. Their aim was to own about 30 hectares of prime vineyards in each of three German wine regions: Mosel-Saar-Ruwer, Rheinpfalz, and Rheingau. The company they have set up to buy and manage the vineyards is three-quarters owned by Suntory and one-quarter by Graf Matuschka. The managing director, responsible for buying and managing all the vineyards, is Matuschka himself. Rumours are going round the surprisingly bitchy German wine world that Matuschka intends, eventually, to sell Vollrads to Suntory. When the Black Death, the Thirty Years' War, and Hitler have failed to dislodge the Greiffenclaus from the castle in the valley among the vines, with the oak and wild cherry woods behind, I somehow doubt that the 27th Knight of Greiffenclau is planning to hand over to the makers of ersatz Scotch from Tokyo.

Weingut Lingenfelder

Weingut K & H Lingenfelder 6711 Grosskarlbach

Produce of Germany

1985

SPÄTBURGUNDER

Trocken · Dry

Deutscher Tafelwein · Rhein

Erzeugerabfüllung · Estate Bottled

0.7 l

Lingenfelder
of
Grosskarlbach

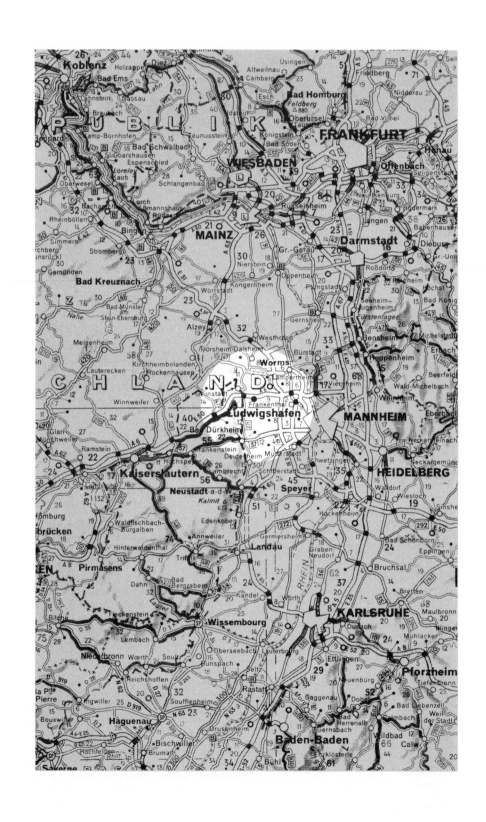

Early october: vintage time in the Rheinpfalz or Palatinate, the southernmost part of the Rhineland, a flattish 80-km-long strip of intensively cultivated land between the Rhine and the wooded Haardt mountains. The climate, protected by the Haardt (which further south become the Vosges, and keep Alsace dry and warm), is one of the sunniest and driest in West Germany. They say lemons and almonds grow here (though I have never seen lemons); certainly grapes ripen more consistently than anywhere else in the Rhineland, and the architecture, with its ochre plaster walls and weathered, beaver-tail tiled roofs, has a southern warmth.

The Pfalz is a perfect microcosm of West Germany's mixture of industrial might and continuing small-scale agriculture. Not only are the two juxtaposed, but many industrial workers go home in the evening to tend an acre or two of vines. Despite its climatic advantages, it has not—with the exception of the small area around Forst and Deidesheim—enjoyed a reputation as one of Germany's top wine areas. Its production is large (ten times as great as the Rheingau's), and diverse, in both character and quality. It may be significant that the Rheinpfalz does not boast many aristocratic estates or monasteries.

I arrived at Mannheim station, in the centre of what was once a cultivated eighteenth-century city-state and is now, with Ludwigshafen the other side of the Rhine, an industrial city of 500,000 inhabitants, dominated by the big BASF works. Waiting to meet me was Rainer Lingenfelder a tall, slim, bespectacled man in his mid-thirties. Until recently Rainer had been working as chief oenologist for Sichel, the Blue Nun people; he had won the International Wine & Spirit Competition Winemaker of the Year Award in 1984; now he was wine-maker at the family wine estate, Weingut Lingenfelder, in Grosskarlbach.

Driving swiftly in his sturdy Volkswagen we were soon out of the industrial sprawl of Mannheim-Ludwigshafen. The small village of Grosskarlbach is in the northern part of the Pfalz, in vineyard and orchard country rolling gently at ninety degrees to the Haardt, which rise to 2000 ft 3–4 kilometres to the west. 'Let's go straight out to look at the vines,' Rainer suggested.

Having parked the car in the village, we set out on foot: the weather was still and mild but disappointingly overcast. 1988 had had the promise of a really great vintage: now perhaps it would turn out just to be a good one. As we parked the car, the peace of the quiet village was shattered by a low-flying phalanx of American fighters. 'That's one of the disadvantages of living in the middle of Europe,' Rainer commented. There are also a number of advantages: Rainer can jump in the car and be in Alsace in less than two hours, in Paris or Burgundy in five.

We walked along the main street, lined with sixteenth-, seventeenth- and eighteenth-century houses, all with plastered walls and sandstone arches leading into courtyards. One house, newly renovated, stood out with its cream walls criss-crossed with black and red beams, and the sandstone and window surrounds painted blue-grey. The arch leading into the courtyard—a double one, a large arch for the horse and cart and a small one for the people—had the date 1598 carved above it. Much older is the Protestant church with its massive square sandstone tower and lowish spire: 'The tower and chancel date from the second half of the thirteenth century,' said Rainer. We went inside, to find the local organist practising Bach chorale preludes on the pretty organ, which retains some baroque pipes.

Leaving the church we went down a narrow alley; at the end is a broader street with several old houses, and running along one side, a busily flowing brook. 'The village is named after this stream—it used to be called the Karlbach, but is now known as the Eckbach, the corner stream. It may look very small, but it was central to the economy of the village; there used to be seven mills on this stream, for grain, paper and tools. One of them, a flour mill, is still just about in operation. We could go and look round if you like.'

The entrance to the Pappelmühle is a broad stone double arch dated 1867. Inside was a cobbled courtyard with the tall brick mill-building facing it. We went in and, after Rainer had shouted up, were greeted by a strong-looking youngish man with a blond moustache. He and Rainer had the familiarity of contemporaries who have lived in the same village all their lives, and they spoke the local Pfalz dialect, quite unlike the Hochdeutsch I learnt at school. We climbed up some rather perilous stairs—the whole building had an air of decrepitude—into a Piranesian hall full of massive, ancient machinery, twisting pipes and vents, everything covered in fine off-white dust. There were five beautifully engineered milling machines, with meshes of different grain. Once the mill must have produced flour of the highest quality.

A stooped old man wearing a blue beret and a dusty pale-blue overall was tinkering with one of the machines. It was the miller, now seventy-three: he still kept the mill going, on his good days, but he was too old to be able to maintain the machinery. His son, our guide, wanted to follow his father's trade, went to technical school and became an apprentice miller. The flour dust gave him asthma and he had to stop. He was now a factory worker.

Before we left, the old miller took us down to the basement, where an antique diesel engine, coated in a noisome mixture of grease and soot, hunkered among huge cobwebs like a geriatric toad. It was obviously his pride and joy, capable of powering all the milling machines with energy left over to provide heat and light. At the back there was a weir where the tinkling Eckbach used to turn the massive millwheel, and between the weir and the mill a strip of well-watered, fertile garden where the miller's wife, bent double, was tending dahlias.

Taking our leave of the miller's family, we turned left out of the Pappelmühle up a steepish road. Just on the fringes of the ancient, sleepy village, nestling in its hollow surrounded by vineyards and orchards, we passed an installation like a miniature petrol refinery. Grapes from large plastic hampers were being sucked up a huge tube and through a cyclone into a crusher-destemmer. Outside sat a row of large fibre-glass tanks. Rainer explained the process:

'The must has to be kept in these fibre-glass tanks before going on to the press. It needs to stirred around all the time. This turns it into pea-soup. It means high phenol extraction, which gives body, but not elegant body: it makes the wine coarse and harsh. We are talking here about throughput per hour, minimum man-hours, efficiency: these people are engineers, not wine-makers.'

This operation was not, of course, the Weingut Lingenfelder, the estate run jointly by Rainer Lingenfelder, his father Karl and his uncle Hermann. 'One of the two guys who runs this is a known crook: he has been in gaol for wine fraud: the other is just a suspected crook.'

If Rainer spoke with a certain bitterness, it was not surprising. In Grosskarlbach, and in the Pfalz as a whole, the two sides of the German wine industry, large-scale, low-price mass-production and high-quality, single-estate wine-making rub shoulders. There is no doubt which, at the moment, has the upper hand.

Beyond the installation, we turned off the road and into the vineyards, which, interspersed with apple orchards, surround Grosskarlbach on every side. 'This slope faces south—it's the best site in the village for vines. As you can see, the north slope opposite is planted with apple-trees—our apple-trees. That is the traditional pattern of agriculture in this region.'

What makes this particular slope good for vines?

'Well, apart from facing south, it is good for frost drainage: the cold air flows off. Air-flows are very important here. Though the Pfalz has quite a warm climate for Germany, we are on latitude 49'30" north, pretty near the limit for the cultivation of the vine. Just a few miles north of here there is a big side valley opening into the Haardt, and the westerly airstream brings cold air. You cannot grow vines there.

'Grosskarlbach is a very old-established area for viticulture: the first reference to Grosskarlbach wine comes in 763, from the records of the Kloster Lorsch abbey, which owned vineyards here. In 776 there is another reference, from the records of Kloster Weissenburg. The Romans must have planted vines here, because if you go to the Speyer museum you can see a Roman wine-bottle, which was found when they were digging the drains in Grosskarlbach. Apparently it was half-full when it was found but the workmen drank the wine.

'In 1391 the records show that more red wine was produced here than white, but that the red fetched a lower price. Grosskarlbach was never one of the most highly rated wine villages: we have an account-book for 1822 which shows Grosskarlbach fetching 130 thaler, less than a third as much as wine from the best Pfalz villages, Forst and Deidesheim.'

Moving among the vines I followed Rainer's example in tasting grapes. In this vineyard several varieties were planted: Scheurebe, Kerner, Müller-Thurgau and Spätburgunder, the German name for the burgundian Pinot Noir. All the grapes we sampled were full of flavour and sweet to taste, the Scheurebe especially aromatic, and the Spätburgunder beautifully balanced between sweetness and acidity.

'We will take a closer look and measure the must weights tomorrow,' says Rainer; 'now we are a bit late for my mother's lunch.'

From the vineyard we could see clearly the most prominent house in the village: a yellow-painted neoclassical building of 1830 on three floors, with a pediment on each side. This is the headquarters of the Weingut Lingenfelder, though the Lingenfelders do not own, but lease, both the ground floor of the house and the 10 hectares of vineyards and several more of apple orchards which go with it. Backing on to the house is a courtyard surrounded by farm buildings, with three shapely Lindenbäume planted in the middle.

We got back in something of a hurry to find Frau Lingenfelder waiting for us at the back door. Lunch consisted of home-made tomato soup, followed by boiled beef with Frau Lingenfelder's special horse-radish sauce. Her excellent cooking owes nothing to the finicky kind of *nouvelle cuisine* fashionable in the new foodie Germany. After lunch there was time for a short wander round the rest of the house and the garden. The gravestones of the original owners, the Fitting, Hilbert, Webel and Stoffel families, can be seen in the front garden. The present owners, a brother and sister in their forties, have no interest in the wine side of the estate.

But though the Lingenfelders are not natives of Grosskarlbach, they emphatically are Pfälzers, imbued with the local pride which seems endemic in this southern part of the Rhineland. I have heard a wine-grower from the Rheinhessen, 40 kilometres to the north, lamenting his neighbours' lazy and careless attitude, and contrasting it to the Pfälzers' pride. 'Here if people have a tree growing by their house they'd rather cut it down than bother to clear up the leaves: they'd never dream of such a thing in the Pfalz.'

The Lingenfelder family originated in the small town of Rhodt in the southern Palatinate, 40 kilometres south of Grosskarlbach. I was to visit the town later, and find it one of the prettiest even in this region of exceptionally attractive towns and villages. The gently rising main street is lined with seventeenth- and eighteenth-century wine-growers' houses whose double archways, leading into the working courtyard, are artfully hung with vines. Just outside Rhodt is a vineyard planted with Gewurztraminer, said to date from before 1618.

Anstatt Lingenfelder, the wine-growing 'patriarch' from whom the family traces its descent, was born in Rhodt in 1520. The family was a prominent one, because Anstatt's brother Hans became mayor of the town.

Two hundred years later, after the murderous campaigns of Louis XIV, Johannes became the first of many Lingenfelders to emigrate to North America. He settled in York County, Pennsylvania, in 1738. In 1752 his cousin Abraham took up residence in Frederick County, Maryland. Things were not necessarily safer on the other side of the ocean: in Lancaster County, Pennsylvania, another cousin, Catherine Lingenfelder, was scalped and killed by Indians in 1757. But the American Lingenfelders survived to become numerous and widespread: it is thanks to the genealogical researches of Bob Downs, whose maternal grandfather Lingenfelder was Governor of Kansas, that so much is known about the family history. One of the family's most notable members was the idealistic doctor Julius Lingenfelder: his book *Der Artzt als Fuhrer der Neuzeit*, written in the 1920s, makes an eloquent plea for a peaceful future, with the doctor, in the manner of Plato's philosopher, as king. Just one American Lingenfelder is known to have grown grapes: not in California but in the mid-western state of Missouri. Prohibition brought an end to that story, but the Lingenfelders' involvement in wine in the United States has recently been revived by Mark Lingenfelder, vineyard manager at the Chalk Hill winery in Sonoma, California.

Rainer is proud to count himself a thirteenth-generation wine-grower, from a Lingenfelder line which, with the exception of seven years from 1938 to 1945, has stayed in the Pfalz. 'Grape-growing became very difficult in the 1920s and 1930s because of the great inflation and the economic crisis. My grandfather Karl Heinrich had a small winery in Edenkoben, near Rhodt, and in fact he was one of the founder-members of the Co-operative there. But times were so hard that he decided to sell up: he went east, to farm—not grapes, of course—near Breslau in Silesia; it was the time when Hitler was promoting the idea of "Lebensraum im Osten".'

This eastern connection was unexpectedly and romantically repeated when Rainer married Elisabeth Franke from Halle in June 1989. What had started as an arrangement of convenience—Elisabeth wanted to emigrate to the West—turned, over three years of meetings, into something deeper.

'My father was born in Edenkoben, and remembers helping with the harvest when he was a child, but he was brought up mainly in Silesia. He had a reputation for being exceptionally strong when he was fifteen or sixteen—a very good farm-worker.' Karl Lingenfelder, a compact, wiry man with steel-grey hair, has a granite-like strength and toughness still, at the age of sixty-four, though serious illness laid him low a couple of years ago. 'But the war came and my father volunteered for the Wehrmacht when he was only seventeen, in September 1942. He missed being sent to Stalingrad because he had flu: nobody in that battalion came back.'

Karl Lingenfelder met his wife in Silesia, where her family originated. At the end of the Second World War, of course, Ostpreussen became part of Poland, and the Lingenfelders became refugees.

'Fortunately my father had relations in Edenkoben, and he came back to work in the Pfalz. After a while, he found time to study at the wine school in Neustadt and then in 1951 he leased the estate here in Grosskarlbach.

'I was born here in Grosskarlbach and feel very much a native. I went to the village school, now closed down, like the branch railway-line. After that I went to the Gymnasium [grammar-school], first in Grünstadt, then in Ludwigshafen, where I specialised in economics.

'I was not at all interested in wine-making or vineyards at that time. When I was fourteen I joined a gliding club, and later got a pilot's licence. German airspace is very busy and limited: I wanted to fly without limits, and that meant leaving Germany. Growing up in the 1960s and 1970s I was a member of the early post-1968 generation from which the Baader-Meinhof group recruited their supporters. I read

Heinrich Böll—*The Lost Honour of Katherina Blum*; I liked Fassbinder's films, and also *Jonathan Livingstone Seagull*—all that free flying, I suppose. I also saw a film about Thor Heyerdahl, the man who sailed the Pacific on a raft, and I developed this dream of going to Polynesia. It was all very romantic, coconut palms and beautiful girls.

'So when I was meant to do my military service and join the Bundeswehr, I bought a VW van together with three friends and set off overland to India. I had decided I didn't want to be German, and would not return to Germany. The military police turned up at Grosskarlbach after we left and my mother became extremely worried.

'It was 1975, and we were lucky that it was possible then to go overland, through Iran and Afghanistan. When we got to India there was a bureaucratic hassle which meant that it wasn't possible either to keep the van or to sell it, so we just had to leave it there. At that point the four of us decided to go our separate ways. After five months of travelling—I had set out with two thousand Deutschmarks—I had just enough money for a plane ticket to Perth, Western Australia.

'I started working in a petrol station, seven days a week, twelve hours a day. Then I hitchhiked to Adelaide, and started getting jobs in the wine industry, which was the only thing I knew about. I worked for Basedow, Kaiserstuhl and Penfold's, where I did the harvest in February and March. I spent two years working in the wine industry in Australia, and became increasingly interested in wine. I decided that I would like to go back to Germany and study at Geisenheim. So I wrote to the Bundeswehr and said that I had changed my attitude and was prepared to do my military service, so long as I wasn't disciplined.

'I flew in to Luxembourg because my parents thought Frankfurt was too dangerous—I might be arrested! My father, my brother and my sister collected me at the airport and smuggled me across the border.

'The Monday after I got back I presented myself at the State Prosecutor's office. The usual State Prosecutor was not there, but a lady named Barbara Just-Dahlmann was standing in for him. That was a stroke of luck for me because she was a very sympathetic person. She listened to what I had to say and her conclusion was that she didn't see any reason to press charges. I later discovered that she was the kind of lawyer who stands up for the underdog, and that she had written books on the philosophy of law and individual rights. She also wrote to the Military saying that she didn't see any reason to prosecute me and would be glad if they let the matter drop. They replied that they would not prosecute but might impose military discipline.

'That sounded as if it might be rough, but I had a second stroke of luck when I joined up in October. I went to see the Captain in charge of discipline, and when he had heard what I had to say, he told me he wished he had done the same thing when he was my age. I was not disciplined.

'In fact my change of attitude was entirely genuine. I now believe that defence is essential: to live in peace and liberty, people must be prepared to defend themselves, with arms if necessary. The Germans should have stood up for themselves against Hitler.

'Then came my third stroke of luck: I asked for early release from military service, which normally lasts sixteen months, so that I could start studying at Geisenheim in October. The general who saw my application was Herr Bastian, who later resigned from the army and became a Green politician [and the consort of Petra Kelly]. I was able to work through the holidays and was given my release.'

Rainer is a modest man, but it is clear that he stood out as an exceptionally gifted student. He went on to do research work on the role of phenolic compounds in wine, which has turned out to have had an important practical bearing on the wine-making at Weingut Lingenfelder.

Before taking up his present post in the family estate, Rainer continued to widen his wine-making experience by doing further work in Australia, at the huge Waikerei Co-operative which taught him valuable lessons about bulk wine-making (the Co-operative handles 10 million litres of grape-must a year), in the Médoc, where he did a stage for the Borie family at Château Grand-Puy-Lacoste, and in that most fashionable of cool-climate wine countries, New Zealand, where he worked for Montana at Gisborne.

The most bizarre of Rainer's overseas wine jobs, however, was in Egypt, where he worked for eighteen months as supervisor on a winery modernisation project in the Nile Delta. Eighteen months on this job was, Rainer admits, more than enough.

He was very pleased when he received the offer of the job of chief oenologist to the big shippers and blenders H. Sichel Sohne. Sichel are an old-established family firm with branches in New York and London, dominated for half a century by the personality of Walter Sichel, creator of Blue Nun. Sichel started work for the family firm selling German wine in Britain after the First World War, which he did very successfully despite the virulent anti-German feeling of the time. Just before the Second World War Sichel and his family, as Jews, were forced suddenly to leave their home town of Mainz without their possessions. After the War, during which he worked as an ambulance-driver, Walter Sichel, based at the London offices of Sichel in the Adelphi, rebuilt the German side of the business by concentrating on

Ronald Barton of
Châteaux Leoville- and
Langoa-Barton *(Barton)*

Anthony Barton in the *chai* at Langoa-
Barton *(Barton)*

Chartreuse-style Château Langoa-Barton *(Author)*

Médoc landscape with Château Langoa-Barton in the distance *(Author)*

Châteauneuf-du-Pape:
view of vineyards near
Château Fortia *(Author)*

Stony vineyards of
Châteauneuf-du-Pape
(Author)

Jean and Etienne Grivot tasting in the cellar below the family house and domaine in the Vosne-Romanée *(Grivot)*

Jean Grivot (left) and Etienne Grivot (right) *(Grivot)*

Christian Pol Roger and Christian de Billy *(Pol Roger)*

Sir Winston Churchill admiring his filly Odette Pol-Roger *(Pol Roger)*

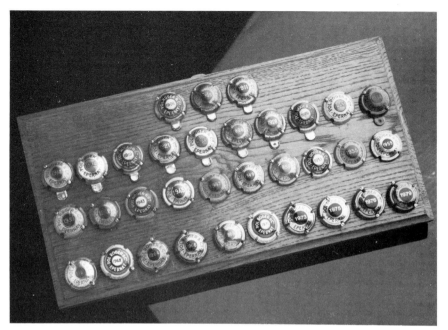

Metal capsules for champagne corks in the collection of Pol Roger of Epernay *(Pol Roger)*

The Pol Roger headquarters in Epernay *(Author)*

Erwein, Graf
Matuschka-
Greiffenclau, with
his wife Sabine and
daughter Francesca
(*Matuschka-
Greiffenclau*)

Schloss Vollrads in the Rheingau (*Author*)

Rheingau: the most prestigious of Germany's wine-growing regions
(*Author*)

Schloss Vollrads, with vines growing in the distance (*Author*)

Rainer Lingenfelder being presented with the International Wine & Spirit Competition Winemaker of the Year Award, 1984 *(Lingenfelder)*

Palladian-style headquarters of Weingut Lingenfelder in Grosskarlbach, Rheinpfalz *(Lingenfelder)*

Rainer Lingenfelder with his father Karl and uncle Hermann *(Lingenfelder)*

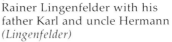

Weingut Lingenfelder cellars containing *barriques* *(Lingenfelder)*

The Antinori's working buildings at Pèppoli *(Author)*

Pèppoli vineyard with poplars and vines *(Author)*

Palazzo Antinori, Florence: home of the Antinori family *(Antinori)*

Three generations of Antinori: Niccolò (grandfather), Piero (father) and Albiera (daughter) *(Antinori)*

Mas Rabell de Fontenac *(Author)*

Torres vineyards in the snow *(Author)*

Don Miguel Torres
checking export shipments
at Barcelona *(Torres)*

Sr. Miguel A Torres
of Vilafranca *(Torres)*

Office party at Vinicola Hidalgo, Dec. 1959 *(Hidalgo)*

(l–r) Juan Luis Hidalgo Alvarez (Pres.), Manuel Hidalgo de Argüeso,
Javier Hidalgo de Argüeso; *(seated)* Simón Sanchez Lopez (Hidalgo rep. in
Seville) in office *(Hidalgo)*

Juan Luis Hidalgo Alvarez with barrels in the Hidalgo *bodega* at Sanlucar *(Hidalgo)*

Javier Hidalgo de Argüeso with barrels *(Hidalgo)*

The Upper Douro near Tua *(Author)*

The Quinta dos Malvedos, the Symingtons' family villa *(Author)*

Maurice and Eileen
Symington in their
vineyard at Bomfim
(Symington)

A J Symington with
associate under the
vines *(Symington)*

(Back row, l–r) John Symington, Ron Symington, Michael Symington;
(seated) Maurice Symington, Elizabeth Symington (Michael's wife) *(Symington)*

the branded, blended, medium-sweet hock which, under that strange ecclesiastical label, was to become the world's biggest-selling wine. Sichel's other activities, as shippers of high-quality estate-bottled German wines, became subsidiary to the big business of the Nun.

It seems rather strange on the face of it that Rainer, strongly committed to high-quality, estate-bottled production at his family estate, should have become involved in making a mass-produced blended wine. But he says there was no conflict of principles: 'Blue Nun is a high-quality product, and I was proud to be associated with it. Not all Liebfraumilch is bad, you know. It was a fascinating challenge to select a few wines of solid quality from hundreds of samples, and then blend them to create something more harmonious and better balanced than any of the components. There is certainly a place for a well-made blended wine on the market. Not everything can be from a single vineyard and estate-bottled.'

When I drove with Rainer, on the last morning of my stay, to visit the big new Sichel plant at Alzey in the Rheinhessen, 48 kilometres from Grosskarlbach, I was impressed by its air of hygiene and efficiency. Parked outside in the forecourt was the most glitteringly clean lorry I had ever seen, polished down to parts no ordinary lorry-driver, at least in Britain, would consider worth touching. The hub-caps and bumpers shone like shaving-mirrors.

Inside, the vast 240,000-litre blending tanks, the Kieselgur and the plate filters were equally spotless. I was shown the laboratory equipped with a gas chromatograph linked to a mass spectrometer—a piece of equipment costing over £50,000 which is used for aroma analysis. No diethylene glycol or ethyl carbonate, a suspected carcinogen, could ever find its way into Blue Nun. The three bottling-lines have a capacity of 30,000 bottles an hour.

Rainer says he found Sichel an agreeable place to work—for a time. The managing director, Riquet Hess, is a man of wide culture and engaging humour. His offices in the hangar-like plant are decorated with lacquer panels, cane furniture and Chinese screens. When Rainer decided, a couple of years ago, that he wished to leave Sichel to concentrate on the family estate, the company, and Hess in particular, were reluctant to let him go. They persuaded him to work part-time for a year, but Rainer found it an unsatisfactory compromise. 'I think I am a person who needs to be fully committed to one thing. I find it unsatisfactory to be only partly involved. You are not listened to with the same attention, for a start.'

So it was that in autumn 1988 Rainer left Sichel, taking a considerable cut in salary and moving into a family business with what might seem to an outsider an uncertain future. The reputation of fine German wine, as I have mentioned, has never been at a lower ebb. And unlike Graf Matuschka, secure in an estate owned by his family for 700 years, Rainer found himself working on an estate whose lease had to be renewed. It was a situation requiring nerve and faith. Both were shaken by the devastating hailstorm on 27 May, which destroyed more than half of the estate's production for 1988. It was a severe blow, but worse things had happened in thirteen generations of wine-growing. The Lingenfelders are made of durable stuff.

So much for the background. The foreground, as the second day of my visit began, was the 1988 harvest, and the day-to-day, minute-to-minute work of monitoring the state of the grapes and deciding when to pick. The first excitement of the day, after a substantial German break-fast, was a bird-scare. We had heard a number of muffled explosions, like distant military practice, then a telephone call from a neighbouring grower confirmed that there was an ominous build-up of avian intruders. 'Let's get over there quickly,' said Rainer. He meant it. Having grabbed a blank-firing pistol and a couple of other implements, we ran to the car and hurtled through the village and out to the vineyard. I felt rather like a character in Hitchcock's *The Birds*, but it was a false alarm. Perched high up on the steel cross-bars of the huge pylons which stride across the vineyards were rows of smallish black birds, distinguishable only as specks. 'They're starlings,' Rainer said. 'They can be a very serious nuisance, because they love the ripe grapes. Just now they don't look too dangerous.' All the same, he fired a couple of blanks, sending a flock of fifty or so wheeling out of range.

'Now we can measure the must-weights.' He instructed me to go through a line of vines, picking grapes from different parts of the compact bunches. These were Scheurebe grapes, just turning a freckled gold, firm but ripe, aromatic and sweet with an appetising acidity. The starlings had good taste. Rainer had given me a small hand-press—a hinged metal instrument with a perforated lid, like a garlic crusher. When the tiny basket was full, I pressed down the lid and the bowl filled with mirky, greenish-yellow must. Rainer then produced a pocket spectroscope, a small cylindrical instrument like a tiny telescope. We carefully deposited a drop or two of must on one end of the lens, then held it to the light and looked through the other end. A black line became visible, measuring the specific gravity of the must in Oechsle degrees, which compare the weight of the must with that of water. These Scheurebe grapes measured 89 degrees Oechsle: one litre of this must would weigh 89 g more than a litre of water. More importantly, when fermented, these grapes would produce wine with rather more than 11 degrees of alcohol by volume.

'They are into the Spätlese, or late-gathered, category: the second of the grades of QmP, quality wine with specific attributes. It's rather a long-winded way of saying the grapes are nicely ripe. To put this level of ripeness into perspective, we expect to make a reasonable amount of Spätlese every year: in the Rheingau or the Mosel-Saar-Ruwer they get a Spätlese vintage only once every three years.' One might add that in the Médoc, in moderate vintages, the Cabernet Sauvignon grapes can struggle to reach 10 degrees potential alcohol.

We performed the same operation on a row of Spätburgunder vines. There was a complication here: the hailstorm of 27 May, which ripped through the buds of the original crop, and left great calloused scars on the shoots, had created a secondary crop of grapes. These were less ripe than the pitiful remains of the first crop—Rainer reckoned only 5 per cent of normal production—but not so much so that they were immediately easy to differentiate. Still, picking with care, and tasting when in doubt—the primary crop grapes were beautifully sweet, the secondary ones sweet-sour—I filled the hand-press and moistened the spectroscope: 90 degrees. Left on the vines for another week or two, these grapes could well reach 13 degrees potential alcohol. At the Domaine de la Romanée-Conti in Burgundy they would be happy with that.

'It's a great shame, because I think we would have made our best ever Spätburgunder this year. The grapes have a beautiful balance. But now we've got a problem: is it worth picking the primary crop separately, and how will we instruct the pickers to separate primary from secondary?' In the event, no one would ever know how good the 1988 Spätburgunder might have been, because primary and secondary crops were picked together, and the wine downgraded from Spätburgunder to simple Grosskarlbacher *Rotwein*.

'Now we had better check that the starlings are not eating our Riesling grapes,' Rainer said. We got back in the car and drove down the gentle slope of Grosskarlbacher Burgweg, through the village and up the slope the other side. This north-facing slope was covered with fruit-trees and scrub, not vines. Half-way up, we stopped by what looked like a large sandpit. It was time for a little geology lesson. I picked up a handful of the pale greyish soil and found it light and extremely fine. 'This soil is called loess: it is a wind-borne deposit, blown here from the peri-glacial till and moraine areas, perhaps from as far away as central Asia. It's very rich in minerals and holds water well—excellent soil for vines. Our main problem here is drought: the average rainfall is 450-500 mm. Unfortunately because of the way the wind blew we have loess only on the north slopes. The south slopes have sandy, calcareous soil which doesn't hold water so well and so gives only about half the yield. We would be quite a lot richer if the wind had blown the other way.'

We drove on over the top of the ridge, down another vine-planted south slope, up another north slope of orchards, and stopped the car where the vines began on the way down. It was a sheltered, peaceful place with a thriving bird-life—goldfinches, warblers, tits—but, at that moment, no massed squadrons of starlings.

'This is our best vineyard. We have just crossed into the parish of Freinsheim, and this vineyard is called Freinsheimer Goldberg.'

From the crest of the slope it is possible to make out the solid bastions of the medieval walls which still surround Freinsheim. On this steeper slope the vines are terraced laterally, unlike those in the Grosskarlbacher Burgweg, to avoid soil erosion. Rainer points out a neighbour's vines, planted straight down the steepish slope. At the base of the rows there has accumulated a thick layer of washed-down sand. 'Another few heavy rainfalls and there will be no soil at all. You can see that many of his vines—the ones with the brown, shrivelled, leaves—are badly stressed already.'

Apart from nearly three hectares in Freinsheimer Goldberg, where they grow Riesling and Scheurebe, the Lingenfelders own just a few rows in the celebrated Musikantenbuckel, or musician's hump, vineyard. 'Our part of the Goldberg should really have been included in Musikantenbuckel, when they reorganised the vineyards in 1971 and changed the boundaries. However, the people in Freinsheim didn't agree with my father's idea about planting laterally, and so they left our part as Goldberg. It's an easier name to say, and I'm not sure it's a disadvantage.' Once again, we proceeded through the vines with hand-press and spectroscope. The Riesling grapes measured 88 degrees Oechsle. If the rain held off, and there was a little more sun, they would make good Spätlese. Or even Auslese...

Only now, after seeing all the vineyards where the Lingen-felders grow their grapes, was it time to return to Grosskarlbach and inspect the cellars, where the wine is made. Like everything Rainer does, the order was carefully thought out for an educative purpose. 'The Lingenfelders have always been grape-growers first and wine-makers second—though now perhaps the two are more equal. There is a German word *bodenstandig*, which means, literally, standing on the soil.' This word implies an Antaeus-like rootedness in the soil rather than the notion of having one's feet on the ground. 'My father is bodenstandig, like his ancestors. Even though I have done a lot of technical oenology, I consider myself bodenstandig too.' Here surely is the real reason why Rainer decided to leave Sichel.

'We believe it is possible to make premium wine only from premium grapes: quality begins in the vineyard. My father was the first person in this area to use high-wire trellising and the wide, two-metre spacing of vines, which has now become standard. When I was in California recently I saw Robert Mondavi's Opus One vineyard and found the same system used there.'

Yields on the Lingenfelder estate are relatively low, at least by German standards: 83 hectolitres of wine per hectare of vines, as opposed to the Rheinpfalz average of around 120.

Back at the estate house, we found the courtyard bustling with activity. A tractor, driven by Rainer's uncle Hermann, was delivering a trailer-full of grapes to the press-house, located in the corner of the outbuilding nearest to the house. Several cars were parked in the courtyard: two Ladas with Polish number plates contrasted with a slick Audi estate. The Ladas belonged to the two families of Polish pickers who, Rainer told me, had just turned up at the doorstep ten years before, and returned for the harvest every year since. The Lingenfelders provide them with decent, if Spartan accommodation on the first floor of the outbuildings: they cook their own food. They are paid the same rate as the German vineyard workers: 8.50 DM per hour.

'The Poles are becoming as important to the German wine industry as the Spanish migrant workers in Bordeaux and the Mexicans in California,' Rainer explained.

The Audi belonged to a long-standing customer from the north of Germany who comes down every October to buy his annual supply of Lingenfelder wine and Lingenfelder apples. Just on the left as you enter the courtyard is the apple shop, manned by Frau Lingenfelder as part of the myriad duties of a wine-grower's wife. Further round is a wine-shop, or wine-bar: customers are encouraged to taste and drink before purchasing. These doorstep sales are important, representing nearly half the total: the apples are a useful source of cash just when it is needed to pay pickers.

This time it was Frau Lingenfelder who was delayed: but the lunch of Wurst and Sauerkraut which she somehow managed to pre-pare was as tasty and satisfying as ever. Afterwards, we went down to the cellars. The contents of the tractor trailer—Morio-Muskat grapes, going to make a cheapish, aromatic litre wine sold independently by uncle Sieghart (married to Karl Lingenfelder's sister Hermine)—were now revolving gently inside a Vaslin press.

'With white wines our aim is to preserve the purity and the aroma of the fruit. So, we try to keep our hands off the grapes as much as possible. The pressing, as you can see, is gentle; we use natural yeasts for the most part; we clean the must by cold settling rather than centrifuging. We don't use a fining agent and we hardly ever de-acidify. When you start playing around technically, you have to make so many adjustments to correct the things you have unbalanced before. Despite the fact that we don't fine and pasteurise, we have never had a protein instability. We know our own vineyards, and so we can trust the grapes.'

A door led through from the press-house to the tank cellar, lined with two rows of fibre-glass and stainless-steel fermentation tanks topped with glass S-valves. Bubbles of CO_2 were passing through them at a regular, not frenetic pace. 'Fermentation should be slow, but not too slow. If it gets too hot, above say 22 degrees, we can cool the tanks either by sprinkling water over them with hoses or by a more sophisticated heat exchange system.'

Lingenfelder white wines see no wood; after fermentation in fibre-glass or stainless steel they are kept in large concrete or steel tanks before bottling in the spring after the harvest. So what explained the presence in the old cellar below the house—a fine vaulted affair built out of massive block of sandstone—of sixty barriques stamped 'Château Grand-Puy-Lacoste'? Had I hit upon an unlikely wine scandal involving the production of ersatz claret in southern Germany?

'When I started maturing our red Spätburgunder wine in these barrels, my father was not impressed. We had some arguments about it, I can tell you.' Red wine from Germany sounds improbable enough in itself, even without the claret barrels. There is the pink, scented, usually sweet stuff from Assmanshausen in the Rheingau: fine in its own way, but not red wine to any except a German mind. Lingenfelder Spätburgunder, I already know, is not like that at all: it is deep-coloured, full-bodied, meaty.

'Historically, as I told you, this was more of a red than a white wine area. But the art of red-wine-making was lost. People here tried, and still do try for the most part, to make red wine as if it were white wine: preserving primary fruit character and aroma. But red wine is not about those things: it is about secondary, evolved characters, which develop in wood.

'I have always had a good feeling about wood—it's a very subjective thing. But when I did my research on phenols at Geisenheim I discovered that wood has a very important influence on the colour of red wine.'

The second time I visited the Lingenfelder estate, in November 1987, Rainer gave an impressive proof of this point. I was presented with two samples of red wine. The first had a good deep colour, a rich Pinot Noir nose, lively fruit and good body on the palate. The second, on the other hand, was much paler in colour, and showed some brownness round the rim. It tasted thinner in the mouth—altogether rather pale and wan compared to the first. Two different wines, obviously. No, these were two samples of exactly the same wine, the Lingenfelder 1986 Spätburgunder, but the first had been matured for a year in small oak barriques, the second in large, old German oak casks. Rainer explained: 'In small barrels phenolic compounds polymerise, giving deeper colour. Pasteur said, "C'est l'air qui fait le vin," and in burgundy it is usual to give red wines several rackings in air.'

Another practice, common in Burgundy but almost unheard of in Germany, which Rainer adopted for the Lingenfelder Spätburgunder, was malo-lactic fermentation, induced immediately after the first fermentation by raising the temperature to around 20°C. Once again he faced opposition from his father, who favoured a fruity style of red wine with the same fresh acidity for which the Lingenfelder white wines are so notable. The 1985 vintage won him round. This splendidly rich, velvety-warm wine soon had a cult following. Almost the only body it did not convince was the local wine authority, which refused to give the wine an AP number, the official recognition of quality, on the grounds of lack of typicity. So much the better for it, was the response of drinkers in Britain.

Apart from red wine-making, there is one other issue on which Rainer and his father do not always see eye to eye. They have different ideas about marketing. 'I would not like to say that marketing is all-important,' says Rainer, distancing himself from the philosophy of Graf Matuschka. 'All the same, I do think it is important to get our wines internationally known and recognised, especially in Britain where, historically, the reputations of all the world's great wines have been made. I have devoted a good deal of time to building up our sales in Britain,and it is now beginning to pay off. At the beginning my father said it was a waste of time, and I would do better to concentrate on the home market which is our bread-and-butter. That shows a generation difference: my parents are people who like to feel they have done something concrete at the end of a day, ploughed a field, pruned a vineyard. Working on a long-term marketing strategy does not pay off immediately. But just as you can only expect a vineyard to produce good grapes if you look after it personally, you can expect the market to open up for you only if you cultivate it and nurture it.' In the autumn of 1989, Rainer spent a week visiting thirty-five Oddbins shops in the south of England, making contact with the managers and monitoring the way his wines were sold and presented.

Winning the International Wine & Spirit Competition Winemaker of the Year award in 1984, as well as being an impressive personal accolade, gave a considerable boost to Rainer's plan to build up the Weingut Lingenfelder's reputation outside Germany. The Lingenfelders also won the Metternich Trophy for the best botrytised wine (for a Freinsheimer Musikantenbuckel Scheurebe Trockenbeerenauslese 1976, a wine as magnificently rich and concentrated as its name is long). In 1988 the Metternich Trophy became the Karl Lingenfelder Trophy. The first winner was Newland Vineyards in the Napa Valley for their 1982 Johannisberger Riesling Late Harvest. Another useful way of making his wines known, Rainer considers, is to invite journalists, from Germany, England and other countries, to come and taste wines at Grosskarlbach. Not just Lingenfelder wines, but also wines from France, California, Australia, are tasted blind, to prove Rainer's contention that his Grosskarlbach wines can compete in the international market.

One of these tastings took place on the last evening of my stay, in the airy, well-proportioned dining-room of the estate house. Present, apart from the Lingenfelders and myself, were a Pfalz wine-maker, Hardy Werlé from Forst, two wine-makers from New Zealand, a German journalist and the English wine writer and expert on German wines, Stuart Pigott. The first wine tasted had a subtle blend of oak and fruit on the nose and was quite lean but stylish on the palate. Chardonnay, certainly, and from a good source in Burgundy, I guessed. The second had a more obviously fruity style (there was a suggestion of grapefruit) but with similar qualities of style and balance. The third wine, oxidised and toffee-nosed, I ruled out. As for the question of which of the first two was the better wine, opinions were divided. One of the New Zealanders liked the oakiness of the first wine; and so did I, because it was artfully integrated with the fruit. The Germans found it difficult to accept that oak should be an element in the flavour of white wine. But both wines were extremely well made and satisfying, albeit in different styles. The wines turned out to be Pouilly-Fuissé, Château de Fuissé, 1984 (top-class grower, average year) and the Lingenfelder Scheurebe Spätlese Trocken 1983.

A number of points had been made. First, dry German wines can work, at least in this part of the Rheinpfalz. About half the Lingenfelders' production is Trocken (containing less than 9 g per litre residual sugar), and a quarter each Halb-Trocken (between 9 g and 18 g) and the traditional style, not really sweet, but balanced between sweetness and acidity. The doubts I have about dry German wines made in other regions, especially the Rheingau, Mosel-Saar-Ruwer and Nahe, tend to disappear in the case of the best dry wines from the Pfalz. It is a matter of body. As Rainer says, 'With 11.5 degrees alcohol achieved without chaptalisation and a high level of glycerol, natural of course, our wines are sufficiently ripe not to need sweetness.'

Secondly, the Scheurebe grape is capable of making fine wines. Both Rainer and his father believe that this grape, a crossing between Silvaner and Riesling developed by a Dr Scheu at Alzey in 1916, can match and even surpass Riesling when grown on the best sites in the best years. I am not convinced that Scheurebe can match Riesling's elegance, but it can certainly produce stylish, intense wines which go notably well with German food.

The final conclusion I draw is that it can be only a matter of time before the best German wines, made with intense dedication and skill, are once more recognised as among the world's finest. Rainer Lingenfelder, at least, is optimistic. 'Despite the generally bad image of German wines, small estates such as ours have a good future. I am convinced that we make wines of the highest international standard. But we must go out and tell the world about them. Nothing will happen if we just sit here complaining that nobody understands us.'

Antinori

of

Florence

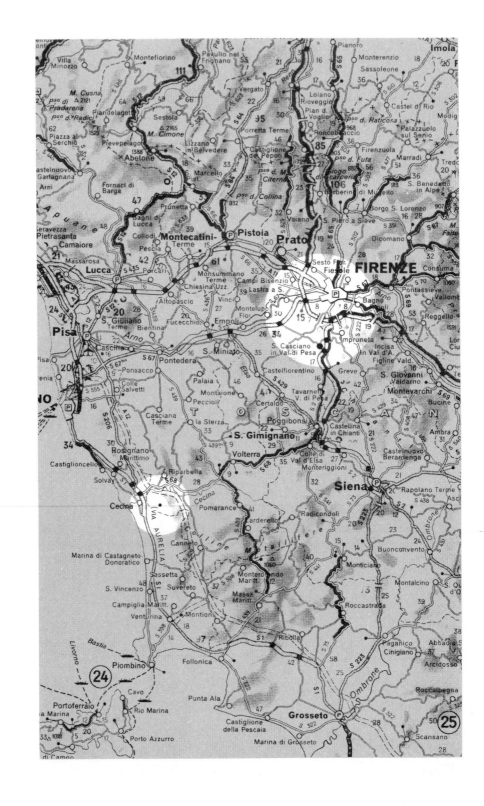

T|HE CENTRE OF FLORENCE is closed to traffic. Coming from the south, if you try to enter the city through the Porta Romana, laid-back students acting as part-time traffic police and brandishing little red lollipop sticks direct you away up the switchbacking road to the Piazzale Michelangelo where all the tourist buses stop. It is an eight-kilometre detour and may seem a nuisance, but the glimpses of the city through the roadside cypresses tempt you to stop too. The Piazzale probably only figures as a five-minute photo-opportunity on the coach-tour itinerary, but the view remains breathtaking. Spread out with red tiled roofs, tawny rough stone towers and the white and green marble smoothness of the cathedral and Giotto's campanile focusing it all Florence seems more perfect than any medium sized city in the late twentieth century has a right to be. Where are the factory chimneys, the gasworks, the ugliness? Florence's miraculous state of preservation, despite war and more disastrous flood, is a tribute to both the overriding Italian concern with aesthetics and the value of tourism. But it is also an indication of a city whose most active, dynamic days are long behind it.

Bernard Shaw spent a few weeks in Florence in 1894 studying religious art, then returned to Birmingham for an exhibition of Pre-Raphaelite painting. 'On the whole Birmingham was more hopeful than the Italian cities,' he wrote, in the Preface to *Candida*, 'for the art it had to shew me was the work of living men, whereas modern Italy had, as far as I could see, no more connection with Giotto than Port Said has with Ptolemy.'

True continuities between the Florence of the Renaissance and the contemporary tourists' city are few and far between. Fifteenth-century Florence was the prototype of modern capitalism, a city-state built on trade and banking. Its modern equivalents would be New York and the City of London, or Tokyo and Seoul. I wonder though whether tourists will make pilgrimages to those cities in 500 years' time as they do now to Florence. The first great Medici, Cosimo, was under no illusions about the stability of his family's power: 'I know the men of this city. Fifty years will not pass before we are driven out.' Some of that power, though, had been invested in the works of Brunelleschi, Alberti, Donatello, Della Robbia. Cosimo was right when he went on: 'Our buildings will remain.' The Medici are a name now —a name which will live because of the great artists they patronised—but not a going concern. The same is true of most of the great Florentine banking clans, the Strozzi, the Bardi, the Acciaiuoli. In one area, though, there has been an extraordinary continuity: Antinori, Frescobaldi, Guicciardini, Ricasoli are all still in the wine business after more than 500 years.

In the early days wine was an unimportant side-line. The Antinori, like almost all the great Florentine clans, made their fortune as traders in fabrics (silk in their case) and as bankers. It is stirring to walk down the Via Tornabuoni (past the headquarters of another Florentine dynasty, Gucci) and find yourself in a small square, called the Piazza Antinori, facing a stern-looking *palazzo* built of great rough-hewn blocks of stone, the Palazzo Antinori (the side chapel of the church with the splendid baroque façade opposite is the Capella Antinori). If this makes you think that nothing has changed for 600 years, of an immemorial tradition of wine-growing, that is not exactly the truth. The reality, as always, has been more dynamic and unstable.

The palazzo was not always the Palazzo Antinori, for a start. The present building, dating from 1461, was designed, probably by the architect Giuliano da Maiano, for the young scion of a leading banking family, Giovanni Boni. Boni died five years later, never having lived in his grand new property. Neither did the next owner Carlo Martelli (for whom the palazzo was purchased by order of no less than Lorenzo il Magnifico di Medici), who rented it out and was apparently just preparing to take up residence when he died in 1498. The sale to Niccolo di Tommaso Antinori, then one of the richest men in the city, finally took place on 2 February 1506, for the price of 4000 florins.

A period of 480 years in the same family is impressive enough. Such continuity is made possible only by constant adaptation. As you enter the massive doorway, the first thing you notice, on the right, is a sign saying Cantinetta Antinori: inside, it could be a London or New York wine bar, clean rather impersonal decor, small rectangular tables, a place to meet for a business lunch or early supper (last orders 9.30 p.m.). The wines, of course, are all from the Antinori stable.

Proceeding further, you find yourself in a classic Florentine Renaissance courtyard, like a secular cloister, the freshly whitewashed walls and simple vaults counterpointed by the grey *pietra serena* of the columns and Corinthian pilasters. There is an old grey stone well in one corner. Everything is immaculately clean. Ahead, through a glass door, is a light-filled waiting room lined with eighteenth-century portraits— cardinals, soldiers, bewigged senators. The waiting room backs on to a fair-sized lawn with bright flowering borders and a driveway—a welcome breathing space amidst the dense stone solidity of central Florence.

Marchese Piero Antinori is as handsome and classically proportioned as his ancestral home. In a face of regular features, his frank, friendly blue eyes stand out; his hair gives no sign of thinning though it is beginning to turn grey. He looks young for his age (late forties), a man in his prime. The Antinoris seem to be a long-lived family: Piero's father Niccolò celebrated his ninetieth birthday in 1988, and still comes into his office in the Palazzo Antinori every morning. Even more striking than Piero's appearance is his ease and charm of manner: few ambassadors, or kings or princes come to that, could better the refined courtesy, said to be a distinguishing mark of the old Florentine aristocracy.

'Our family has been involved in wine-making since at least 1385. We had a big celebration in 1985 for the sexcentenary. We thought then we were the oldest family with a continuous tradition of wine-growing, but I got a letter from a man in Germany, Graf Matuschka, saying that they were 175 years older. It was all very friendly and we had a good dinner together. Anyway, it was in 1385 that we have the first record of an Antinori, Giovanni di Piero, being enrolled in the Florentine Guild of Wine-makers. Wine-makers were quite low down the social scale in those days; they came under the "lesser guilds", below the seven corporations, which were professions like law and various forms of trade. Wine was a side-business for the Antinori then: they started in silk trading and became rather international, establishing other divisions outside Florence. As a consequence of that they started to be active in finance and banking. After that they began to farm and to buy land and villas outside Florence, and to produce wine, as a hobby rather than a main activity. The main purpose was to have beautiful houses and villas around Florence: the agriculture and wine-growing sprang out of that. Afterwards, in the sixteenth century when the Medici started to lose power, Florence went through difficult times in trade and banking, especially in banking: all the prominent families got into difficulties, and that was when the agricultural properties became their main concern—they had lost all the rest. I think since that time we have continued in wine production with no interruption.'

In his poem 'Bacco in Toscana' written in the mid-seventeenth century, the pharmacist-poet Francesco Redi cites Antinori as a source of good wine. In the next century, Donato Maria Antinori (whose portrait, haughty and aquiline-nosed, hangs in the hall of the Palazzo Antinori) numbered the Pope among his customers. A letter written to his cousin Niccolò on 6 March 1729 testifies to a meticulous care and refined connoisseurship, not common at that time. 'Not only have I tasted the "Leatico" you sent me, but I have had it tasted by those who will be drinking it...we have found it to be of the best quality, and we are of the opinion that after standing for a little more time it will become even better...I, myself, would have liked it to have a little more of the bouquet of "Leatico", but since it was liked by those (the Pope) to whom I am sending it, for their own consumption, this opinion of mine is superfluous.' (Quoted in Pellucci, *Antinori: Vintners in Florence*, 1981).

'The reason why we have developed and grown', Marchese Piero explains, 'is that in every generation there has been at least one member of the family who has been active and totally involved in the wine production—sometimes more than one, but always at least one. There has been a continuity whereas in other families there have been interruptions. I think in this business, like any other business, perhaps more than other businesses, you need to be very dedicated all the time. You cannot really leave it alone, even when it starts to become bigger and more important. You can be very organised, you can have a fantastic structure and good managers but there is no substitute for the personal dedication of a member of the family. It is necessary for the maintenance of quality, for keeping an image.'

It is as a result of careful attention to both quality and image that Piero Antinori has turned his family company's fortunes round, from a low point in the 1970s when there were newspaper reports of a take-over by the vast American-based Villa Banfi group, to a high-point in terms of both reputation, and judging by big new purchases in Chianti, of profitability. That is quite an achievement, in a country where the saying goes that there are three ways to lose a fortune: women (the pleasantest); gambling (the fastest); and owning an estate in Tuscany (the surest). True, Antinori is not entirely family-owned: the large English brewers Whitbread have a 49 per cent share. This arrangement 'helps with foreign markets', says Marchese Piero, but is very far from meaning that Antinori have sold out to the English, as a front-page headline in *La Republica* claimed in October 1988. Marchese Piero was incensed and considered suing the paper. After all, he himself controls Antinori with a personal holding of 51 per cent of the shares.

He gives the impression that it has all come very easily. 'For me it has been a very natural thing to work in the business. I grew up in this kind of environment, talking all the time about wine, about the family problems of wine production. So for me there has never really been any other particular interest in my life. I have one brother and one sister. My sister, who's older than me, has never been interested in business. She lives in Chianti Classico [the central zone of Chianti between Florence and Siena: *classico* in Italian wine parlance refers to the oldest-established part of a region, not to any special refinement of wine-making]; she loves the country and the wines, but she doesn't want to pursue the wine activity directly. Then I have a young brother—four or five years younger than me—who has done many things, including working in the company on the commercial, marketing side. He has spent many years in the States and in other parts of the world. He had a sort of interruption with other interests and now he is looking after a small, very high-quality vineyard on our estate at Bolgheri near the Tuscan coast. It is going to be something independent yet integrated into our company.

'I suppose you could say my own progression in the firm has been very smooth. My father, who, as you know, is still very active, handed over control of the firm to me when I was very young, in 1966. He was always very good at delegating, so there was none of the usual problems of the father wanting to continue controlling things. In fact it was a little bit the opposite: I think he handed over control too early, though he was in his late sixties at the time. It was not because he wanted to give up responsibility, but because he had confidence in me. Before that, I went to university here in Florence to study economics and business science rather than agriculture. I began working part-time for the firm before I finished at university and at that time I worked in the marketing and sales department, which was especially difficult and important for us then. But more and more, gradually, I started to devote myself to the technical side, viticulture and oenology. I'm not a trained oenologist but I think right now at my age I devote much more of my time, out of preference, to the technical, production part than all the rest of the business.'

This progression from marketing and commerce to production could be seen to reflect, in a curious way, the development of the Antinori dynasty itself, from general traders and bankers with only a passing interest in wine to a family which puts wine at the very centre of its activity. But there is a more practical explanation for Marchese Piero's decision to absorb himself in the details of wine production.

'It was a very critical moment, the beginning of the 1970s, in terms of wine production. I thought it was essential to make a change in the style of wine—to try to introduce a new style, new types of wines. I began to realise that here in Tuscany we had an extraordinary potential to produce different wines from all those which had been produced by our fathers, grandfathers and so on. I found this situation so exciting that I became more and more involved in this side of the business. And I am still becoming more involved because I think we have a long way to go, in terms of improving the quality of the wine. I am convinced that we have the right soil, the right climate, except today'—my arrival in Florence had coincided with a terrific thunderstorm—'and now we have the technology. The potential is all there.

'I always say I consider myself lucky to be involved in this business *in Italy* now, especially in Tuscany. In other parts of the wine world there are countries and areas which have already reached the top, in terms of quality, in terms of reputation. Certainly in Italy this is not the case. We may have one of the oldest viticultures in the world but for centuries we have been so conservative that we have never really developed the potential we had. That is changing now. We form a group of producers in Italy and especially in Tuscany who are working to change things. I think we can say that Antinori played an important part at the beginning of this new evolution which I sometimes even call a revolution in the Italian wine industry. Now, fortunately, there is a really big group of serious producers spread all over Italy, in Piedmont, in Campania, in Friuli. But I like to think this revolution started in Tuscany, as the Renaissance of the arts had its heart and centre here. I believe that centuries later Florence has been the heart and centre of the renascence of Italian wines.

'It's a change of spirit, of mental attitude. Instead of believing that we should continue to do exactly what was done in the past, we now see that we can change things. I learnt a lot of this new spirit from the Californians. I started going to California in the early 1970s; their attitude of constantly trying to produce something new, and better, their belief that anything was possible, was a great influence on me personally. I would say that the Californians have been the biggest influence on the Italian wine renaissance in terms of attitude; technically we have learned more from the French.'

Marchese Piero's admiration for California has recently taken a concrete form: Antinori have a 5 per cent share in the ambitious, 1650-acre Whitbread/Bollinger/Antinori vineyard and winery development at Atlas Peak high in the hills above the Napa Valley.

These claims about the Italian wine renaissance and Antinori's role in it need to be set in context. In the last forty years a series of major upheavals has occurred in the Italian wine industry, and particularly in Chianti. In the 1950s and 1960s the system of *mezzadria* or share-cropping, by which tenant farmers kept half their produce and gave the other half to the landowner, was dismantled. At the same time, there occurred a mass migration from the Chianti hills to the industrial towns of the north. Chianti became in parts quite deserted.

Share-cropping, a system of immemorial antiquity, encouraged mixed cultivation of vines with other crops—olives, corn, vegetables—which allowed the small farmers to be more or less self-sufficient. With the end of share-cropping came the change from this antique style *coltura promiscua* to specialised cultivation of vines in vineyards planted in vertical rows, previously little seen in Tuscany. It sounds like a step forward for quality production, but the snag was that this extensive planting took place at a time when the future of Italian wine was still seen in terms of the bulk market. The theory went like this: the quality market had been cornered by the French; rather than compete with such a formidably successful rival, let the Italians supply the quantity. Selection of vine-plants for this massive replanting was empirical and based, if anything, on high yields rather than high quality. Flatter land, easier to work but not conducive to the best, most concentrated vintages, was planted wherever possible.

The result was a distinct drop in quality, given the benefit of the doubt for the first few vintages but increasingly recognised by people such as Antinori as a grave problem in need of urgent solution. The reputation and price of Chianti plummeted. By the late 1970s the price of basic Chianti was so low as to be uneconomic.

It was time, clearly, for a fundamental rethinking of the philosophy of a wine whose modern formula had been laid down by Baron Bettino Ricasoli, wine-grower and second Prime Minister of Italy, in the 1860s. One of the problems generally admitted was that the addition of white grapes, laid down in the original DOC decree of 1967, was making Chianti unacceptably weak and light in colour and flavour. The worst offender, Trebbiano, a generally somewhat insipid white grape which could legally make up 30 per cent of the Chianti blend, had never, according to Piero Antinori, been included in Ricasoli's formula.

A reduction in the permitted percentage of white grapes was finally enshrined in the DOCG laws of 1984, which laid down 2 per cent, a rather absurd bow to tradition which is generally taken as a tacit admission that white grapes need not be used. That seems to be the way it is taken by a number of top Chianti producers, including Antinori.

The drastic reduction in the role of white grapes in Chianti was only part of the solution. The main red grape, Sangiovese, posed a considerable problem too. It was not a question of replacing Sangiovese, for this grape was clearly essential to the character of Chianti. However, the character in question often verged on the astringent, for Sangiovese is a tannic grape which produces wine with an almost bitter finish. The Italians have become used to this taste, and indeed it seems to harmonise with the local food, cutting through the richness of the sauces and providing a stimulating bite to offset the blandness of pasta. On the export markets, however, the astringent character of Chianti was undoubtedly a drawback. So at least it appeared to Piero Antinori.

'This roughness or bitterness was considered a typical character of the area. In my opinion it was a bad character. Bitterness or harshness is not something which is pleasant.'

His solution was threefold. 'We started doing some research on the vinification of red wines and we discovered something which seems very simple and almost obvious, namely the malo-lactic fermentation. This converts the tart malic acid into softer lactic acid [the acid which exists in milk and yogurt], making a smoother, rounder wine, and is taken for granted as an essential step in the making of red Bordeaux and Burgundy, but in Tuscany—you may not believe this—it was not known until fifteen or twenty years ago. In Tuscany there used to be something called *governo*, not used very much now. Governo is a secondary alcoholic fermentation using partially dried grapes, but it sometimes induced the malo-lactic fermentation. And at the end of governo the wines were more supple and softer, but people didn't understand why. Now that we know how to induce and control the malo-lactic fermentation the governo doesn't have the importance that it used to. We don't use it any more, because a secondary alcoholic fermentation can aggravate some of the weak aspects of Chianti, especially the colour. Any fermentation takes out colour, and we have some problems anyway with colour with the Sangiovese grape. Sangiovese is not like Cabernet, always full of colour.'

Here Marchese Piero anticipates the second, more controversial ingredient of his recipe for the transformation of Chianti. In 1971 he brought out the first vintage of a wine which has influenced the whole subsequent development of the Tuscan wine industry. It was called Tignanello and made from a single vineyard of the Antinori's Santa Cristina estate planted with 80 per cent Sangiovese and 20 per cent Cabernet Sauvignon. Antinori were not the first people in Tuscany, let alone Italy, to experiment with the classic red grape of Bordeaux. There is a considerable amount of Cabernet in the northern provinces of Trentino-Alto-Adige and Friuli, and in Tuscany an important Cabernet enclave was staked out decades ago at Carmignano in the Montalbano hills north-west of Florence by the enterprising Contini Bonacossi family. However, Antinori's larger scale and marketing power made Tignanello a seminal wine. The reaction from fellow-producers was, and in some cases continues to be, by no means always welcoming. The criticism could be summed up as 'C'est magnifique, mais ce n'est pas le Chianti'. The market, however, responded with immediate enthusiasm.

Tignanello, together with the 100 per cent Cabernet Sassicaia produced by Antinori's cousin Incisa della Rocchetta at Bolgheri on the Tuscan coast, became the first Italian equivalents of the Bordeaux first and second growths or the top Cabernets of the Napa Valley: wines not just for drinkers but also for investors.

Marchese Piero defends Tignanello with his characteristic modesty: 'It was the first example of a Cabernet/Sangiovese blend and it has been relatively successful. It has become almost a classical blend of grapes now—there are many other producers in other regions, even in Southern Italy. It differs according to the microclimate and the soil but it is always rather a successful blend. Tignanello has been the consequence of our feeling that in order to produce more elegant wines it was indispensable to use other grape varieties in addition to Sangiovese. Our basic philosophy is to try to produce wines with a certain personality in which a local grape variety has a part—more or less important, but always giving a fundamental character. Our latest wine, a white called Cervaro from our estate in Umbria, is based on Chardonnay but has 20 per cent Grecchetto, a local grape which we believe is interesting and which we are trying to develop. But as you know, to do the clonal selection, to rediscover old Italian grape varieties which have been forgotten, all that takes a lot of time, years and years, maybe generations. And therefore to do something more rapidly we were almost obliged to use some other varieties of grape.

'Our long-term ambition, though, is to produce wines which are perhaps not entirely made from Italian grapes, but mostly—to keep our Italian character. Tignanello, for instance, is very definitely a Tuscan wine. It cannot be confused with a French or Californian or Australian wine. And that is why we are rather proud of this wine, because it is the result of this philosophy.'

The third prong of Antinori's tridental thrust follows on from the use of Cabernet Sauvignon. To go with the Bordeaux grape, and on the advice of the ubiquitous Professor Emile Peynaud of Bordeaux University, came the Bordeaux method of maturation in barriques bordelaises, the small oak barrels now spreading over the wine world from California to New Zealand and threatening to wipe out the French oak forests. Previously Chianti was matured in largish barrels called *botti*, of from 250 litres up to 1500 or more, usually made of chestnut rather than oak. Small barrels are more expensive and lead to greater evaporation, but they also have a softening, smoothing effect on the wine, clearly desirable to someone such as Piero Antinori who considers that the old, traditional character of Chianti was unpleasantly harsh. Not just the top wines like Tignanello and Sassicaia, but Antinori's standard Chianti

Classico Riserva, Villa Antinori (whose label carries an etching of the Antinori's ravishing baroque villa outside Florence, completely destroyed in the war), spends a certain amount of time in barrique. Once again, reactions from fellow-producers are mixed. Some consider Antinori has betrayed Italian tradition and produced an international-style wine in the French mould which could come from anywhere. The market, on the whole, has reacted favourably. Villa Antinori is the UK's best-selling Chianti Classico Riserva. And whatever they think in private, all ambitious Chianti producers sell a barrique-aged Sangiovese/Cabernet blend at a premium price.

Next day I had an appointment at the business end of the Antinori operation, their big bottling and ageing cellar at San Casciano in the heart of the Chianti Classico country. The road south from Florence, narrow and with no central markings, takes curious twists down deserted back-streets; only stone signs handsomely carved with Roman letters (Via di Greve) reassure you that you have not been led astray. After busy Grassina, the urban is left behind: you begin to climb into rolling hills, the lush valley bottoms cultivated with maize, the slopes striped by unpromiscuous rows of vines: this is the beginning of the Chianti Classico vineyard.

Chianti is both a wine and an area: a wine called simply Chianti can come from six sub-regions stretching over a large swathe of central Tuscany from Pisa to Arezzo. When Tuscans talk about the region of Chianti, though, they mean the hill-country between Florence and Siena—a 70,000 hectare heartland which is the delimited area of the wine called Chianti Classico. Fought over for centuries by the rival powers of Florence and Sienna, it is an area of fortified hill-villages and isolated farms. Almost all the buildings are constructed from the rough, grey-tawny limestone which is the country's bones. An elaborate baroque villa such as Vistarenni stands out as an anomaly—an imported piece of Venetian finery in a stony, medieval world. For all its connotations, to northern minds, of idyllic Mediterranean warmth, Chianti is a tough country: there are very few expanses of flat, easily worked land; much of it lies 1500 ft or more above sea-level; the winters can be severe. Two things soften the contours of the landscape; first, the great wealth of trees, not just the silvery grey olives (terribly ravaged in the great freeze of 1985) and the dark punctuation of cypresses, but also forests of oak and chestnut. And secondly there is the light, an intense luminosity (shared by the rather different wine area of Penedés in north-east Spain) which inevitably makes you think of the backgrounds of Renaissance paintings, and more practically aids the photosynthesis of the vine.

San Casciano Val di Pesa is a bustling, working small town without a trace of an aesthetic pose: likewise the Cantina Antinori, built originally from 1898 onwards by the brothers Piero and Niccolò Antinori, though it is as immaculate in its own way as the Palazzo, is essentially a functional place.

I arrived somewhat late to find myself among a small group of visitors, being shown round by a very elegant blonde with a look of Italian high fashion but the vowels of Brooklyn. This was Bette Ann Scavetta, Antinori's half-Italian, half-American head of public relations. The group consisted of two couples: a boutique wine-maker from the Napa Valley, Michael Fallow, and his girlfriend, Ellen Carucci, who sells advertising for the *New Yorker*, and a Dutch paediatrician, Gerrit Smeent, and his teacher wife, Marike. Gerrit and Marike were enthusiastic wine drinkers but had never visited a winery before; Michael knew most of the European wine regions intimately and could perhaps have taught Piero Antinori himself a few tricks about the making of Cabernet Sauvignon.

Bette Ann Scavetta did not let herself be deterred by the niceties of mixed-ability teaching. Her stock in trade was dynamic, up-front enthusiasm. On a bottling line (much like other bottling-lines) a procession of bottles of a very pale white wine was rattling along, being adorned with a deep purple capsule and elegant label, which set off the insipid colour of the wine most artfully. 'That's Galestro,' said Bette Ann. 'Boring wine but a brilliant marketing idea. When Antinori and the other Chianti producers cut down on the white grapes in Chianti, there were all these white Trebbiano and Malvasia grapes lying around and no one knew what to do with them. So Piero and some other guys came up with the name *galestro*—that's the white stony soil around here—and this sexy packaging, and the wine sells brilliantly.' Next door to the bottling line a robot, with what seemed to my untrained eye rather fumbling, uncertain movements, was wrapping stacks of cases with cellophane.

The most interesting aspect of the San Casciano cantina is the ageing facilities for red wines. There are not only a variety of sizes of cask, from 225-litre barriques through larger 550-litre to 1400-litre botti, but, among the barriques, also a variety of types of oak: some French (the most expensive), some American (which gives the strongest oak character), some Yugoslavian. Villa Antinori spends 18 months in barriques; Santa Cristina, which used to be the basic Chianti Classico, but has now been down-graded to *vino da tavola* to allow more flexibility in the use of grape varieties, is matured in the 1400-litre Yugoslav botti.

Our trip continued in reverse order from the maturing cellar to vineyards—in this case a recently purchased Chianti Classico estate formerly called Villa Terciona, renamed by Antinori as Pèppoli. A modest group of stone buildings—farmhouse, screened by cypresses, courtyard, chapel—half-way up a gentle slope overlooking a quiet valley, almost entirely planted with vineyards: Pèppoli exudes a slightly mysterious, almost melancholy calm and stillness. 'We're all madly in love with this estate,' said Bette Ann with unabashed acquisitive ardour; 'it's a little corner of paradise, without any doubt at all. We'd had our eye on it for some time, then the owner died conveniently just in time for our six hundredth anniversary.' Marika Smeent and I exchanged glances of Old World consternation. 'His widow still lives in the villa, by the way. Meantime we've hung our family shield a couple of places.' In the fifteenth century, I suppose, they might not have waited for the owner to die.

Pèppoli does seem to have a particularly favourable micro-climate: the 1985 winter which killed an estimated 80 per cent of the olive trees of Chianti claimed scarcely any casualties on this estate, long noted for the quality of its oil, pressed on the premises, as well as its wine. One part of the cellar is still lined with the great Ali Baba ceramic jars which were used formerly to store the oil.

Antinori are marketing the wine of the estate separately under the Pèppoli label, at a premium price: an opportunity to taste the '85 vintage (a scorchingly hot summer followed the icy winter) came at lunch. The immediate impression was of big, rich fruit—a bold, vivid character which made me think of Australian Shiraz. Giacomo Tachis, Antinori's celebrated 'wizard' wine-maker, decided on a very different style of wine-making from that used for Villa Antinori: Pèppoli sees no barriques, but spends a shortish time in 500 litre barrels of older oak. Otherwise it is kept in stainless-steel vats to emphasise the ripe juici-ness of the fruit. Perhaps the most significant feature of Pèppoli is that it contains no Cabernet. It represents, therefore, a step back from Anti-nori's revolutionary, eclectic approach of the 1970s, and a return to the tradition of the region.

The venue for lunch was the Santa Cristina estate—an Antinori property of long standing, this time, situated only a few kilometres to the south of Pèppoli, on the western fringe of Chianti Classico. Before reaching the farm, we stopped to admire a large south-facing slope reaching up to the very top of the hillside, 1400 ft above sea-level: this was the Tignanello vineyard, though it is no longer big enough to provide all the grapes needed for Tignanello.

Santa Cristina is an eighteenth-century villa, with simple iron-balustraded steps leading up to a front entrance on the first floor, which stands in a small garden with an almost English front lawn. Below the entrance is a ground-floor archway leading to what were cellars, but are now kitchens and dining-rooms. The Antinori use it as a summer holiday house, when they are not entertaining visitors.

The peace of this secluded spot was disrupted one night in August 1944 when Marchese Niccolò woke up to find a German officer standing by his bed shining a torch into his eyes. The Germans were then in retreat from the advancing Allies. They too seemed to have used Santa Cristina as a temporary resting-place. When the time came for their final withdrawal, they wanted to take Marchese Niccolò with them. 'Somehow or other,' he recalls, 'I persuaded them to leave me here.'

At the back of the villa, now restored to peaceful pursuits, are modern facilities for the vinification and maturing of Tignanello and the 100 per cent Cabernet Solaia, which is produced only in certain vintages.

Sitting on the lawn, in the hot May sunshine, we tried as an aperitif the new Antinori baby, the white wine called Cervaro della Sala. Cervaro comes not from the Antinori's Tuscan vineyards but from an estate in the neighbouring province of Umbria. This is based at the Castello della Sala north of Orvieto, a building clearly designed for grimmer purposes than the peaceful cultivation of the vine.

Orvieto's white wine, traditionally made sweet (*abbocato*), has always been one of Italy's most famous (even if it is difficult for non-Italians to understand why), more highly prized than any white wine of Tuscany. The Antinori had for many years been involved in selling Orvieto: their practice was to buy grapes from local growers, have them crushed at the farms, then transport the must to San Casciano for vinification. Marchese Niccolò was dissatisfied with this system, which involved him in numerous journeys between Florence and Orvieto in his Spider Balilla sports car. In 1940 he found out that the Castello della Sala, then in a ruinous state, was up for sale with 700 hectares of land. He bought the lot for 3,300,000 lire. The medieval fortress of the Monaldeschi family, with its massive circular keep, its courtyard and the huddle of red-roofed farm-workers' cottages clustered feudally around its skirts, has been meticulously restored. As for the vineyards, there are now 100 hectares in production, planted with the traditional Procanico (the local clone of Trebbiano), Verdello, Grecchetto, and small quantities of Drupeggio and Malvasia Toscana, together with the untraditional Chardonnay, Sauvignon Blanc and Pinot Blanc.

Cervaro (first vintage 1985) is a blend of the traditional Grecchetto and the international Chardonnay (proportion roughly 20/80), fermented in new oak barriques from the French Massif Central. Another example of the Antinori philosophy, based on traditional indigenous Italian grapes, enhanced by French and international refinements? I am not so sure. The big rich buttery and oaky flavour suggested Californian Chardonnay rather than a typical Italian wine. On the other hand, its light gold colour and amply proportioned yet fresh, clean lines were hard to resist—far more to the modern international palate than the majority of neutral, yet heavy Italian white wines.

After sipping Cervaro and nibbling *crostini*, the little bits of toast spread with a delicious purée of chicken livers, olive and capers, we moved on to more serious things. Three red wines had been chosen to accompany the veal main course, served at a table on the gravel under a shady broad-leaved tree: at regular intervals the big shiny leaves fell on to the cloth with a heavy slap. After Pèppoli, and in striking contrast, we were served the Villa Antinori Riserva Particolare 1982, the top Chianti Classico in Antinori's range, this time aged in barriques. This was a silky, velvety wine of great refinement, suggesting Bordeaux rather than Chianti on the nose. I could not believe that it contained no Cabernet Sauvignon. Whether it is typical of Chianti is a moot point: there is none of that astringency which can so often be harsh and raw, but which is surely part of Chianti's character. Too smooth, then? Perhaps, but on its own terms this is a very fine wine.

Last of all came Tignanello, of the 1983 vintage. Although making up only 20 per cent of the blend, Cabernet Sauvignon announced its presence forcefully with that minerally, irony tone on the nose which makes me think of human blood. The colour was blood-red too, several shades deeper than the Villa Antinori. To taste, though, Tignanello was no tiger: the first flavour was almost sweet, the wine was smooth and open, immediately appealing, much less tannic and stern than a comparable Bordeaux of the same year. 'Tignanello's just a little guy—a simple little table wine,' said Bette Ann Scavetta. She was being ironic, of course, in referring to the strange Italian wine regulations which outlaw such undeniably distinguished, and high-priced, wines as Tignanello from the official appellation system (DOC and DOCG), because they contain grapes not traditional to the area. Tignanello is classified as vino da tavola. At £12 plus a bottle it is not exactly plonk.

Before returning to Florence to meet the youngest member of the Antinori dynasty, I had to make a substantial detour. Bolgheri on the Tuscan coast does not look so distant on the map, but it is a two-and-a-half hour drive, admittedly through some of the loveliest countryside in Europe. The road climbs past the towers of San Gimignano—a kind of medieval Manhattan—into high airy meadows, speckled with poppies. The views are commanding: you can understand the strategic importance of the gloomy fortress town of Volterra, perched on an isolated hill, which even now requires a laborious 15-minute, first-gear climb from any direction.

Between Volterra and Cecina on the coast, the landscape changes: the hills become more thickly wooded and darker green with evergreens, the valleys lusher. This is a hidden, empty part of Tuscany: it seems not to have been discovered by the wealthy Romans and Milanese—and British—who have colonised Chianti Classico. Parts of the Maremma, as this coastal district is called, were plagued by malaria until the beginning of this century, as D.H. Lawrence's *Etruscan Places* attests.

The area around Bolgheri, though, has long been known for its fertility. The climate, moderated by the sea, is milder than that of Chianti, though drought can be a problem. For over a thousand years, the strip of coast between Bibbiona and San Vicenzo, several kilometres thick, has been farmed by the Counts della Gherardesca. The Antinori connection goes back to 1931, when Marchese Niccolò married Contessa Carlotta della Gherardesca. At around the same time, Carlotta's sister Clarice married Count Mario Incisa della Rocchetta. The combination of Incisa's vision and Antinori's commercial expertise was to make Bolgheri an internationally known name in the wine world.

Wine has always been produced on this land, but its reputation, before the coming of the Antinori and Incisa, was indifferent. The farms were better-known for their cereals, sugar-beet, peaches and livestock, which continue to occupy 90 per cent of the land. Better-known still was, and is, the double avenue of cypresses stretching four kilometres in a dead-straight line from the Via Aurelia to the tiny fortified village of Bolgheri. They are the subject of Carducci's poem 'Davanti San Guido': 'Come and sit down in our scented shade,' they whisper to the poet, returning to a scene of his childhood, 'where the north-west wind blows in from the sea: we do not grudge those stones you threw against our trunks: they do not hurt us any more! We still carry the nests of nightingales—Why do you run away so fast?'

Just at the lower end of the avenue, whose trees, unaffected by the Tuscan cypress blight of the early 1980s, are as tall and straight as they were in Carducci's time, stands an insignificant grey building. This converted tulip shed houses an impressively tidy, well-integrated and unshowy winery—crusher, press, fermentation tanks, assemblage tank and barrique store—which produces Sassicaia, described by Hugh Johnson as 'perhaps Italy's finest red wine'.

Sassicaia could also be described as the Italian red wine for those who do not like Italian red wine. It is made entirely from Bordeaux varieties, 80 per cent Cabernet Sauvignon and 20 per cent Cabernet Franc, and is the brainchild of a man, Mario Incisa della Rocchetta, who wished to emulate the great growths of Bordeaux.

'My father did not like the traditional styles of Italian wine,' says Mario's son Niccolò, a shy, courteous man in his fifties with a prominent, Bardolphian nose. 'He liked the special aroma of Bordeaux—particularly Château Margaux.'

It was a truly pioneering move, in 1942, to plant a mini-vineyard of 1000 Cabernet vines on the hillside of Castiglioncello, 400 metres up behind Bolgheri. He selected the site because the exposure, north-east, was similar to that of many vineyards in the Côte d'Or and the Médoc.

The first efforts were made in tiny quantities: just enough to fill one barrique, which Mario Incisa was already using in his estate in Piedmont. Of all those who claim to have been the first to use barriques in Italy, he seems to have the best authority. The local farm managers were not impressed: 'It's gone off,' said one. 'You can't drink this,' said another. Incisa persevered, and found that his wine improved with keeping.

In 1963-4 he planted Cabernet in another vineyard (the original one was very exposed to the sea wind), this time the one called Sassicaia because of its stony soil, only 50 metres above sea level. 'Amidst the general undrinkability of the wine of Bolgheri,' wrote one Italian authority, 'Sassicaia was known as the vineyard which produced a decent wine.'

The first Sassicaia proper was made in the fine (in Tuscany, not in Bordeaux) 1968 vintage, and turned out to be very much more than decent. But Niccolò Incisa realised that experienced help was needed to get the wine properly marketed. Such help was at hand in the person of Niccolò's first cousin Piero Antinori, who took over the distribution, and for a while the bottling, of Sassicaia from 1971. The Italian wine critic Luigi Veronelli was sent a bottle of the 1968 and immediately penned a eulogy in his influential column. Sassicaia's reputation was made. Other critics compared the wine to first-growth Bordeaux. The price became comparable also. I remember being given some of the 1972 to taste blind and guessing that it was Château Haut-Brion. I felt better when I read that the leading authority on Bordeaux, Edmund Penning-Rowsell, considered Sassicaia to have a Graves-like character. There was never any doubt about its high quality.

Enthusiasm spread to other countries, sometimes in more extreme forms. Canadians queued all night in sub-zero temperatures for the first release by the Maison du Vin in Montreal in 1981. Those who secured a bottle (the shipment sold out in twenty minutes) had a badge printed: 'I froze my ass for a bottle of Sass!' Production increased many times over, to 60,000 bottles in 1980 and then to its present figure of 80,000–100,000 bottles.

The arrangement with Antinori, although undoubtedly beneficial to both parties, was not always free of friction. The old Marchese Mario was always arguing with the Antinori wine-maker, and fellow strong-minded Piedmontese, Giacomo Tachis, about details of wine-making. Eventually he started producing a small quantity of his own Sassicaia, made in a more artisanal way without Tachis' assistance. It was labelled *vino diverso della Sassicaia*, different wine from Sassicaia.

Now the marketing arrangement, though not the assistance of Tachis, has ceased altogether, partly because Marchese Niccolò has decided to devote much more of his time to wine and less to his first love, horse-breeding. Incisa's Dolmello Olgiata stud is probably the most celebrated in Italy, and Mario Incisa is remembered by more people as the breeder of Ribot, the famous Italian race-horse who never lost a race, than as the creator of Sassicaia. His son sees the two activities, horse-breeding and wine-making, as analogous. 'In both cases one is matching things together to achieve the ultimate perfection.' Niccolò Incisa does not plan further increases in production. 'I would like to average about 80,000 bottles per year. The first consideration must always be quality.'

Another reason for the break with Antinori could be competition. Tignanello and more especially Solaia, Antinori's 100 per cent Cabernet wine from the same vineyard, are perhaps too close to Sassicaia for comfort. Now Piero Antinori's brother Lodovico is developing his own version of Sassicaia, from a vineyard right next door on the other half of the divided Bolgheri estate.

From the other 50 hectares or so of vineyards in their part of Bolgheri Antinori produce a pink-shaded rosé, made mainly from Sangiovese with about 15 per cent Cabernet. Called Scalabrone, it is light and freshly scented. Since 1984, unlike Sassicaia, it has been entitled to a new DOC, Bolgheri Rosato.

I returned to Florence for a meeting with the person who is set, one day, to take over control of what is now a large, international and, to all appearances, flourishing concern. Piero Antinori has three children, all daughters. The eldest, Albiera, in her early twenties at the time of writing, has already decided to join her father in the wine business.

I met Albiera back at the Palazzo Antinori. Dressed in unpretentious student's clothes—jeans, a baggy jumper—she looked even younger than her age. I had asked to see the living quarters of the

Palazzo. 'We rent out the piano nobile—the first floor with the biggest rooms. One half is rented by an American university, the other by a gynaecologist.' On the second floor, leading off a wooden-roofed gallery with views of the Duomo, I saw a still fairly grand drawing-room and Marchese Niccolò's study-library. This long room is dominated by a huge Tintoretto of the Pellegrini family: a Venetian scene of ladies and hunting-dogs, glowing with subdued, rich green and gold. Albiera almost shrugged it off—'I believe it's quite important.' There are other hunting pictures ('We all like shooting,' Albiera confirmed) and a beautiful Annigoni portrait of Albiera's aunt Ilaria.

Like her father, it seemed, Albiera had never desired to do anything except work in the family wine business. She did not want to go to university; she was taking a series of sandwich courses in wine and commerce while working on the domestic sales side, and accompanying her father on trips abroad. Being a member of such a grand and successful dynasty has its privileges, but also its obligations.

Torres

of

Vilafranca

del Penedés

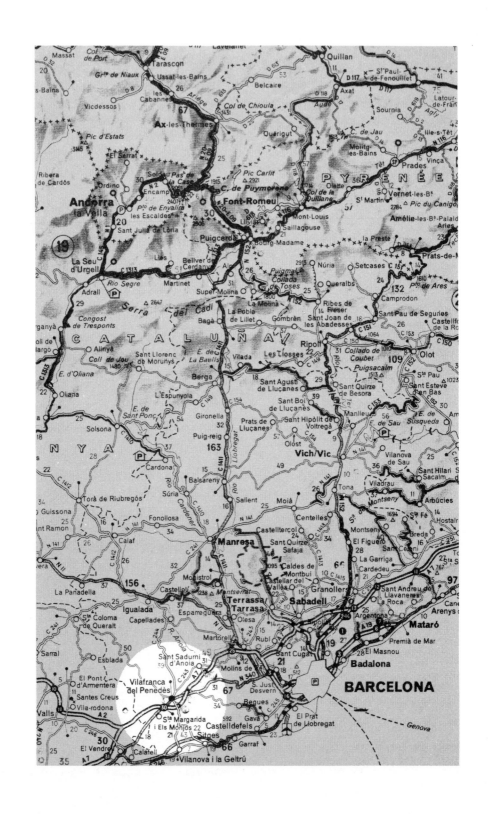

THEY HAVE A RHYME IN SPAIN, 'los catalanes de las piedras hacen panes': the Catalans make bread from stones. The independent-minded people of the north-eastern corner of the peninsula are regarded within Spain, not always with affection, as shrewd, money-grubbing, business-minded—not typical Spaniards at all. But it is notable how many of Spain's best-known exports come from Catalonia; the composers Albéniz and Granados; the architect Gaudí; the painters Miró and Dalí (and by adoption, Picasso); and, heading the list of Spanish wine exporters, the family-owned wine and brandy firm of Torres. Perhaps not so unexpected, when you remember the great Catalan trading empire of the fourteenth and fifteenth centuries, which made Barcelona one of the great mercantile capitals of Europe, a role she has been struggling to resume ever since the Catholic kings relegated Catalonia to the status of a distant province in the grand Castilian scheme.

The Torres family come not from Barcelona—though they have close connections with the city—but from the town of Vilafranca del Penedés, 40 kilometres west. Vilafranca is the prosperous capital of the Penedés wine-growing region—a town whose stone medieval core is surrounded by rather nondescript turn-of-the-century tree-lined avenues, with a rundown industrial area of warehouses by the railway line. At least, this area was rundown until Torres started to buy it up a few years ago. Their offices, marked with a wrought-iron sign depicting a bunch of grapes, are discreetly situated in a side street. Inside, there is a tiled, cork-lined waiting room with a late-nineteenth-century air, and when the frosted glass sliding doors open, a view of a distinctly low-tech bottling-line.

This is one aspect of Torres: the old-fashioned family business, staffed by loyal retainers. It is by no means the whole story. My appointment at the offices is with Albert Fornos, Torres's head of public relations, who has learnt to speak fluent English and German without ever visiting Britain or Germany and has a deep knowledge of local geography and culture: we are to drive to the ultra-modern winery at Pachs, a few kilometres outside the town. Vilafranca stands between the coastal Garraf hills and the high Penedés uplands, in a wide bowl of vineyards and orchards. Presiding over the scene, on clear days, is the isolated, blue, strangely indented ridge of Montserrat, rising to over 4000 ft 30 kilometres north. Its bare rock formations have been compared to organ pipes: those who wonder about the sources of the weird architectural inventions of Gaudí need not look much further. 'There is a lot of light in the Penedés,' Albert, a good-looking, humorous man in his fifties, comments; 'too much light sometimes. It is very dry here in summer.' It is a crisp, lucid landscape; the shapes, of the compact town and the hills, are clearly defined, the colours predominantly blue and red-ochre, with orchards of almond, in flower in early March, adding a skein of incongruous pink-like smoke.

The new winery, entered through an 'Open Sesame' electronic gate, stands on a hillside, looking down on the town: a typically Mediterranean view with the church's campanile in the centre, suffused with light. But the winery hardly comes out of the Mediterranean tourist gallery. Lines of gleaming stainless-steel tanks and a concrete forecourt are positioned on the hillside in a stark, abstract geometry. They could have been designed for any place and indeed for a variety of purposes—a small oil refinery, a gas depot, or some more sinister military installation. At harvest time, the red-wine grapes, from Torres's own vineyards and from two dozen local farmers who supply on contract, are brought in to the forecourt in plastic hampers provided by Torres and weighed. They are emptied on to a revolving screw which takes them to a crusher/destemmer, from which they are moved into the nine-metre tall fermentation tanks. We climb up aluminium steps on to a catwalk to look down into the tanks.

'We use an automatic system of pumping over, or remontage, to extract maximum colour from the skins. When the fermentation is over—it takes about a week—the skins and pips at the bottom are removed and pressed. The press wine is a little harsh but has good colour; if used properly it adds something.'

There is a further installation of tanks for the more delicate white wines: here control of temperature during fermentation, a technique pioneered in the New World and used by Torres since the early 1970s, long before it was common in the rest of Spain, is crucial for preserving freshness and aroma. Skin contact time has been increased to intensify flavour. 'The whole fermentation system is now computer controlled,' says Albert, taking me into a clinical room full of dials and digital displays, watched over by two technicians in white coats. 'They can monitor and change the temperature of each tank by remote control.'

We walk down from the computer room past a building site— yet more tanks—to a doorway in a rustic stone arch built into the hillside. There is something of a hiatus in our guided tour here, as we stand outside in the spring sun and hear about plans for a new cellar to be built in the hillside above the existing one. We are waiting for Sr Torres sen., something to which Albert is accustomed, as the relaxed way in which he lights up a cigarette makes clear. 'He is, how do you say, a law of his own.' After a considerable while, we move inside: the temperature seems warm after the brisk March air: it stays at 15–16°C all the year round. It is very quiet, and humid, and rich with the smell of oak and the vapours of wine. This is the barrel cellar where the Torres red wines mature in 300-litre oak casks for 18 months to two years—the same length of time as the great wines of Bordeaux and Burgundy. Traditionally, Spanish wines have been aged for as long as five or even eight years in oak. One of the most important elements of the Torres revolution has been the rejection of excessive oak-ageing. The thousands of casks represent a huge investment: a new one now costs £250.

'We want to sell red wines which are mellow and ready to drink,' Albert explains, 'and that means maturing them ourselves. But we are interested in the idea of a barrel which is mainly metal but has a wooden end; as far as I can see, that would give the same effect as a wooden barrel at a much lower cost.' Constant experimentation, even with ideas that sound barmy, is a Torres trademark.

There are rapid steps in the distance. A small, spruce, elderly man is not walking but running along the treacherous wet floor, hands flapping out partly for balance, partly in apology. 'How do you do, so sorry I am late, how is your visit?' The torrent of words leaves no time for reply; the man's energy is breathtaking. He is quite short, but dapper in the Latin manner, with a clipped moustache; his most striking features are a pair of very pale blue eyes. 'What would you like to see, what have you seen already?' He insists on taking us round the new fermentation tanks for a second time, and proudly points out the computer control room. He is a man who does not like to be left behind the times.

As a guide, he is both authoritarian and capricious. 'We have had enough of this visit, yes? Shall we have lunch?' He directs us into his car, a turbo-charged Citroën CX—and despite warnings about his driving, it is impossible to refuse. As we reach the end of the winery drive, a bus comes into view, crossing a narrow stone bridge on the main road back to Vilafranca. This is the kind of challenge Sr Torres relishes. The Citroën shoots forward, turning 90 degrees to the right and missing the oncoming bus by a couple of yards. There are rumours that Torres employs one person mainly to deal with Sr Torres's driving offences.

We head back to the town centre; not to the offices but to a tall, stone, nineteenth-century town house in the truncated square by the railway station. The proximity of the railway line reduces the attractions of the house as a dwelling, but Sr Torres has lovingly restored it as a museum of wine and of the Torres family. Above the door is set a plaque honouring Sr Torres's father as President of the Water Company of Vilafranca: 'Some people think this is ridiculous, but I like to keep it,' says Sr Torres. I am not sure whether he sees it as a joke, turning from wine to water, or just another public testimonial to the family's power. As we enter, there is a loving reunion between Sr Torres and a large silky-haired Alsatian. Since the death of his beloved and reputedly ferocious Doberman, this dog is Sr Torres's friend and protector. He is reputed to live in fear of kidnapping by terrorists.

The rather gloomy ground floor and patio house an impressive collection of wine artefacts: several wine presses, including one from the seventeenth century with pressure supplied by a gargantuan oak treetrunk 12 metres long, a barrel, dated 1511, with staves nine inches thick, pruning knives, and, in the patio, a beautiful, tall, Gothic cross found in one of the Torres vineyards, with a carved crucifixion mounted on an octagonal pillar. On the first floor are more recent, but equally fascinating exhibits: barrel labels marked 'Malaga Seco' (not a product Torres would sell these days), bottles in straw labelled 'Spanish Chablis' and 'Torres Port—Very Old Tawny' (relics of the bad old days before Spanish wine gained an identity of its own). There is also a carved oval sign in the form of a tray, with rope edges, advertising the shipping company, Willoughby & Tyler, which operated 'fast clippers to all parts of the world'; a collection of hand-blown glass *porrones*, the Catalan drinking carafes with a handle and a horn-like spout (difficult to use, I find); and a dictaphone and a movie camera, which were the first seen in Vilafranca when Sr Torres bought them in the early 1930s. We are taken up the neo-Renaissance stone staircase to the top floor; here in an appropriately light-filled setting is a collection of Catalan painting from the late nineteenth and twentieth centuries. The big *Allegory of Autumn* in grisaille by José-María Sert used to hang in the Waldorf Astoria Hotel, New York. The vivid vineyard scenes by Monzó beautifully capture the intense Penedés light in different seasons.

The time is getting on; it is about ten past two, and the walk around the winery has given us hearty appetites; there is no hurrying Sr Torres, however. Back downstairs, we stop at the first floor this time, which gives us a tantalising glimpse of the dining room before passing into an ante-room filled with cabinets displaying precious glassware, including a blue-tinted Roman jug of extraordinary delicacy. Above the cabinets are photographs; one of a vast wine vat, destroyed when the Fascists dropped bombs on Vilafranca in January 1939; another of a large family group, posing in front of the same vat. 'That is my father and his cousins,' says Sr Torres; 'he bought all their shares in the business.' It is understandable that this dynasty-consolidating moment should be prominently displayed and should still give satisfaction to Sr Torres. It also reminds him of a ceremony which must be performed before lunch. 'Where is the photographer? Now come here—not like that, you behind.' Sr Torres's son, Miguel, physically very similar to his father, with darker hair receding from a high, long forehead, and exactly the same disconcerting pale blue eyes, has joined us and stands deferentially back from his father in the photograph. The father's features compose themselves into a practised, proprietorial smile; the son looks wary, a trifle tense. The process has to be repeated several times before Sr Torres is satisfied; then finally we can go through into the dining-room, painted dark green and hung with severe family portraits, floored with the kind of tiles which Gaudí smashed up and made into the mosaic benches of the Parque Güell in Barcelona.

Lunch is worth waiting for, a starter of Coquilles St Jacques, with which we drink Torres's Gran Viña Sol, the white wine which contains a proportion of oak-aged Chardonnay in addition to the native grape Parellada. The wine is a successful conception: fresh and crisp, with an underlying hint of buttery richness from the Chardonnay. It is not the top white wine of the Torres range: that is Gran Viña Sol Green Label, made from Parellada with Sauvignon Blanc, aged in new oak, a curious wine which divides opinion (I like its very individual character) and can age for several years in bottle.

The main course is tender, undercooked beef with *cèpes*: its relative simplicity is designed to complement Torres's top red wine, Gran Coronas Black Label, made from the Bordeaux grape Cabernet Sauvignon. The vintage is 1981: the colour is deep ruby; the nose has the classic Cabernet combination of cedar and blackcurrant; the flavour is long, deep and subtle. This is undoubtedly a wine of the highest class, with a subtlety and refinement rare in hot-climate Cabernet Sauvignon wines. The 1970 vintage created a sensation at the 1979 Gault Millau Wine Olympiad in Paris by winning first prize above such luminaries of the French wine scene as Château Latour 1970. 'It is very good, your wine,' says Sr Torres magnanimously to his son; turning to me he adds, 'This wine is his brainchild, you know.'

'Yes, Black Label is improving all the time,' Miguel replies, 'but the 1982 will be even better. That is the first vintage to include a proportion of wine from our new Cabernet vineyard near Poblet. It is producing very concentrated, powerful wine.'

The atmosphere at lunch is a mixture of the formal and informal. It is both a business lunch and a family lunch (no distinction between the two in this family): apart from the Torres, father and son, myself and Albert, there are two other employees of the firm, Sr Torres's assistant, Montse, and his private secretary, Painous. Painous is a curious figure, of indeterminate age, dressed in a black suit, with the highly trained, subservient expression of an assistant undertaker. His job is to be with Sr Torres on all occasions, to take down his master's words, not to speak unless spoken to. 'Painous!' Sr Torres shouts out every few minutes, 'make a note of this!'.

Despite the almost absurd paternalism, there is a familiarity about the relationship between Sr Torres and his staff which partly validates his claim that the staff are treated like family. 'If one of them is ill, I pay for him to go to the best doctors in Barcelona,' Sr Torres told me. I heard other stories: 'I do not like that red jersey,' one employee was told, 'it is a foolish colour for a man of your age.' It may have been pure coincidence that the autonomous election campaign had just begun, with the Socialists threatening to win the local seat. Another employee was given a gruelling schedule of overseas visits, which meant that he would be away for Christmas. 'My wife is expecting our first baby at that time,' he complained. He received the following poser in response: 'Sr X, which is more important to you, your family or Torres?'

The relationship I wished to explore was that between father and son. Rows between the two have been publicised in the past; at one point Miguel left the firm. The reason was reported to be his father's absolute refusal to relinquish control, combined with his increasing annoyance at the wine press's attribution of all the company's dynamic new ideas to his son. These bones of contention have not been entirely buried. An English wine merchant who made a special offer of Torres wines, praising Miguel's work with new grape varieties in the introduction, was taken on one side during a visit to Vilafranca and told that the success of Torres was due first and foremost to the genius of Sr Torres sen.

Things have been patched up. Relaxed was not the word which sprang to my mind when I talked to them together after lunch, but they have clearly sorted out some kind of working compromise. Their physical similarity may be the clue to their stormy relationship; despite Miguel's outwardly more diplomatic, less autocratic exterior, they are probably too similar to be able to work easily together. When I asked one of their employees who had worked for both which was the easier boss, he replied, 'The father, without doubt. He tells you to do things, then he leaves you alone, but the son is on your back the whole time.' Miguel's sister, Marimar, the ambassadress of Torres wine to the USA, has said: 'My father is into control. He will not let go until he dies. But we are all like that—it runs in the family.'

She has also said that she greatly admires both her father and her brother—indeed regards them both as geniuses. A disinterested observer must also find a great deal to admire in both, and would have to attribute a great deal of the company's success to the father.

He inherited the business when he was twenty-three on the death of his father, whom we saw in the photograph, having bought out the rest of the family's shares in the business. The Torres wine concern had been founded by his great-uncle, Jaime, who was born in the village of Sant Pere Molanta near Vilafranca in 1843. Jaime, the youngest of many brothers, went to Barcelona in 1860, and got a job as cabin boy on a ship bound for Havana. In Havana he found work in a grocery shop: apparently he was so poor that he had to sleep under the counter. With typical Catalan determination he saved his money, then had the inspired idea of writing to an American oil company suggesting they sell their oil in Cuba. They agreed; he became their distributor. In ten years he had saved 200,000 pesetas, a very considerable fortune, and he was still only twenty-seven. He decided that the oil business was becoming too competitive, and returned to Spain. He persuaded his brother Miguel, who was working as a wine farmer, to start exporting wine to Cuba. By 1873 the company Vinos y Licores Torres was in business. Initially, Jaime Torres did not purchase vineyards, but bought in wine from small local growers, and sold in barrel, not bottle. The quality was no doubt rather ordinary: as Miguel explains in his scholarly book *The Distinctive Wines of Catalonia* (1986), an archaic and oppressive system of land tenure meant that Catalan farmers had no incentive to produce high-quality wine. The majority of farmers held their land on the system called *rabassa morta*, which gave them a right to cultivation for the lifetime of a vine. In the old days, the Catalan peasants had managed to prolong the life of their vines to about fifty years, thus securing their livelihood for a working lifetime. The coming of Phylloxera, the devastating vine aphid which gnawed its way through all the European vineyards, starting in the 1870s, wrecked that compromise, but greatly enriched the Torres family.

Phylloxera struck France before Spain, and in doing so gave an enormous boost to the Spanish wine industry. Between 1871 and 1881, exports of wine from the port of Barcelona rose six-fold from 201,461 hectolitres to 1,269,896 hectolitres. Looking at the 1881 figures, one can see that slightly more than half the total volume went to the Americas, but nearly double the value. Jaime Torres was doing good business at that time. In 1886, at the height of the Phylloxera crisis in France, 397,427 hectolitres were exported to France alone.

By that date, however, the aphid had begun to ravage the Spanish vineyards. In the last years of the nineteenth century, Catalan wine-growers were reduced to the desperate measure of planting hybrid vines, crossed between the American *Vitis labrusca* and the European *Vitis vinifera*, which were resistant to Phylloxera and produced high yields, at the expense of quality. There was widespread poverty, which led to at least one armed uprising, in 1883. When the solution to Phylloxera—grafting European vines on to resistant American rootstocks—was finally discovered, it brought a further problem. The lifespan of the new, grafted vines was very much shorter than that of the old pre-Phylloxera vines—no more than twenty-five years. The *rabassaires* (holders of land under rabassa morta) had their livelihood cut by half. Social unrest continued until the time of the Civil War: indeed, the Law of Cultivation, passed by the Catalan Generalitat in 1934, then revoked by the central government in Madrid, deepened the rift between Catalonia and the rest of Spain and could be regarded as one of the Civil War's many indirect causes.

Juan Torres, son of Jaime's brother Miguel (the founder never married), died in 1932. It was in those terribly troubled times for Spain that Sr Torres took charge of the family wine business. While still a very young man, he achieved two major goals, either one of which might have sufficed for an ordinary mortal. First, he kept the firm going during the grim years of the Civil War when there was very little to eat, especially in Republican sectors such as Catalonia. 'In this part we had good clothes but no food. On the other side, they had enough to eat but nothing to wear,' recalls Sr Torres's wife Margarita.

The real damage was done right at the end of the war when the Fascists jettisoned bombs which reduced the bodega to ruins and smashed the immense assemblage vat, making the streets run red with wine. This was probably not a calculated move on their part. Margarita Torres remembers that the 'liberating' Francoist general had lunch with them in Vilafranca. 'We were all speaking Catalan, and he told us that we should not speak that language in the Spanish motherland. I said, "Excuse me, General, but in our house we will speak the language we have always spoken." '

On the whole, the Torres' relations with the victorious Franquistas were more diplomatic. 'I managed to negotiate a loan for the rebuilding of the winery at a special interest rate—three per cent,' Sr Torres told me: 'but I had to deal directly with Madrid—nothing was available from Barcelona.'

The Torres family are great supporters of Spain's new constitutional monarchy. Photographs in the family museum show Sr Torres shaking hands with both King Juan Carlos and his cousin, Queen Elizabeth II. Although the Torres family speak Catalan among themselves, they have no truck with the more extreme forms of Catalan nationalism. The Torres consider themselves Spanish first, Catalan second.

One of the most courageous things the Torres ever did was to take ship in 1940 for the United States in the middle of the U-boat blockade of the Atlantic shipping routes. It proved to be a farsighted and decisive move for the company, and led directly to Sr Torres's second great achievement: the move from selling bulk wine in barrel to selling quality, branded wine in bottle. For 18 months Sr and Sra Torres travelled round Central and North America selling wine to countries starved of their traditional European supplies. Seeing the success of branded products in America, which could command a premium price and customer loyalty because of their known, consistent quality, enforced by advertising, Sr Torres decided to go in the same direction.

'Selling branded wine in bottle means a shared commitment to quality on the part of the producer and the bottler; this was what I had to build up.' At that time, and indeed until the 1960s, Torres still did not own significant quantities of vineyard, but the third phase of the Torres master plan was in preparation. Phase three involved the new generation of the family, and especially his son, Miguel.

'I trained as a chemical engineer and started work as a pharmacist. In those days you could not study oenology. But in the 1950s, when I was going round Europe, I started looking out for the best places for my son to study. People told me you cannot make good wine in Penedés. In my little Renault I went to Burgundy, I went to Montpellier. I invited his future professors to come back to see me in Vilafranca. I met Professor Peynaud and he took me to Sauternes. At that time I did not know much about their wines and when they asked me what wine I would like with dinner I said, "anything except sweet wine". But Professor Peynaud was very kind, very generous. I owe a lot of gratitude to those French professors.'

During this conversation, Sr Torres had been playing down his own role—most of the material about his early years with the firm I have gleaned from other sources: he did not seem particularly keen to talk about them. The achievement of which he seemed proudest was his foresight in mapping out his son's brilliant career—not an entirely selfless gesture, to be sure, but characteristic of his desire to look to the future. 'What has been important in the success of the firm has been to look for all the new improvements.'

Miguel is Sr Torres's second son: the elder, Juan María, decided not to join the family bodega. 'He was always a bit of a rebel,' Marimar Torres recalls. 'He went into business and was very successful, but the sector he was in, plastics, just got wiped out.' At that time the future of the wine business probably did not look especially exciting. Juan María is now back in the family business fold, working mainly in international sales.

Miguel admitted that he did not particularly want to go into the business either. 'There were other interests—girls, for instance,' he said, his features relaxing into an engaging grin. 'Miguel has always been the diplomat, the non-conflictive person,' says Marimar. 'Perhaps because he was always in the middle: I was my father's little girl and Juan María was my mother's darling. Miguel was in the middle.'

In any case, Miguel has followed the course his father determined—a science degree at Barcelona University followed by oenological studies in Dijon and Montpellier. Wine began to seem quite attractive in Burgundy. At Montpellier he stood out as one of the most gifted in his class at France's most prestigious school of wine-making. He came back to Spain with a host of new ideas to try out on what was, in many respects, virgin territory.

'The first new idea was the use of foreign grape varieties—Cabernet Sauvignon, Chardonnay, Sauvignon Blanc, Pinot Noir. This was in the mid-1960s. There was a lot of land available for planting and we bought a good deal of vineyard.' The firm now own about 600 hectares of vineyards, which cover almost half of their requirements for grapes. Apart from those mentioned, Torres have planted such unlikely grapes as Gewurztraminer, Muscat d'Alsace and Riesling with notable success. 'The second major new idea was temperature-controlled fermentation. We introduced that in the early 1970s. We did it by rather primitive means before that—just using a hose-pipe to pour water over the tanks. It has become more sophisticated.' As Miguel points out in his book, a major difference between the traditional fine wine areas of France and a Mediterranean area like Penedés was always the temperature at the time of fermentation. In Burgundy October is a fairly cool month—the nights can be freezing—and this means that the wine ferments slowly. In Penedés, on the other hand, October is still warm and without temperature control the fermentation can be so swift and tumultuous that the finer nuances of flavour are lost. Temperature-controlled fermentation has meant first that good quality commercial white wine can be made in Spain (and other warmer wine-producing regions) and secondly that it is possible to produce red wines to match the finest from France.

'Not all my experiments were successful, I should tell you,' said Miguel. 'I tried a new strain of yeast with one batch of Viñā Sol (the crisp, dry white wine made from the local Parellada grape) and ten thousand bottles all went cloudy.'

Such set-backs have been outweighed by Miguel's many successes. But he, like his father, is always looking to the future. 'At the moment we have achieved the goal of producing a good quality range, using some foreign varieties, in reasonable quantities. The next step is to achieve perfection in the matching of grape variety to vineyard site. We are getting there with Gran Coronas Black Label, or Mas La Plana as it is now called, which is now generally agreed to be one of the world's very best Cabernet Sauvignon wines. This year we will be releasing a single-vineyard, barrel-fermented, 100 per cent Chardonnay called Milmanda, of which I have quite high hopes.' Miguel is also interested in ecological viticulture. Since 1975, he has used other insects rather than insecticides to kill pests.

It is obvious that Miguel has interests outside the family wine business. 'Oh yes! I would like to write a novel. There is not time at the moment, it is very heavy, too heavy. I am planning my retirement.'

This is only half a joke—and something one can never imagine his father saying. His father's view is that retirement is fatal: 'The people I was at school with, when they retire, they die. They pass away.'

'But more seriously,' Miguel adds, 'I definitely plan to go back to university in one year's time. Going back to university could be fun.'

'To study more oenology?'

'Yes, day-to-day involvement in the business does not allow one time to keep up with all the new developments. Things are changing so fast in wine.'

The father is showing signs of restlessness. 'Have some brandy: this is our very special brandy, called Honorable. It comes in this cut-glass decanter—nice presentation, don't you think?' For upwards of £50 a bottle, both brandy and bottle should be rather special—and they are. It is a much subtler spirit than most Spanish brandies (generally heavily coloured and sweetened), more in the style of Cognac XO. It is made from local Parellada grapes and double distilled in a Charentais pot-still—exactly the way cognac is made. Torres have been making brandy for a long time; until the last twenty years the firm was probably better known for its brandies than its table wines. Torres brandies are a special interest of Sr Torres, maybe because of his son's increasing control over the table wine-making. 'How do we sell our brandies in England?' he asks, with a businesslike look in his eyes. 'We have some sample advertising material. I would like your comments. Painous!'

His personal secretary, Jeeves-like, disappears and reappears with a sheaf of papers. We settle down to a detailed discussion of the advertising copy: family lunch, business lunch, author's lunch, it all boils down to the same thing with Sr Torres: the further success and glorification of Torres.

After about three-quarters of an hour's serious discussion ('Painous! Take that down,' Torres cries, whenever I say anything he considers interesting), he looks at his watch. 'I have an appointment now. I am being made President of the Chamber of Commerce of Vilafranca. It is in our new reception centre. Perhaps you would like to come. I think it would be interesting, no?'

Torres's new reception centre stands across the road from the offices. It has a severe, four-square look from the outside, but the cool marble hall is impressive. Up the marble stairs there is a very beautiful painted wooden high relief of the nativity, by a Catalan artist of the sixteenth century. A large conference room is lined with intriguing, vaguely mystical panels, peopled by angels with multiple wings, sprouting from arms, legs and bottoms as well as shoulders, by the early twentieth-century Catalan artist Galí (closer in spirit to Chagall than his surrealist near-namesake). Along one wall of the dining-room runs a magnificent sixteenth-century Flemish tapestry depicting a Bacchanalian vintage scene.

After the tour of the building, I make my excuses: the prospect of an assembly of commercial pillars of the Vilafranca community followed by interminable speeches in Catalan is hardly alluring, but I compliment Sr Torres on his great energy and stamina in taking on new responsibilities at an age (late seventies) when most people have long shaken them off. 'Oh, many people my age are just wearing their slippers and watching the TV. That is boring. I still play forty or fifty holes of golf a week at El Prat.' The man has more energy than I do: I need to get back to Barcelona and put my feet up for an hour or two. Watch TV, maybe.

Day two starts with a tour of the vineyards. Once again, Albert Fornos is my guide. We drive past the new winery and through some gently sloping vineyards. The Torres vineyards stand out very obviously from the others in the area: whereas the vast majority of the vines which cover most of the Penedés are little unsupported bushes, looking black and stunted in the bright March sun, Torres's vines march in lines, trained on wires supported by concrete posts in the French Guyot system. It would take a more expert eye to notice that the density of plants is much higher than the average: 5000 as opposed to 2000–3000 per hectare, planted in narrower rows. The unspectacular, gently sloping land Albert points out is part of Mas La Plana, the Cabernet vineyard which produces most of the great Black Label; but then most of the great Bordeaux vineyards are unspectacular too. A couple of kilometres further on the land becomes hillier and a little village with a rustic campanile perched on a rock comes into view. We stop by a small vineyard with an umbrella pine in the middle: this is San Martí Sarroca, a lovely peaceful place which seems to belong to a different age from the ultra-modern winery. We drive on deeper into the countryside, and climb through thickly wooded hills, backwards in time too, because Albert points out a sturdy farmhouse built out of irregular blocks of limestone like a dry stone wall. 'That is the oldest inhabited *masía* [fortified farmhouse] in Catalonia. From the tenth century.' Shortly afterwards we are in a landscape of snow-dusted pine-covered hills, which might be in some romantic part of Germany or Alsace—the Schwarzwald or the Vosges. In clearings among the trees are a few lonely hectares of vineyard, the highest in Catalonia, and among the highest in Europe, at 2500 ft above sea level. A savage Alsatian, appropriately enough, tied on a chain, guards the old farmhouse where Torres's vineyard manager lives. 'This is where we grow Gewurztraminer for Vinã Esmeralda, and some Parellada,' says Albert. 'Yes, it is pretty cold up here. It snows almost every year.'

What this trip has shown is the extraordinary variety of vineyard sites which the Penedés region offers within a small compass: Torres's lowest-lying vineyards near Vilafranca rate as Area Four on the scale of vineyard climates drawn up by Davis University in California; in layman's languague, a hot Mediterranean climate suitable for sturdy red wines or sweet Muscat. Here, in the high Penedés, the accumulated number of degrees above 10°C in the growing season is not enough to qualify for Area One—the coldest climate suitable for wine growing. This is the explanation for the extraordinary width of Torres's range, from the fruitily aromatic Viña Esmeralda (60 per cent Muscat d'Alsace, 40 per cent Gewurztraminer), more like Alsatian wine than anything else produced in the Mediterranean, to the hearty, warm-flavoured red Sangre de Toro (literally, bull's blood).

Time for lunch—for all Torres's un-Spanish business acumen and unceasing search for technical improvements, they have the proper Spanish regard for the midday meal—but this time we go not to Vilafranca but, instead, to a masía tucked away among the vineyards near the brandy barrel cellar. The Mas Rabell de Fontenac is a fourteenth-century building, once part of an abbey, restored by Torres with excellent taste and lack of pretension as a venue for less formal entertaining and tasting. They have left the flagstoned floor untouched but uncovered a Gothic arch in the upstairs dining-room, where you eat on trestle tables covered with simple red check tablecloths. Before lunch there is a tasting for which we are joined by Miguel. We taste the wines blind and the first (white) has the unmistakable gooseberry and crushed nettle nose of Sauvignon Blanc. This is surely not from the Penedés—it smells like Sancerre. 'You are right, it is not Penedés—this is the Bellaterra Sauvignon from our estate in Chile.' After this it is not so hard to guess that the red with its blackcurrant and tobacco nose and piercing fruit purity is the Cabernet Sauvignon from the same estate.

The Chilean operation is Miguel's responsibility, and he is clearly excited by the quality and potential of these wines. 'We spent a lot of time doing research on many factors, climate, costs, and so on before deciding on Chile. First of all the climate in the Maipo Valley, as people have known for a long time, is particularly good for fruit growing of all kinds. There is a long growing season and, just as important, a very big difference between daytime and night-time temperatures. Then the costs are extremely reasonable; we calculate that it costs six times as much to grow a ton of Cabernet in the Napa Valley as it does in the Maipo Valley.'

How about the political climate?

'I think the problems have been greatly exaggerated,' Miguel replies diplomatically. 'Clearly, if we thought the political situation was dangerously unstable, we would not have made a big investment in Chile.'

After we had tasted some distinctive single vineyard varieties from Penedés—an impressively deep-coloured, if rather sturdy Pinot Noir, a marvellously intense, almost opaque Cabernet from Poblet, and the rich, buttery Milmanda Chardonnay—Miguel had to move over to a neighbouring table for a business lunch with some Spanish distributors. Albert and I settled down to an unpretentious lunch of lamb casserole and a bottle of Gran Coronas '82 (the splendid blend of 70 per cent Cabernet Sauvignon and 30 per cent Tempranillo, which I consider Torres's single most successful wine), and a discussion of Catalan poetry. A somewhat one-sided discussion, because my knowledge of Catalan poetry is extremely limited, but an enjoyable one nonetheless. In a corner of this rustic dining-room, I noticed an old-fashioned pottery stove with an air-vent which might have been designed by Heath

Robinson. 'Oh yes,' commented Albert, 'we tried more modern technology but found that this gave out more heat.'

If Torres owes much to the commercial, marketing genius of Sr Torres and the scientific brilliance of his son, success in the export markets has been aided by the family's female members. I had heard much about the Torres women, but during my visit to Spain I did not get a chance to meet them. The opportunity came back in England, when Marimar and her mother converged for a party at the Spanish Embassy to launch the English-language edition of Marimar's book on the food and wine of Spain. The evening before I was to meet both at a dinner party held by Torres's public relations person in London, Catherine Scott. Eight o'clock came and there was no word from Margarita Torres. Then the telephone rang: Sra Torres had just arrived at Heathrow. No, she would have no trouble getting to Peckham, she would just hail a taxi and hope for the best. At nine o'clock she arrived, immaculately turned out, a handsome woman in her mid-seventies, less flustered than most people after a short journey on the tube. There is steel, energy and vitality on both sides of the family, I discovered. Two or three times a year Sra Torres travels to Prague, East Berlin and Budapest to sell Torres wines into demanding, new markets. 'People wonder how an elderly lady like my wife can sell wine in Eastern Europe,' her husband told me, 'but she has no trouble.'

Her daughter Marimar is not yet so formidable, but she is a forceful woman nonetheless. In her mid-forties she is youthfully attractive and vivacious. The most striking thing about Marimar, though, is the way she straddles two cultures, Spain and America. It is not just that her English twangs with American vowels ('eeand', 'yeeah'), but that she radiates a peculiarly American attitude of self-improvement combined with self-advertisement. You hardly need to be told that she runs five miles every day before breakfast and cycles in to work. Marimar is engagingly frank about the dissatisfaction with herself and with Spanish society which, in consequence, compelled her to travel to the United States. 'I never really fitted in to Spanish society. I was not rebellious—in fact I never questioned what my father told me. What he said was the Bible, Truth, God. But I gradually became aware that something was wrong.'

She took the more ambitious of the options her father offered her—a business studies degree rather than a secretarial course—and worked at weekends on the accounts in the family bodega. Her father inadvertently set her off in the direction she was eventually to take by asking her to accompany him on a selling trip to the United States when she was nineteen. Other trips followed: in 1969 she went for the first time on her own to Canada, to sell the family wine.

'I was young and I enjoyed doing it and I was very successful. I made the most of the advantages I had. Those guys at the Liquor Board, they were very tired with just seeing boring old men and I achieved more than a guy probably would have done with the same qualifications.'

The most fateful trip was to San Francisco in Easter 1973: she went with her father but decided to stay on and take a holiday. That is when she met the wine writer Bob Finigan, who was to become her husband. 'It was strange, you know, when I was nineteen, and doing a very meaningless job at the winery, the daughter of one of my father's best customers came to stay with us in our summer house in Sitges. And she said to me, Marimar, you will never marry a Spanish man, you will marry an American. She was the typical Californian girl. She got married and then divorced.'

Marimar's marriage to Bob Finigan lasted four years. 'It was good while it worked. It was just that I changed. I see it as a period of transition, breaking the mould and going to live in America. The great thing about the structure of society there is that you have options: if you want to stay married, you stay married. If you want out, you get out, and it does not mean you are a bad person. We never had any money. We were living in a small apartment and I was getting a rather meagre salary—fifteen hundred dollars a month plus five hundred dollars expenses—that was in 1975. Sales in America were very low then—only 1500 cases. I remember Miguel coming over in 1976 and telling me, "This market is not worth bothering about. Settle down and start a family." '

It was advice she did not take. Gradually things picked up: she got a raise in salary and was able to buy the house in the smart Bayside suburb of Sausalito where she still lives.

'When the marriage broke up, there was a kind of expectation that I would go back to Spain, and I must say that I was tempted. I thought I would be living in an empty house—all the furniture was Bob's—with no friends. I did go back—it was December 1979 and after a month with the family I started missing America. I went back and made a very important discovery: Bob's friends were my friends too. I never had friends like that in Spain.'

We were talking the day after the launch party for her book on the food and wine (Torres notably prominent) of Spain, *The Spanish Table*. 'That was a major chunk of my life. I mean I had no social life for two years.' I knew what she meant. The party was a glamorous occasion in the palatial Spanish Embassy in Belgrave Square. The 200 or so guests were ushered in and directed in a line to be received by the three Torres ladies, Margarita, Marimar and Mali, wife of Juan María. Wearing tiaras and dressed in long, glittering satin dresses, the three had an almost regal appearance.

Marimar has ended up as the most unconventional of all the Torres children. Far from marrying a vinous nobleman, she married a wine writer and got divorced. She has recently had a child. Asked about the identity of the father, she has said, with humour probably unappreciated in Vilafranca, 'The Holy Ghost'. On the whole, though, she has managed to win the family over to her individual way of life.

'I had a party the other day for all the family in my flat in Barcelona and my mother said, "You are the one who has managed to bring us together." ' Marimar has also, incidentally, managed to push Torres's American sales past one million bottles a year. And though Marimar may not have added legitimate offspring to the family tree, she has persuaded her father to graft on to the family holdings in Penedés and Chile. Torres have bought 20 hectares of prime vineyard in the Russian River area of Sonoma County, which Marimar is personally managing. The first releases were expected in 1989 and are eagerly awaited.

So Torres stands at the apogee of its might as a dynasty, spread across three continents, with sales—over 20 million bottles—and critical acclaim at an all-time high. The family's combination of commercial flair, vitality, determination and scientific brilliance have achieved success on a scale seldom matched in the world of wines. Their influence within the world of Spanish, and specifically Catalan, wine is hard to exaggerate. Though Sr Torres's labelling policy has been to minimise the importance of Penedés (he would not use the official *denominación de origen*, or appellation system until recently) and to maximise that of Torres, a host of Torres imitators has sprung up in the area. None has yet come close to challenging Torres's supremacy, though the Raventós family have produced some notable Cabernet Sauvignon and sparkling Chardonnay on their vast estates of Raimat, near Lérida. To say that the Torres family have singlehandedly put Spanish wine on the international map would be unfair to the best producers in Rioja, but otherwise it would not be an exaggeration.

The pressures and frictions, probably inevitable in such a talented family, seem to have been largely resolved. It is difficult to imagine a dynasty more firmly based, more sure of itself and its future. And yet, and yet...'Vineyards, like empires, have their rise, their glory and their fall,' said the Elder Pliny: perhaps the same rule holds for vineyard empires. Who will carry on the Torres succession? Miguel has let it be known that he does not wish to be involved in running the business for ever: his talents, as one of the world's most gifted wine-makers, do not lie in the field of commerce. He and his German wife, Waltraud, an accomplished painter, have two daughters: the elder has already decided to become a doctor. That leaves his second daughter and the children of his elder brother Juan María. Whether any of these will prove to have the business flair of Sr Torres must be a moot point. Some of the most consummate wielders of power prove to have one mortal weakness: the inability to let it go.

Hidalgo

of

Sanlúcar de

Barrameda

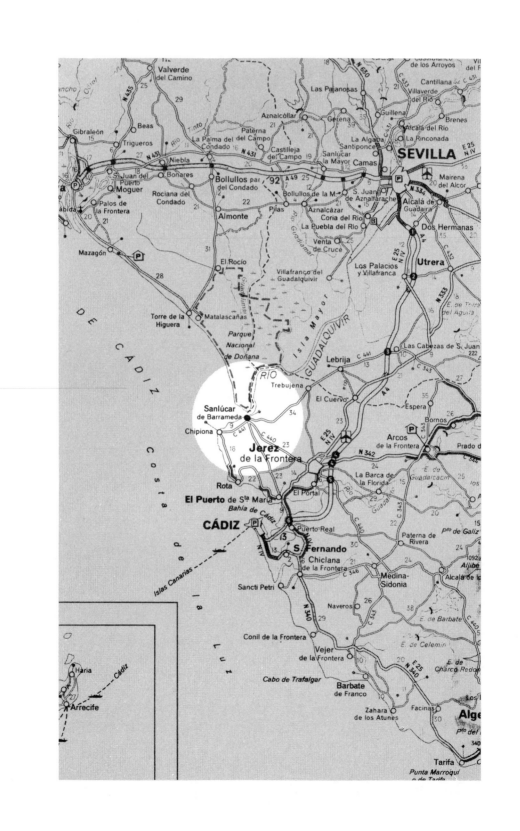

JAVIER HIDALGO LIVES ON A FARM—the Spanish word is *finca*—in the fertile flat land between Sanlúcar de Barrameda and Chipiona, about two kilometres from the Atlantic Ocean in the extreme south-west of Spain. You approach the low, white farmhouse along a short avenue of cypresses, with carnations growing on one side and cabbages on the other. The house is built around a square central courtyard, with the main dwelling part opposite as you enter, buildings for the animals on the left and a guest-room on the right—and a fountain in the middle. Potted flowers and spiky-leaved cacti hang from the white walls, as they do everywhere in Andalusia, creating the vivid contrasts of colour, red against white and the deep cobalt-blue of the sky.

As you drive in through the gateway—designed, two centuries ago, for smaller vehicles than Javier's executive Renault, which squeezes through with an inch to spare on either side—you are greeted by an enthusiastic, not very well disciplined black labrador. 'Hola, Nutria,' Javier says, trying to look stern. He is wearing, incidentally, a tweed cap, a green hunting jacket and cavalry twill trousers, all bought in Pall Mall. You might conclude two things from this introduction: first, that this is an Andalusian trying to look like an English gentleman, and second, that this is a sherry producer whose surroundings give no inkling that he is concerned with sherry.

Most people in the sherry business, whose largest customer by far is Britain, cultivate, to some extent at least, *el estilo inglés*, but with Javier, the 35-year-old managing director (in fact if not in title) of the 200-year-old family sherry firm, Vinicola Hidalgo, the English look is based on something deeper than mere style. He speaks excellent English, and the reverse of the Hispanophilia which affects so many Britons and Americans draws him to the English countryside, whose damp, soft greenness is so utterly different from the light-filled dryness of the south of Spain. He would not only not look out of place at Badminton or Bisley, at a meet of the Pytchley or on a grouse moor in Scotland, he really does hunt (with the West Shropshire) and shoot, in the shadow of the Welsh hills.

After lunch on Saturday afternoon, in bright, clear January weather, like a fine English March, what Javier proposed was not the traditional Spanish siesta. 'Shall we go and make jumps?' he asked, making no sense to me at first. Donning green wellies we plodded out across a field to a straggly copse. When we started balancing tree-trunks on posts, it became clear that we were constructing some kind of rustic show-jumping course.

Javier has four horses, medium- to small-sized (like himself), crossed between Arab and thoroughbred. The farm buildings also house four bullock calves, sleek tawny creatures being fattened for slaughter in the spring, and a black Iberian sow with a litter of squeaking, mucky piglets. 'This is a semi-wild breed. We call them *pata negra* [blackfoot]. If you see hams hanging up in a bar [a common sight all over Spain], look at the feet and make sure they're black. The blackfoot pigs are allowed to run free most of the time. It's very important for the taste of the ham that they should eat acorns.'

But the most unusual denizens of the Finca Santo Domingo are the birds. Through a cage in the back yard I exchanged glances with a honey buzzard: mine admiring, his bright yellow, murderous and mad. 'If looks could kill...' said Javier. 'He's in fine form now. When we found him he was half-dead.' I looked twice at the pale pink vertical bird standing by the pool in the back garden with its impossibly elegant neck and coral legs before realising it was not a statue but a real flamingo. 'Somebody brought it in with a broken wing—he said it had had an accident but he'd obviously shot it. I'm afraid people still do shoot flamingos around here.'

The stray flamingos are ones which have flown across the Guadalquivir river from the Coto Doñana, Spain's premier national park and one of Europe's most important nature reserves. A visit there is as essential an introduction to Javier Hidalgo as a tour of his sherry bodega (the word means both the warehouses in which the barrels are matured and the offices). It is also a bizarre experience. You set off from a reception centre masquerading as a hunting-lodge in a fifteen-seater jeep, and drive for a few kilometres down a straight road. Suddenly by a wire fence the jeep plunges off the road into thick tussocks of seagrass: on one side of the fence are a host of half-built, prefabricated holiday villas, on the other are dunes and then the white sand of a deserted beach stretching as far as the eye can see. 'There are thirty-three kilometres of empty beach from here at Matalascañas to the Guadalquivir estuary,' says the driver, who doubles as guide. The Spanish people on the jeep duly gasp, in wonder that their country can still contain such a stretch of unexploited beach. The non-Spanish visitor may be equally amazed that a vast new tourist development could be allowed right on the edge of the country's most important nature reserve.

There are other surprises. The Coto, the former hunting preserve of the Dukes of Medina Sidonia, still supports a great wealth of fauna in its varying environment of shifting dunes, pine scrub and marshy wetland. You need to be exceptionally lucky to catch a glimpse of the elusive European lynx (though visitors are encouraged in the vain hope that they might), but deer and wild boar, and, above all, migratory birds, are plentiful. You may find, however, that the driver's attitude to the wildlife is not quite in the David Attenborough or Tony Soper mould. Spotting a fallow deer hiding among reeds, our driver slung the jeep off the road in pursuit of the creature until it leapt away in terror. Shortly after, he pursued a wild boarlet a hundred yards down the track to disconcerting cries of 'Oink, oink!' from various excited fellow-passengers.

The moment when our noisy safari seemed most like an incursion came when we were faced not by shy wildlife but by a group of men with white handkerchiefs hung from broad-brimmed hats poking long sticks up into the pine trees. The pine kernel gatherers were a reminder of a traditional human way of life which still, just about, survives in the Coto: people live in thatched wooden huts, burning charcoal and keeping bees. That way of life and the one implied by our motorised excursion can never really meet.

There are better ways of visiting the Coto Doñana, but they are open, for most of the year at least, to very few people. One of them is Javier Hidalgo. Javier's business may be in Sanlúcar but his heart, one feels, is across the river in the Doñana. He was a director of the Park for seven years. 'I used to spend a week at a time in the Coto. I still go over when I can.' Although the Coto is only 600 metres from Sanlúcar, if you or I want to get there we must go on a hugely circuitous journey, returning to Seville then going on to Matalascañas. Javier has a more direct route: 'I just cross over with one of the fishermen, and my horse swims behind.' If it sounds romantic, it was also, undoubtedly, hard work. Javier trained, at Seville University, as a biologist, and when he was a director of the Park he conducted many technical conservationist projects: monitoring animal and bird populations, studying and protecting the marshes' crucial water sources. He writes regularly on wildlife for several Spanish nature magazines.

Just across the Guadalquivir estuary from the eastern edge of the Coto is the white-washed town of Sanlúcar de Barrameda. It was once a leading port for Spain's trade with the Americas—Columbus set off from Sanlúcar on his third voyage—but it seems to have gone gradually to sleep since the sixteenth century. In the mid-nineteenth century the outspoken travel writer Richard Ford called it 'dull and decaying'; James Michener, in *Iberia*, paints a lurid picture of its filth and squalor (beneath which, it is true, he finds a heart of gold). These days Sanlúcar is known mainly as the only place in the world which produces the lightest, driest, some would say the finest kind of sherry—manzanilla.

The Hidalgo bodega is a couple of hundred metres from the river estuary, well placed to receive the sea breezes which freshen the summer heat and supposedly freshen also the taste of manzanilla. As you walk into the bodega, past the statutory decorative barrels, there is a lovely patio vivid even in January with geraniums and red hibiscus, with its trumpet-shaped flowers. 'The patio used to be much bigger,' says Javier, pointing to a photograph from the 1920s, 'but my grandfather reluctantly decided the space had to be used more profitably.' Space in Sanlúcar is limited. One wall of the patio is decorated with *azulejos* (painted tiles) depicting vineyard scenes, and beneath them are bird-cages enclosing canaries and delicate collared doves.

You step momentarily into the great darkened expanse of the main bodega building with its earthen floor, dark wooden-beamed roof supported on whitewashed pillars, and row upon row of barrels stacked three high, before turning left into Javier's office. Cool, high-ceilinged, dark, also decorated with tiles and warmed in winter by an open fire in one corner, this office feels suspended in time. On the walls hang various maps, some of the sherry country, but one showing the fox-hound hunts of Great Britain. It does not, on the whole, seem a bad place to work.

Some might say it does not seem like a place to work at all. 'My family formerly used the bodega mainly as a place to entertain friends. They'd invite people to come round at about one o'clock, have a few glasses of sherry. Some members of my family still seem to regard it in that way. There's one of my cousins, wearing a beautiful camel-hair coat. He also has a very nice collection of Hermès ties. The other members of family seem to be cleverer than I am. They just sit around drinking *copas* and I work all the time.'

Behind the sarcasm lies a social commentary. The philosophy in this part of Spain is that once you have made enough money to live comfortably, you do just that. It is a relic of the old Castilian attitude, well described in Luis Buñuel's autobiography *My Last Breath* (1982), that work is fundamentally ignoble: a gentleman should be able to live without doing anything much more strenuous than curling his moustaches, going to his club, chatting with his friends, perhaps reading the occasional newspaper and conducting the odd romantic intrigue. And the sherry industry is, in some ways, peculiarly adapted to this manner of life.

Many of the great sherry houses were started by immigrants—in the case of Domecq, an immigrant from France; in the case of Barbadillo and Hidalgo, immigrants from the more industrious north of Spain. The first Hidalgo of Sanlúcar, Don José Pantaleón, arrived from the Cantabrian mountains in the second half of the eighteenth century. Like many *montañeses* (natives of Santander province), Don José set up a shop selling colonial merchandise: Sanlúcar was then one of the main ports for ships plying trade with the South American colonies.

Don José sounds like the classic founder of a dynasty: energetic, hard-working, with an eye'for the advantageous marriage. His alliance with Doña Fermina Verjano, whose father Roque had founded the sherry bodega which was to become Vinicola Hidalgo, established him among, not exactly the aristocracy, but the comfortably off landowning class of the area. Most important of all for the future of the dynasty, it gave him both the bodega and top-quality vineyards, in the chalky slopes of Miraflores, outside the town, and in the Balbaina hills half-way to Jerez.

Not much seems to be known about Don José's domestic life, but two paintings, one almost a miniature, the other life-size, of a doe-eyed, soft-fleshed gypsy girl, like the denizen of an Ingres harem transferred to Andalusia, hang in the bodega offices. La Gitana has become the brandname of Hidalgo's most successful manzanilla, her portrait printed on every bottle. Attempts to change the label have met with fierce resistance from the local market. Whether Doña Fermina Verjano would have been amused to see how the products of the vineyards she brought as her dowry would be marketed is anybody's guess.

Don José and Doña Ana's son, Eduardo Hidalgo Verjano, consolidated the family fortune and was then able to turn his attention to more public matters: he established the railway line—now sadly defunct—between Sanlúcar and Jerez and was active in local politics as a Liberal. Despite being, *ipso facto*, anti-monarchist, he invited the King, Alfonso XII, to stay in Sanlúcar. Showing admirable broadmindedness, and appreciation of Don Eduardo's public spirit, the young monarch offered him a marquisate. The offer was refused. 'There is always a Liberal in every generation of our family,' commented Javier. The current representative is his sister, a Communist deputy in the Cádiz provincial government.

Don Eduardo's fourth son and Javier's grandfather was an engineer by training but a sportsman by passionate avocation. He built roads as a hobby but shot very seriously, snipe amd partridge, often in

Doñana, every day of the week except Sunday. The bodega offices he visited once a week, to sign papers. 'As I've said, my family used to regard the bodega more as a place to meet people and have a drink than a serious business. The serious business was the farming.' All the same, when the wine journalist Henry Vizetelly visited the sherry country in 1875, he was obviously impressed by Vinicola Hidalgo; he describes meeting 'Señor Hidalgo, one of the principal growers of Sanlúcar and the largest holder of manzanillas, including the very finest qualities of this delicate, aromatic wine'.

Javier's father was a judge and amateur ornithologist, as well as being legal adviser to the family firm. In those days, one feels, the firm was left largely to run itself. And, once the initial capital investments have been made—the vineyards bought, the bodega constructed, the stock amassed—it is a business which can seem to run and, equally important, sell itself. For what sherry requires to become itself is principally time, peace and quiet, shade. Once the wine has been made— and this often takes place in vinification plants out in the vineyards—it rests in the bodega, admittedly having to be moved through the stages of the solera system for anything from four (in the case of the basic manzanilla sold to bars) to a hundred years.

But what is manzanilla? If you ask for a manzanilla in a Spanish bar anywhere except Sanlúcar, the chances are that you will be given a camomile tea. Manzanilla is the lightest and driest of all sherries, with an almost bitter tanginess which has led to its (unfair) association with the herbal infusion. Wine writers used to ascribe manzanilla's 'salty tang' to the proximity of the Atlantic Ocean, conveniently forgetting that one of the other sherry towns, El Puerto de Santa María, is just as close to the sea. It seems much more likely that manzanilla's special character comes from the quality of *flor*—literally 'flower'—which grows, more thickly than in the other two sherry towns, in the bodegas of Sanlúcar. Flor is a white yeast, with the not very attractive look of bleached porridge, which grows on the surface of some barrels of sherry. Flor feeds on the alcohol and glycerine in the wine, rendering it lighter, almost sharp, and, owing to the formation of acetaldehyde, pungently aromatic. Because of the thicker growth of flor in the cooler, more humid air, levels of acetaldeyde are higher in Sanlúcar than in the other sherry towns. New research being carried out at the University of Cádiz also suggests that one of the three main strains of the flor yeast, *Saccharomyces beticus*, is more prevalent in Sanlúcar than Jerez or El Puerto.

Some barrels develop flor, but not all: the growth of flor is natural, and uninduced, if not entirely haphazard. Flor is certainly fickle: it grows better in some parts of the town than others, even in some parts of a single bodega. People in Sanlúcar will tell you that it grows better in the lower town, nearer the river and the ocean, than the upper town (where, incidentally, the largest producer, Barbadillo, has most of its bodega space). But then those people always turn out to have bodegas in the lower town. No doubt in California they would synthesise and induce it, but here in southern Spain they leave things to God, or chance.

In practice, however, despite centuries of wine lore, sherry producers know pretty well that the barrels containing the first pressing of grapes from the best vineyards will develop flor. The growth of flor marks those barrels out as the élite—those destined to produce the finest, lightest sherries, called fino in Jerez and El Puerto, and in Sanlúcar, manzanilla.

From here on, the process involves a kind of dynamic ageing—the passing of the wine through a series of stages, consisting of flights of barrels, known as the solera system. By the time the wine reaches the final stage, called the solera, it will have been moved up to fourteen times, at intervals ranging from a few months to a year or more. The stages can be seen, in a simplified model, as rows of barrels. The wine is drawn off to be bottled—never more than a third at a time—from the bottom row. The bottom row is then topped up from the next-to-bottom, called the first *criadera*, and so on up to the top, which is filled with the newly fermented wine. The point is that the character of the older wine is preserved, and a consistent style maintained.

It is thus imposssible to know the exact age of any sherry: some of the wine in an old-established solera can clearly be a century old or more. Sherry is the only top-class wine not to carry a vintage date. In Sanlúcar, soleras tend to have more stages (Javier's La Gitana is a 14-stage solera) and to be moved through them at quicker intervals than finos from Jerez or El Puerto. This means more work and, Javier would claim, greater finesse. The job of tasting every barrel, and deciding whether it belongs where it is or should be transferred to another stage, is in the hands of the *capataz*, or head taster—the most important man in the bodega, proprietor included. The instrument he uses for sampling resembles a candle-snuffer with a cylindrical cap at the end of a long, flexible shaft. In more lordly Jerez the shaft is made of whalebone and is called a *venencia*: in Sanlúcar the material is cane and the name simply *caña*. In both places the action of inserting the instrument through the bung-hole, penetrating the layer of flor, whipping out the small sample and pouring it into a *copita* is dramatic grace and gesture, very much more difficult than it looks to perform.

If something seems a little cockeyed about this definition of a wine, that might be the omission of what is usually considered the *fons et origo*—the vineyards. For unlike almost any other wine, manzanilla is defined not by where it comes from, but by where it is made. The grapes which go to make manzanilla are not necessarily any different from those which become fino, though the area of Miraflores just outside Sanlúcar has always been known to produce delicately flavoured grapes especially suitable for manzanilla.

The Hidalgos own vineyards in Miraflores, but also in Balbaina, one of the most famous areas for fino. Very unusually among sherry producers, they rely almost entirely on their own 260 hectares to cover their requirements for grapes to make manzanilla. 'I prefer to be able to control the whole process: with other people's grapes you never know exactly how the soil has been treated, how the pruning has been done,' said Javier, who managed to complete an agriculture degree while doing his military service.

El Cuadrado vineyard in Balbaina is 10 kilometres outside Sanlúcar on the road to Jerez. The land is smooth, treeless and largely flat, but soft rounded hills, hardly hills at all, just gentle undulations, rise up in places. On them, the brown clayey soil of the bottoms becomes dappled, as if by the shadows of clouds. This is chalk, the *albariza* soil essential for the Palomino grape to produce high-class, delicate-flavoured fruit.

You enter El Cuadrado by a gate off the main road, and climb up 100–150 feet through the vines before reaching the vinification plant and manager's house at the top. Nothing much, but it gives you eminence in this low-lying land, great views over the hollow in which Jerez nestles to the jagged Sierra de Cádiz in the northern distance.

The January day I was there it was bright, almost dazzling, with a cool but not piercing wind. 'Normal weather, good weather,' said Javier. 'We call it good weather if it's not raining. It's either like this, bright and sunny, or it rains. We don't have your English shades of grey.' The rainfall in this part of Spain is surprisingly similar to that of southern England, but it falls in much more concentrated bursts, in late autumn and winter. From April to September, when the vines are growing and the grapes ripening, there is very little rain at all.

Walking among the vines, Javier pointed out two methods of pruning: one a severe training down to one short and one longer shoot, the other a riot of shoots growing in all directions from the low, bush-like vine. The latter is not as careless as it looks: 'We leave the old vines like that, to exhaust them more quickly.' Uprooted blackened stumps lay around in sad, superannuated piles: vines are replaced roughly every thirty years, when their vigour and yield start to decline.

Like most buildings in Andalusia, the little winery is low and sparkling white. Two araucaria trees, natives of Argentina but naturalised citizens of Sanlúcar, spiky evergreens with stiff branches like a child's drawing, stand guard on either side: between them are gnarled, silvery olives, with a weathered sensuousness which points up the outlandish rigidity of the araucarias. On one side of the winery is a meadow, almost unreally green, the pasture of a splendid white mule, with much more about him of the horse than the donkey. All around stretches the softness of this surprisingly gentle land, much less harsh and austere than Spain's céntral tableland. The only intense element in the landscape is the light, which seems to dissolve the solidity of the distant hills.

The winery consists of a pressing hall and a cluster of tall concrete fermenting jars called *tinajas*, modern versions of an ancient concept, still exuding a faint air of *The Arabian Nights' Entertainments*. At this time of year they are full of the newly fermented wine: we climbed up some rather perilous wooden ladders to sample a future manzanilla, with attractive, quite delicate fresh fruit aromas, but soft and broad in flavour, and a future oloroso, made from second pressings, much heavier and harsher in flavour.

At the back there is a small bodega, containing a solera of fino — not manzanilla since we are outside the boundaries of Sanlúcar. Watching over this is a big, tall, gentle-looking man of about forty, called José Antonio and nicknamed 'el chico' ('the kid'). He lives in this isolated spot with his wife and pretty dark-haired daughter of five, who sat outside, dressed only in pyjamas, during our visit, playing with the dog. I asked him if he found it lonely, but he only shrugged and smiled. His wife goes out shopping during the day, and he has plenty of work with the vineyards.

There is a no-nonsense quality about the vineyard management at Hidalgo. In other parts of the wine-making world people agonise over the choice of grape variety best suited to the soil, the density of planting, the type of pruning: here it seems remarkably clear-cut. There is no argument over grape variety, for a start: the Palomino, which produces flat, indifferent table wine, but is magically transformed by flor and the solera system, reigns supreme in the sherry country. All the other technical questions likewise seem to have been solved with the minimum of fuss.

The explanation for this must lie partly in the fact that what makes manzanilla, and all sherry, special is not so much the base wine (though that is clearly an important factor) as what happens to it in the bodega. Here sherry is closer to the great spirits, which metamorphose from a very ordinary wine or wash into something rich and strange simply by lying in a barrel, than the great wines, where the quality of the grapes is paramount. Time, in both cases, is of the essence.

We drive back to the bodega, and have a chance to taste not only the various stages of manzanilla, but also some of the older rarities. The *amontillado viejo* is not so much an aged manzanilla as a wine which started out with more the characteristics of a fino (somehwat heavier and less delicate) and has aged over twenty years or more to a pale copper colour, with a pronounced oily nose and concentrated, very dry flavour. Hidalgo's Napoleon amontillado is a slightly (but only slightly) more commercial version of this: very light and dry, yet concentrated for an amontillado, with something of the tangy, pungent manzanilla character. This is worlds away from what is generally known as medium sherry, and also very different from a top-class dry amontillado from Jerez like Valdespino's Tio Diego. But the pride of the bodega is an even older wine, which in Jerez would be called Palo Cortado but in Sanlúcar, in defiance of common sense, is known as Jerez Cortado. This is a deeper copper in colour, very aromatic on the nose, with a wonderful dark nutty flavour, extremely dry in the finish. This wine, Javier estimates, could average 80-100 years in age.

These old, heavier wines probably have only a connoisseur's following these days—just as well considering that they exist only in tiny quantities. We live in a world which craves lightness. Here is one reason for the current fashion, especially in Seville, for manzanilla, the lightest of all sherries. It is also a reason for the move from *manzanilla pasada*, aged from seven to twenty years, still pale and dry but pungent and characterful, to the lighter, younger style called *manzanilla fina*. It is fascinating to taste samples from the different criaderas of the manzanilla solera. The wine at one, two and three years old is still soft and fruity, and lacks the pungent tanginess, and delicacy, of true manzanilla. Only at about five years old does it start to take on its proper character, which then goes on intensifying, at the expense of primary fruit freshness.

Javier's La Gitana is carefully poised between the two styles, but closer to the younger, fina one. It is very pale in colour, fresh yet tangy on the nose, both appetising and characterful on the palate. Javier is aware that it is a somewhat lighter wine than the manzanilla pasada San León produced by his uncle, Luís de Argüeso, down the road. 'It is an interesting question,' he says. 'Do you carry on producing what has traditionally been considered the best wine, or do you adapt to the requirements of the market? There has to be a compromise.'

Certainly the British market, a gently declining one in recent years, has responded enthusiastically to the lighter manzanillas. These have started to be shipped at 15.5 degrees alcohol, the strength at which they are consumed in Spain, rather than 17.5 or 18 degrees, as used to be normal practice. The lighter wines are more delicate, and will go off very quickly once opened, but they surely offer sherry's best hope of persuading younger people that it need not be a tired, sweetened beverage kept for too long in a decanter by an aged aunt.

The multi-faceted Javier Hidalgo is an energetic salesman. While other producers in Sanlúcar have not looked beyond the local market, which still drinks more than 90 per cent of all manzanilla, he has travelled thoughout Europe and the United States with samples of his sherry. 'It is really very easy. Once people taste our manzanillas, they usually want to buy them.' He has built up quite a following in Britain for his manzanilla, initially sold only through specialist wine merchants such as the Merchant Vintners group. Just recently, he has sold La Gitana to Waitrose. He has only one serious rival, his much bigger neighbour Barbadillo. However keen the rivalry of their brands, Barbadillo's managing director, Alfonso Barón, is probably Javier's closest friend.

There are signs that Sanlúcar and its unique product, manzanilla, having languished for so long in the shadow of the richer, grander firms of Jerez, are beginning to establish their own identity. The sign on the wall of Barbadillo's huge bodega in the upper town may still say, 'Suppliers to Harvey's of Bristol', but Barbadillo recently took the almost unprecedented step, for a Sanlúcar bodega, of buying a Jerez company, Williams & Humbert. It had formerly been in the clutches of Rumasa, the enormous holding company built up by the Jerezano businessman José-Maria Ruiz-Mateos, which controlled a third of the entire sherry business when it was expropriated by the Spanish government in 1983. Rumasa, it is generally agreed, came close to destroying the sherry industry, selling vast quantities of inferior quality wine at low prices. Sanlúcar's unglamorous image probably saved its best firms from Ruiz-Mateos. As for manzanilla La Gitana, it is, according to Javier, not only the best-selling manzanilla but the best-selling sherry on the important Seville market. Not just the future of Sanlúcar, but that of the entire sherry industry is now seen to lie in the light, fresh, fino style of which it is a distinguished representative. That at least was the conclusion of an economic survey on the future of sherry commissioned by the Spanish government in 1987 from Arthur Young Management and London Economics.

In any case, what has been seen as the traditional British way of drinking sherry, stale, sweet, warm and unaccompanied, has very little in common with the way sherry is drunk in Spain, or at least in Andalusia. To learn about the latter, Javier took me, in the evening, on a round of the tapas bars of Sanlúcar. We were accompanied by his vivacious wife Paula, whom he met while they were both studying at Seville University. Paula used to work as a teacher, but now spends most of her time at home on the Finca Santo Domingo, looking after their young son Gonzalo. 'I found it quite diffiicult at first,' she told me. 'I missed my family and friends in Seville. But I have got used to it. Now whenever Javier goes away on a long trip I go to Seville and see my family. We have a lot of fun.'

Back at the Finca Santo Domingo, before setting out, we are joined by Javier's cousin, Alfonso Hidalgo, Alfonso Barón of Barbadillo, and Lucy Tanner, daughter of Javier's friend and customer Richard Tanner. Lucy, fresh from university, was out in Sanlúcar working for Vinicola Hidalgo—continuing a tradition of English merchants living and working in Sanlúcar which goes back to the fifteenth century, incidentally.

Spanish parties have a tendency to expand, a freewheeling quality which finds its most extreme expression in the great street fiestas of Pamplona and Seville. They also have a tendency, like this one, to be organised at the last moment. On second thoughts, they are not organised in any Anglo-Saxon sense, they simply happen.

Sanlúcar is transformed at night into a humming, buzzing network of bars, too many to count, linked by groups of people progressing from one to another until the early hours. The custom is to eat one tapa, that apotheosis of the bar-snack which is one of the great achievements of Spanish culture, at each bar. In Sanlúcar, whose small, ramshackle fleet of fishing-boats is moored along the Guadalquivir estuary, tapas generally consist of fish and shellfish.

We begin with *cazón*, a fresh slice of shark fillet fried in batter, speciality of the busy bar in the main square. To accompany it, Alfonso Barón orders a bottle of Barbadillo's manzanilla pasada Solear, which has an average age of twenty years. Despite this, it is pale in colour and fresh to taste, though not with the obvious freshness of fruit, but the keen, tangy freshness acquired by years under the protective, refining flor. 'Very fine manzanilla,' says Javier, complimenting his competitor's wine. He adds in an undertone to me, 'They hardly sell any of this. I don't know why.' It is served cool, and the bottle is drunk with the same speed that it takes to dispose of the delicious, firm-fleshed cazón. The first lesson about sherry in Andalusia is that it is wine, not a strange liqueur-like substance to be poured sparingly and kept until long after its goodness is gone.

We moved on to another bar which specialised in shell-fish. *Langostinos* are unfortunately almost as expensive in Sanlúcar as in London, so we ordered instead the sinister-looking mantis prawns. They have a coarser flavour and woollier texture than langostinos, and it is hard work to crack open their spiky carapaces. Still, I knew they were as fresh as could be, having seen them, or their brethren, only that morning still contracting their ridged bellies on the slab in the Sanlúcar fish market. One thing was certain: they were immensely improved by the tangy lightness of La Gitana. Another lesson about sherry: it is almost always drunk with food. No white wine I know goes better with shellfish.

I found myself sitting next to Alfonso Hidalgo, a young but determined character whose business has nothing to do with manzanilla. He has set up an ice-cream factory on the outskirts of Sanlúcar and is now exporting all over Europe. 'Sanlúcar is a sleeping lion,' he said. 'Most people here are content to go around with their thumbs in their waistcoats congratulating themselves that they are Hidalgos or Barbadillos. I don't see the virtue in that. Just because you're born something it doesn't prove you've done anything. That's why I admire Javier—he's made an effort and been active, travelling abroad and developing exports. There are very few people like him around here. Frankly, I am bored by sherry bodegas. I prefer to do something untraditional and quite different.'

It is time to move on. Our final port of call is the famous bar El Bigote, down by the estuary with the fishing boats in front, and across the river, marked by a darker line of umbrella pines, the mysterious stillness of the Coto. One of Bigote's specialities is the giant clams called *almejas*, served in a sauce made with sherry. Once again we drink Solear, an aristocrat among white wines, absurdly undervalued. But the conversation has moved away from sherry. Javier and Lucy Tanner are discussing the El Rocío pilgrimage which takes place every Whitsun. Thousands of people from all parts of Spain converge on the small pilgrimage town of El Rocío, on the western fringes of the Coto Doñana. Some on foot, some on horseback or in horse-drawn wagons, they take about a week to cross the Coto from west to east. At night they camp out in the open. A good deal of sherry, particularly manzanilla, is drunk. 'I do it every year,' Javier says. 'It is a very good way of cleaning the mind.' He meant not only the sherry, but the sherry, the pilgrimage and the Coto combined.

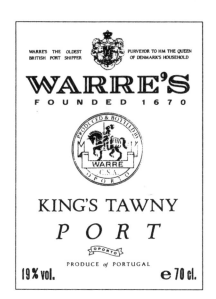

WARRE'S THE OLDEST
BRITISH PORT SHIPPER

PURVEYOR TO HM THE QUEEN
OF DENMARK'S HOUSEHOLD

WARRE'S
F O U N D E D   1 6 7 0

KING'S TAWNY
P O R T

PRODUCE *of* PORTUGAL

19 % vol.   e 70 cl.

The Symingtons
of
Oporto

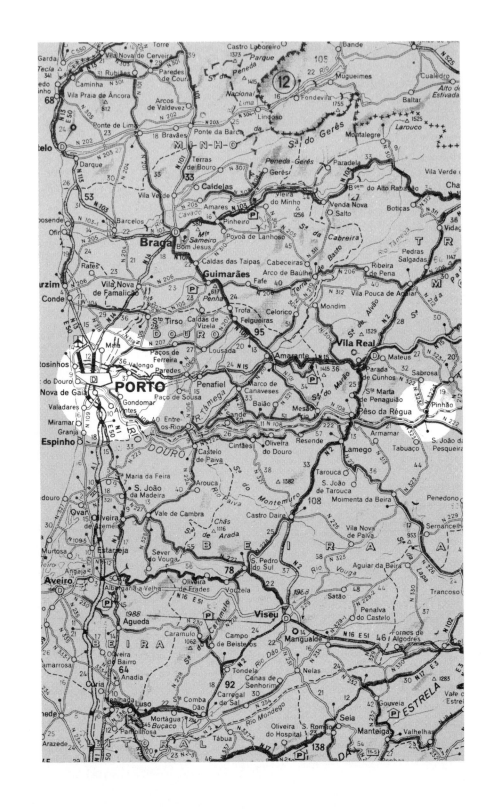

Port is the most British of all the wines which Britain invented. From Bordeaux and Jerez, Marsala and Malaga, the British merchants who once dominated the wine trade have retreated, leaving, in the first two cases, significant but not controlling presences behind. While the British Isles are no longer the largest customer for port, the fortified wine from the Douro valley in northern Portugal (France imports more than three times as much port as the United Kingdom), the quality end of the market still has an incontrovertibly British accent. In defiance of world-historical trends, the British maintain a quasi-colonial presence in a country which has never been a colony. Long after the Union Jack has been hauled down in the former colonies of Africa and the East, the Factory House, the eighteenth-century merchants' club in the heart of old Oporto, continues to hold its Wednesday lunches from which women (completely) and natives (as members) are excluded, and which culminate in the ritual guessing of the decanter of vintage port. The only deference to the tides of history is that the street on which the Factory House stands is no longer called Rua Nova dos Inglezes.

The British grip on Oporto is easy to exaggerate. The community has been in decline for much of this century, and now only twelve or fifteen families remain in the port business. Where other families have declined or disappeared, however, one in recent times has gone from strength to strength. There are now thirty-four members of the Symington family in Oporto, and the Symington group owns no less than five separate port companies, including three of the most prestigious: Dow's, Warre's, and Graham's.

The rise and rise of the Symington dynasty has coincided with a rather unexpected boom in the port business, which for twenty years after the Second World War had seemed to be in irreversible decline. The renewed fashion for a heavy, fortified red wine, over 20 degrees in alcoholic strength, and in the case of its most noble manifestation, vintage port, requiring twenty years to reach maturity, flies in the face of the general trend towards light, dry white wine.

It is perhaps a sign of the easy-going nature of the Portuguese, mildest and most tolerant of colonisers, and almost the only nation in history to have achieved a bloodless revolution, that they have allowed

197

the British to colonise them with no more than the odd flare of resistance. Of course the alliance between England and Portugal, going back to 1373, is celebrated as the oldest in existence. It predates the history of port by some 300 years.

In the late seventeenth century, wars with France and the ultraprotectionist policy of the French minister Colbert forced the English to look to their old ally, rather than their old enemy, as a source of wine. English merchants had for many years been established in the north of Portugal, especially at Viano do Castello, selling mainly cotton, cloth and salt cod. By the terms of the treaty of 1654, they enjoyed an extremely favoured position, with legal privileges, reduced taxes, freedom of worship and permission to participate in the slave trade. The more famous Methuen treaty of 1703 allowed English cloth to be imported into Portugal free of duty, while in return Portuguese wine should always be subject to a third less duty than French wine. The English rag traders turned their attention to wine. Initially, the main selling-point of the new port wine seems to have been patriotism, as Swift's couplets illustrate:

> Be sometimes to your country true
> Have once the public good in view
> Bravely despise Champagne at Court
> And choose to dine at home with port.

The implication is that it was pretty filthy stuff. Gradually, however, the intrepid English traders discovered better sources of wine, and encouraged the Portuguese farmers to plant vines on the steep hillsides of the Douro Valley rather than the lusher valleys of the Minho (source of what is now called *vinho verde*). A certain amount of brandy was probably added to the wine to make it stronger and more robust, but the special method of stopping the fermentation half-way through by adding a considerable amount of strong grape brandy, to make the sweet, strong red wine we know as port, did not become general practice until around 1840. Even after that date, James Forrester, the most distinguished and multi-talented of all British port shippers, argued against fortification. His arguments were not heeded, and now in a world flooded with good table wine, the port shippers should be thankful for it. Their powerful, aromatic fortified wine has few serious international competitors.

As for relations between the British and Portuguese, there should probably be an element of gratitude on both sides. The British shippers may have milked the profit from millions of hours of toil put in by generations of Douro peasant-farmers, but they created, if not the wine itself, then its international market. The Portuguese shippers were able to follow in the footsteps of the pioneering British. I once asked a Portuguese port shipper if he resented being excluded from the Factory House. 'Oh no,' he replied, 'if the British want their club, why shouldn't they have it? It is true that the British here are exaggeratedly British, but they lend the place a certain distinction. I am in favour of them.'

It is not difficult to see why both Oporto, the grimy, vertical, intriguing port city at the mouth of the Douro, and the wine country over 100 kilometres up river, should have such a long-lasting appeal for the British. First, Oporto itself—first because even now it is where the port story both starts and finishes, the vineyard country being more or less inaccessible from any other direction. It is a northern city in a southern country, like Milan and Turin in Italy, but with a climate much milder than that of either. You might call it the Portuguese Manchester, except that its smells of putrefying fish are more reminiscent of Rio de Janeiro, and its blue-and-white tiled houses, its terracotta roofs and its baroque towers resemble those of Ouro Preto, Brazil's rococo capital.

Oporto is damp—47 inches of rain annually—and grey much of the year, but seldom cold. It is therefore a gardener's paradise. In the garden of the Symington offices in Vila Nova de Gaia, which command a splendid view of the old city climbing steeply up from the Douro's gorge, roses grow in almost indecent profusion. There are also camellias, some of the first in Europe, brought over by the Jesuits from Japan in the late eighteenth century, and a magnificent tulip tree. 'This must be a great place for gardening,' I suggested to Penny Symington. 'No it's a terrrible place,' she laughed, 'because everything grows here, much too much of it, much too fast.'

The previous evening, Penny and her husband James, in charge of the Graham's brand, had greeted us (a small group of journalists out for a vintage-time jaunt) in their substantial town house in Oporto. From the street, an arched gateway led into a large, riotously fertile garden with a line of topiary yew. The air was full of the scents of jasmine and canned fish. James, a small, energetic man with an engaging air of boyish enthusiasm, led us past a swimming pool to a double garage which housed a magnificent burgundy-coloured open-top Avis and a sporty AC. Their stone-detailed, classically proportioned house was built in 1859 in a style which had not changed for a century. The ground floor was covered in soft-grained granite slabs, which, Penny Symington remarked, 'sweat like mad in the winter.' She led us upstairs past a lovely double-arched landing to the first-floor drawing-room. James poured generous measures of 1970 Graham's, a big, powerful wine, with firm tannin backing up the rich strawberry fruit. The illusion of an eighteenth- or early nineteenth-century squirarchical existence, subtly modified by a warm, damp, as opposed to cool, damp climate, was complete.

'The Portuguese are very sweet but they are rather slow and not terribly efficient,' said Penny Symington, a slim, attractive woman who has not lost her English complexion after twenty-five years in Portugal. 'The British built almost everything here, the railways, the trams, the sewers. The Portuguese even bought British letter-boxes in the time of Queen Victoria and painted them green. You can still see some of them around and make out the V.R.'

'Things are changing here, though, with entry into the EEC,' her husband interjected. 'As far as we are concerned, we feel very happy about Portugal's membership of the EEC because it makes it much more difficult for them to kick us out—if they ever wanted to, of course.' After 300 and more years of fairly peaceful cohabitation, James Symington's nervousness might seem unnecessary. The 1975 revolution, however, which left the British port shippers miraculously unscathed, also gave them a fright from which they may not have entirely recovered.

The plush, impersonal modern hotel in the commercial district of Oporto where we spent the night certainly bore witness to a city tackling the late twentieth century with some enthusiasm. None of the other guests had anything to do with the port trade: most were textile buyers from Japan.

The next morning's entertainment was a tour of the Symingtons' extensive office and warehouse quarters in Vila Nova de Gaia. Gaia is the suburb of Oporto on the south bank of the Douro entirely given over to port wine. Its official title in Portuguese is *entreposto*, which means nothing more than a bonded warehouse, and suggests an in-between sort of place. Vila Nova is both, a collection of warehouses and the half-way house between the wine's origin, in the Alto Douro, and its eventual destination—historically, northern Europe and especially Great Britain. Vila Nova de Gaia is where almost all the port shippers have their offices and hold their stocks. Bottle manufacturers, cork makers, coopers, label printers have all been established there for over a century. Until 1986, all port had to be exported from Gaia. It was thought that port, aged in the more extreme climate up-river in the Douro, had an undesirable burnt flavour—Douro stink. Now, in the opinion of some shippers who have invested in temperature-controlled warehouses in the Douro at least, that problem has been solved, and port can be shipped directly from the Douro. It is certainly a political move, designed to favour small farmers in the Douro and counter the near-monopoly of the big Oporto-based firms.

Gaia may not be the most logical place to begin the story of port, but it is the place where, for most visitors, it does begin. Down on the quayside in the lowest part of the entreposto you can see a line of elegant, narrow sailing boats with squarish transverse sails, like Viking gondolas. As the port shippers' names printed on the sails make clear, these *barcos rabelos* are now superior advertising hoardings, but they were once the means by which the barrels of young port were taken down the rushing perilous river in the spring after the vintage. Now lorries are used and in any case the Douro has been dammed to make a series of beautiful, placid lakes. The rest of Gaia has not changed much: it is a place of steep cobbled streets, not designed for the grunting, mastodontic lorries which somehow manage to negotiate them, and warehouses built of Cyclopean blocks of granite. These warehouses, which contain thousands of barrels of maturing port, are called lodges. If that sounds like a euphemism, these cool, pleasing stores, with their whitewashed walls, earthen floors and ancient, twisted beams deserve the gracious name. They would have made a good subject for one of those seventeenth-century Dutch painters who specialised in church interiors. The Symingtons own a variety of lodges, one for each of their brands. Since port is a meticulously regulated commodity, all the stock has to be registered to a particular brand. Stock can be transferred from one brand to another, but only with a good deal of paperwork. Bill Warre, last representative of the oldest British port family and now a Symington employee, told me that not all the port in the beautiful eighteenth-century Smith Woodhouse lodge (one of the Symingtons' smaller brands) will come out as Smith Woodhouse port.

The dark barrels which fill the lodges are mainly of 534 litres' (117 gallons' or fifty-six cases') capacity and are called pipes. They are made of oak from different sources, and are up to a hundred years old. A few of these ancient barrels are made of oak from the forests of Estonia, then an independent country, perhaps soon to be one again. Now the main sources are Portugal itself, France and Yugoslavia. The taste of new wood, so sought after to enhance the flavour of some wines, is actively avoided in the case of port. New barrels will be filled first with inexpensive table wine. 'The cooperage used to be the biggest employer here,' said James Symington. 'Now we have seven coopers, working mainly on repairing old barrels. One interesting feature is that they use no nails—reeds are inserted between the staves to keep them water-tight, or port-tight.'

These lodges are filled with many different lots of port of varying age, type and quality. They range from raw, purple wine of the last vintage to venerable *colheitas* (wine of a single vintage aged in barrel) as much as half a century old. By far the greater part of the Symingtons' trade is in so-called wood ports, in two main styles, ruby and tawny. These are aged in barrel for between three and ten or more years, until they are considered ready for drinking. Most wood ports are relatively straightforward and inexpensive wines: their main market used to be British pubs where they were drunk with lemon; it is now France, where port is drunk as an aperitif. The best of these wines are the old tawnies, faded pink to amber in colour, delicate in aroma and nutty in flavour, the type of port most commonly drunk by the port shippers in their farms in the Douro. The style which has made port's reputation as one of the world's four or five greatest wines, vintage port, represents a tiny proportion of the market—about 2 per cent. Only three or four times a decade do the port shippers 'declare' a vintage, setting aside a proportion of the best wine of the year to be bottled, unfiltered, after only two years in the barrel. With the top châteaux wines of Bordeaux, vintage port has the most solid reputation for durability among wines. As a result, it has become a wine for investors (an increasing number of them Americans) as well as drinkers. Indeed, when the 1985 vintage was declared at prices above the prevailing auction values of the previous two declared vintages, 1980 and 1983, I began to feel that vintage port was becoming a wine for investors alone.

In between vintage and wood ports comes so-called Late-Bottled Vintage or LBV. This is the wine of a single year, bottled after four or five years rather than two in wood, so that it is ready for drinking on release, and filtered, so that it does not require decanting. The port shippers themselves admit in private to mixed feelings about LBV. It is the wine which saved their bacon in the late 1970s, before the recent vintage port boom, being not just cheaper but in every sense easier to drink. The problem is the word vintage: LBV has very little to do with true vintage port, whose character comes from prolonged ageing in the bottle.

Probably the most important and fascinating job in the whole port business is that of the blender, who, with hundreds of subtly different lots at his disposal, must maintain a distinctive style or styles, and a regular quality. Blenders do not like to give away their secrets: perhaps they tend to have secretive natures. Peter Symington, the partner in charge of the sample room, a tall man in his late fifties with a fine, aquiline (and doubtless highly efficient) nose, is a reserved character who gives little away. He does, however, admit that the current blend of Dow's Vintage Character contains a certain amount of older colheita wine to balance the assertive, fruity vigour of the two- and three-year-old port. What is it that makes Dow's different from Warre's, say, or Graham's? With the top-quality vintage and vintage character wines it is a matter of the source of the grapes, but there is also a multitude of wine-making and blending decisions. Graham's, for instance, has always been made considerably sweeter than Dow's, with Warre's somewhere in between.

The timeless tranquillity of the lodges is only part of the picture of the Symingtons' operations in Gaia. Emerging into the bright, hot sunshine from the Smith Woodhouse lodge, we were driven up to a large modern installation built on the highest point of Gaia. The new Quinta do Marco bottling and warehousing plant is a slick, functional facility with a high-tech bottling line and loading bays for container lorries. It does have its more human face: James Symington insisted on taking us round the back to the staff canteen, where two sturdy and jolly ladies were busy stirring huge pots of bean-and-sausage stew. At the instigation of 'Senhor James', they ladled some out on to a saucer and we all had a taste. Nourishing stuff, I am sure, though boiled to within an inch of its life.

Our lunch was, I am ashamed to say, a more gracious affair, served in the long, cool dining-room of the Symington offices adjoining the house which once belonged to Baron Forrester and looking across, over a splendidly rustic vegetable garden, an obstinate survival of pre-industrial times, to the Oporto skyline. Not much time, though, to linger over the *bacalhau*, served with delicious mustard-yellow mayonnaise, the very decent modern-style cold-fermentation white wine made by the Symingtons' Australian oenologist, David Baverstock, or the delicious blackberry-scented Quinta dos Malvedos 1978 port: we had a train to catch, one of only three daily which connect Oporto with the Douro.

The train journey up the Douro may not be the dangerous adventure which the old mule-and-boat trek represented for earlier travellers, but it is still something of a ritual. The first stage is arrival at the Estaçao Sao Bento in Oporto, a handsome Victorian structure, its tall ticket hall beautifully decorated with azulejo tiles. It is advisable to arrive in good time, because seats are oversold and the journey, though 130 kilometres, takes nearly four hours, often in stifling heat. The wide carriages have friendly, facing seats, and once we are ensconced, the atmosphere mellows into a feeling of leisurely, summer afternoon relaxation. There is an air of expectation and of holiday: the Douro, after all, is the point of the whole business, the wild, remote, beautiful country to which the port shippers all become romantically attached. They have the same feeling for the Douro that many of the old English ruling class have for Scotland.

The train is no longer drawn by the steam engine dubbed *Paciencia* by a frustrated English port shipper, but it still proceeds at a dawdle. It stops at deserted stations and then, as if resting or meditating, remains motionless for twenty minutes. Nobody minds; the Portuguese are indeed a patient people. The first part of the journey is through thickly wooded, verdant country; clearings among the eucalyptus and pines are planted with maize; vines trained high on concrete pergolas often share ground with vegetables. The wine produced from these exuberantly vigorous plants is the thin, acid stuff called vinho verde. This land is too green and pleasant to produce top-quality port, the scarce fruit of steep, barren, sun-baked slopes. Time stretched out before us into the hotter, deeper, drier interior. The rainfall drops dramatically as you travel east up-river, falling from 47 inches at Oporto to 27 inches at Pinhão in the heart of the wine country. I noticed a fellow journalist named Rafferty, who had accused me the night before of not being combat officer material, ordering four beers simultaneously from the carriage attendant. It seemed a good moment to tackle James Symington on the subject of family history.

'We are relatively recent arrivals in Portugal, compared to families like the Warres, Delaforces and so on. My greatgrandfather Andrew James Symington was the first member of the family to come out to Portugal. His father, also Andrew James, was a well-off man of letters in Paisley, from a line of ministers, who made translations from Icelandic literature. He was one of the trustees for the son of a friend who had inherited a lot of money. The trustees invested all the money in the City of Glasgow Bank, which went bust in 1865. At that time there was no limit on liability, so all the trustees had to cough up very substantial amounts. This case led to the changing of the trust laws in Scotland. A. J. Senior was not exactly on his uppers, but he was a good deal less well off than he had been. The result was that in due course he sent his son off to Oporto to work for a cotton company which belonged to friends of his, the Grahams. Now A. J. Junior was clearly a wheeler-dealer, and he also developed an interest in the port trade, which was only a sideline for Grahams at that time. He left Grahams to become manager of Southards, a port shipper which no longer exists. In 1894, when he was thirty-one, A. J. was asked by the Portuguese government to help conduct the famous Burnay sale. The Burnays were bankers who had speculated in port and gone bust. There were some twenty thousand pipes to dispose of, which represents more than our annual turnover today. A .J. went over to England with a sample case, and as he was able to undercut leading suppliers, he was very successful in selling it. It did not make him popular with the port trade, as you can imagine, but the government was delighted. They offered him a title, Viscount of Alijó, but A. J. turned it down and suggested they gave it to his assistant.

'In 1905 A. J. was invited to become a partner in Warre & Company, the oldest of the British port firms, and run their wine side. Warre's were also the major shareholders in Silva & Cosens, a much larger company which had the Dow's brand. At that time there were no members of the Warre family working in Warre & Company. George Warre, who had been running Silva & Cosens, then came into Warre & Company to run the London side, and A. J. continued to run the shipping side of both Dow's and Warre's. After an exchange of shares with the Warres, he ended up with a third share in each company. He had the difficult job of running the two companies during the depression years after the 1929 crash and preceding the Second World War when business was almost at a standstill. The famous illustration of the depression is the 1931 vintage, generally agreed to be one of the finest ever, which hardly anyone declared. Noval are famous for declaring 1931, but both Dow's and Warre's declared a little also.

'A. J. managed to keep both companies going, and indeed relatively successful. Though he was obviously a good businessman, he was also keen on golf and shooting. He liked to play golf after work in the summer at a course half an hour's drive south of Oporto.

'On one occasion, when a curfew had been imposed during the civil disturbances following the First World War, A. J. returned from the golf course after the curfew. As he drove his Buick over the top level of the double-decker Dom Luis I bridge, he found a company of troops drawn up in the main square. An officer drew his sword and ordered him to stop. A. J. paid no attention and just drove on. The officer retreated. Perhaps he knew something about A. J.'s driving, which was notoriously bad.

'A. J. had four sons. The eldest, Edgar, died when he was twenty-two, then there was Maurice, who was very upright and proper, the father of Michael, and the twins John, father of Ian, Amyas and Peter, who are all in the firm, and Ron, my father.

'A. J. died at the start of the Second World War, in 1939, and the business was run by the three brothers. The twins were identical: they not only looked alike but thought alike. There are many stories told about them: during the war, for instance, they used to swap over halfway through each other's sentry duty. Then in Oporto, at one time there was a law against hooting in the street. John hooted when a policeman was nearby and was reprimanded. A few minutes later Ron came along, in an identical car, wearing identical clothes, and happened to hoot himself. The same policeman, still in the same spot, became very angry this time, and said, 'I warned you before, Sr Symington,' and tried to fine him.

'The twins were very gentle, unpompous people, excellent tasters. They both worked in the sample room, but John was responsible for Warre's and Ron for Dow's. For the history immediately after the war, the person to speak to is Michael, whom you'll be meeting shortly.'

It was time to break off our conversation in any case, because the train had finally left the lush uplands and, through a long tunnel, was approaching the mythical river of gold. The first view of the Douro is always exciting, even now since the four dams have tamed its occasional furies and long droughts. In some ways the damming may have increased its beauty, because the still water, with no perceptible flow, mirrors the steep, scrub-covered hills, some layered with the remains of abandoned pre-Phylloxera terraces, and the sky with its fleece-like clouds. Phylloxera hit the Douro as hard as any region in Europe: it is estimated that up to 300,000 people may have emigrated from northern Portugal at the end of the last century. A. J. Symington must have regretted the depopulation of the wine country, but it was not entirely disadvantageous for him. One of his side-interests was the travel firm of Tait & Co., which held the agency for the Royal Mail boats to South America.

The Douro is a region which has enjoyed a renascence in the last decade. The province of Tras-os-Montes, which includes the Alto Douro, has been declared a priority development area by the World Bank. Special loans, interest-free for the first five years, have been made to farmers intending to plant vineyards. There was new terracing, crudely bulldozed out of the hillside rather than patiently built by hand, to see, as well as the remains of the old. Between the ugly, functional town of Régua, where the high-quality port region, called Cima Corgo, begins, and our destination of Pinhão, every bend of the winding river brought into view another gleaming white, red-roofed *quinta*, or port farm, with citrus trees planted on its terrace and olives and cypresses breaking up the monotony of the vines. For many visitors, this is the most beautiful wine country in the world. For me, Tuscany and Provence, with a more equitable balance between wine and other works of human culture, may have the edge, but for sheer natural beauty, the Douro is hard to beat.

Pinhão, capital of the Cima Corgo, is finely situated on a bend in the river below the great conical hill of Carvalhos, but it is hardly even a one-horse town. Arriving at the station (picking your way over the tracks, for there is no foot-bridge or tunnel), you get an unduly favourable impression of the place, for this, kept neat and clean like most in the Douro and decorated with beautiful azulejo tiles depicting vintage scenes, is by far the town's most splendid building. Port shippers will constantly tell you how prosperous Pinhão is becoming, but only in the Peloponnese in Greece have I seen a European township with less to offer in the way of consumer choice.

We were met off the train by Michael Symington, a tall upright man in his sixties, wearing square glasses and clothes which combined the casual with a faint hint of the colonial. We piled into a minibus for the very short ride to Dow's Quinta do Bomfim, the Symingtons' centre of operations in the Douro. The lane leading to the quinta, only a couple of hundred yards from the centre of Pinhão, was blocked by a line of lorries carrying large plastic bins of newly picked grapes, getting extremely warm in the afternoon sun. We abandoned the bus and made our way up to the quinta on foot, despite the protests of Rafferty, who claimed a history of heart trouble.

Bomfim, built in the early years of the century on the model of a Sinhalese tea-planter's bungalow, is not a beautiful house, but it has several very practical features. Foremost among them is a veranda, on green-painted steel supports, surrounding all four sides of the building. It makes an excellent setting for the pre-prandial snifter, particularly the side looking down, past several rows of vines, to the river a hundred feet or so below. That may seem more than a safe distance, but the highest flood marks of the pre-dam Douro stand an astonishing 50 or 60 ft above the normal level of the river. On 23 December 1909, flood waters reached the lodge immediately below the quinta.

It was not quite the cocktail hour, so we sat on the eastern veranda and on the lawn which abuts on to it, sipping Earl Grey tea and eating lemon cake. Traditionally, the point of quintas like Bomfim was to provide fairly basic accommodation during the vintage time. Now, they are increasingly used as weekend retreats, and to receive guests who, not surprisingly, are keen to visit the Douro at any time betwen May and October. The Symingtons employ a permanent staff of three to clean and cook, primarily for the hundred or so pickers who stay at the property during the hectic month of the vintage. I took a look inside the kitchen and saw several home-made sausages hanging above the huge open fireplace.

'This has not been the easiest of vintages,' said Michael. 'Things looked very good earlier in the summer, then we had an excessively hot and dry three months from June to September. The berries were small and shrivelled when we started picking. Then the weather broke suddenly last week and we had heavy rain—normally a disaster, but very welcome this time, because it swelled out the berries. This sun is the first we have had for a week. So far, touch wood, everything has worked out well and we have had no rot. The only problem is that the harvest has been compressed and we have had great queues leading to the crushers, as you saw.

'Anyway, let's have a quick look round the vineyards before we inspect the grapes coming in and the wine being made.' Michael Symington led our party out of a small gate at the end of the lawn, and down some steps leading to a track traversing the vineyards. 'Take a look at the soil here, if you can call it soil.' The ground, a clayey brown colour, is made up of what look like solid pieces of layered rock. If you pick one up, though, you can crumble it in your hand. This stuff is schist, a kind of slate; the Douro Valley is a long seam of schist sunk into the surrounding granite. Port grapes can be grown only on schistous soil.

'We have a hundred and eighty odd acres [76 hectares] here at Bomfim, and an interesting feature of the property is that it extends from a hundred metres above sea-level, at the river, to over four hundred metres. The wine from down here tastes very different, much bigger and "hotter", than the wine from the highest part. It all faces due south, of course. People used to say that Bomfim was too hot to make balanced port on its own, but now we feel with the new high terraces that we can produce a balanced Bomfim, so we are bringing out a single-estate or single-quinta bottling, starting with the 1978 vintage. This is made in exactly the same way as vintage port, but comes from non-declared vintages and is therefore somewhat cheaper. We are also lucky at Bomfim that the gradient, though it may seem steep to you, is relatively gentle compared to most parts of the valley. The vines are a mixture of what are recognised to be the best Douro varieties: Touriga Nacional, Touriga Francesa, Tinta Roriz and Tinta Barroca. We are particularly keen on Touriga Francesa, which gives a wonderful bouquet.' The Bomfim vineyards had all been picked, but one or two shrivelled bunches of small, dark-skinned grapes still hung from the vines. 'All the grapes looked like that before the rain came,' said Michael.

We turned back from our modest walk and went down, past the level of the quinta, to the working parts immediately below it. The lodge, which in New World parlance would be called a winery, is on two levels. On the upper level there is a large forecourt, a weighbridge and two big metal troughs with revolving screws for receiving grapes. This is all modern, efficient and functional. The most notable aspect of the whole operation is probably the paperwork kept in the small office above the receiving troughs. The Symingtons, as well as using grapes from their own vineyards, buy from over 3000 farmers in the Douro. Some bring no more than 50 or 100 kg, others many thousands. Every consignment must be weighed separately, measured for must-weight and entered in the books, for the benefit of the farmers, who will be paid a few weeks after the harvest, the Symingtons themselves and the bodies which determine the amount of port each farmer can make in any given year, and a minimum price. These are the Instituto do Vinho do Porto, the official government body, and the Casa do Douro, which represents the interests of the farmers. A third body, the Gremio dos Exportadores do Vinho do Porto, representing the shippers, was dissolved after the Revolution.

The revolving screws lead the grapes into a crusher/destemmer, and thence through a system of pipes into the fermentation tanks in the covered lodge building below the receiving area. All the port made at Bomfim is produced by the autovinification system, invented by two clever French Algerians in Algeria in the 1920s. A system of valves allows the CO_2 produced by fermentation in the closed tanks to build up and then be released, causing fermenting must which has been forced out of the tank into an open trough on the top, to fall back into it, breaking up the cap of grape skins and pips. The point is to extract the maximum of colour, a prerequisite of fine port, in the minimum time.

However limited your understanding of their operation, watching the autovinifiers in action is an exciting experience. At the top of each huge tank is an open trough for receiving the excess must forced out of the tank. It builds up, a thick purple froth like blackcurrant ice cream, until you think it must overflow, when the valve suddenly blows with a great whoosh like a diving whale, and the must pours back down the tube in the middle, starting the whole process off once more.

It takes only about twenty-four hours for the sugar level in the must to drop from 12 or 13 degrees *baumé* to 7. At this point the special feature of port, as opposed to red wine-making, comes into operation. The must is run off from the autovinifiers into large oaken vats, and mixed immediately with one part of strong (77 degrees by volume), neutral grape brandy to four of wine. This has the effect of stopping the fermentation at once, leaving a fair amount of unfermented sugar in the port. From then on it is merely a matter of time, allowing the dense, concentrated sweet red wine to marry with the brandy as it ages in the barrel, and, in the case of the very best ports, the bottle.

Nothing, incidentally, is wasted in this highly efficient system. The mass of grape skins, pips and sometimes stalks left in the autovinifiers is pressed several times and then filtered. The first two pressings are generally added to the port. The residue is then used for distillation into the rasping firewater called *bagaceira* (pronounced, indelicately, like 'bugger Sarah'), comfort of Portuguese vineyard workers on cold nights. Even the residue of the residue is used for something, I forget what. That is the modern method of making port, fast, efficient and not much more romantic than the production of milk or keg beer. After supper at Bomfim, we would see the ancient method.

Supper, preceded by an aperitif of white port (pleasant enough, but I agree with the wag who said that port's first duty was to be red), accompanied by delicious, plump, heart-shaped almonds grown on the quinta, was a large, festive affair, featuring more Symingtons than I could take in at one go. I found myself sitting next to Michael and Elizabeth, châtelain and châtelaine of Bomfim, presiding over the family gathering with the practised ease which springs from confidence and authority. Michael was prompted to reminisce about his start in the family firm. 'The situation immediately after the war was very different from the boom of the last ten years. When I entered the business in 1947, I don't know whether it was out of loyalty to my father, out of inertia or out of a genuine belief in the future of the port trade. You would have had to be extraordinarily prescient then to predict the amazing success of the last few years. Most of the families who had alternative interests back in England were pulling out. But we had no alternative. We had always lived in Portugal, we considered ourselves as much Portuguese as English, so we just kept going, without any great faith in the future at the beginning, I must say.'

'You also had a half-Portuguese wife,' added Elizabeth Symington, whose somewhat imperious manner only half-conceals a keen and kindly interest in people from markedly different backgrounds than her own. 'I was born and brought up in Lisbon and Sintra. Normally the north and south of Portugal do not mix, but I fell in love with Michael when I was five and he was ten, because he could write with his left hand.'

The conversation turned to politics, a favourite subject of 'Senhor Mike', as he is known in the Douro. 'The exceptional thing about Portugal after the war was that whereas most other European countries had been through about sixty years of social change in those six years, Portugal had not changed at all. Salazar was not really a Fascist, he was a military man, rigid and inflexible, who let power go to his head. His successor, Eanes, was an enigma— a pompous, self-important character. Soares has had a marvellous touch as president— a Socialist who mellowed and grew up.

'I suppose we were extremely lucky during the 1975 revolution.

If we had been nearer Lisbon, I am sure they would have nationalised us. The Portuguese port firm of Borges & Irmão was nationalised, because it belonged to a bank. There were two things which helped us: first, northern Portugal has always been a conservative region, and there was not a great deal of enthusiasm for the revolution here. Secondly, if we can give ourselves a pat on the back, we have always been careful to fit in to the society here. For example, we have never built a swimming-pool—just imagine, girls in bikinis swanning by the pool while people toiled away in the vineyards picking grapes. Quite unacceptable, in my view. Likewise, we have never bought a helicopter, unlike some of the other big firms. How could you step out of the helicopter, meet the farmer and say, no, I'm sorry, I can't pay you an extra one thousand escudos [five pounds] a pipe?'

The meal—a homely one of the ubiquitous bacalhau with boiled potatoes and salad, followed by some delicious creamy ewes' milk cheese—also provided an opportunity to meet other members of the Symington clan. Michael's son Paul was already preparing to take over some of the reins from his father, officially due to retire in 1989. Paul is a clean-cut, sharp-featured, youthful-looking man in his mid-thirties, impressively involved in and committed to a business he obviously adores. 'I didn't go straight into the firm, which I think would be a mistake. I worked in a bank for a while, and for two years as a buyer for Boots. If you go straight into the business, you will always wonder what you missed. Now of course is a good time to be in this business, and what's particularly encouraging is that there are more younger people coming into the port trade than there were ten years ago. As a family, we are in the position that we could sell out and make a good deal of money, as the Sandemans did a few years ago. Eighty per cent of the shares are owned by the seven of us who work in the company. We sold twenty per cent of the shares in the early 1960s—the time when everyone was selling—to our French distributor, which was then bought by Cusenier, the liqueur makers. Cusenier was subsequently bought by Pernod-Ricard. It is rather by accident that Pernod-Ricard have a twenty per cent share in us—it does not give them the right to have a director on the board. Perhaps they would like to buy us out, but the thought would not cross our minds, because this is the business we all understand and love.

'It is not easy, because as a relatively small family-owned enterprise we face very stiff competition from the big multinationals like Seagrams, who own Sandeman's, Allied-Lyons, with Cockburn's, and IDV-Grand Met with Croft's. They are constantly buying up distributors and retail outlets, which makes it hard for us. We certainly cannot compete with them on a volume basis. But at the quality end, with vintage port, vintage character, LBV, and revivals of old styles like crusted, which in any case is where the big recovery of port sales has come, we believe we can compete successfully.'

However difficult things might have become for the Symingtons, they had recently demonstrated considerable faith in the future by purchasing the largest quinta on the Douro, the historic Quinta do Vesuvio of the Ferreira family in the eastern reaches of the Douro valley, for well over £1 million.

'It's certainly a huge place, a great hillside sweep of four hundred hectares, which were all planted with vines before phylloxera. At the moment there are eighty-five hectares planted to vines and twenty-eight thousand olive trees. The house is a bit of a barracks—twenty-two bedrooms and a chapel. We might turn it into a hotel or something one day.

'I hope we have done the right thing in buying it. We all felt a lot of *soudade*, a sort of homesickness for the place. We used to own the Quinta Sra da Ribeira right opposite, and shot there often. Another factor was that the opportunity to buy a great historic quinta like Vesuvio may come only once a century.

'I know we are often accused of being colonials and exaggeratedly British, but a lot of that is nonsense. I was brought up here, have always spoken Portuguese and regard myself as Portuguese.'

All the same, Paul was obviously educated at an English public school, and when he came to choose a wife, he returned to the English counties rather than Oporto or Lisbon. Janey Symington, from Sussex, pretty, freckled and demure, has obviously settled in to her Portuguese existence, split between Oporto and the Douro, where she and Paul have a summer house. 'England used to be home for the first few years—I would get terribly homesick and rush back whenever I could. But now Portugal is home. We have four small children, and this is a great place to bring them up. The day I am dreading is when we have to send the eldest to prep school. It seems an inhuman system, but apparently if you want them to go to public school, they have to go to prep school first. There is a very good primary school in Oporto, but after that the education system here is less satisfactory.'

Peter Symington has broken with this tradition by marrying a Portuguese wife, Fernanda. Their daughter Natasha looks more Latin than English but feels split between the two cultures. 'I get very bored with my friends in Oporto, but I don't think I could live in England—I would miss the Latin life-style too much.'

Speaking of the Latin life-style, it was time, after the cheese and a glass of Dow's 1975 vintage port, with a firm core of fruit and the dry finish characteristic of the Dow's style, to witness a remarkable survival of a method of wine-making which would not have seemed alien to Bacchus himself. In deference to more modern standards of decency, we were first instructed to put on a pair of old bathing-trunks.

We piled into the minibus and set off in the velvety Douro night, through Pinhão, over the iron bridge which spans the Douro and left down the steep side valley of the Rio Torto. The Torto has probably the greatest concentration of top-quality port vineyards in the entire Douro region. Visiting it on another occasion in the company of James Symington, I was amazed by his intimate knowledge of every parcel of vineyard. After a few kilometres snaking round bends we turned off right down an extremely bumpy track. 'This is the Quinta do Bom Retiro, which is divided into two parts,' Paul Symington informed us. 'One belongs to Ramos Pinto, a leading Portuguese firm, and the other to a man named Serodio, who sells his port to us. With any luck they will still be treading.'

As we neared the winery or adega buildings, we could hear the sound of the treaders, chanting rhythmically to the accompaniment of a wheezy accordion. 'Strip off and hose down, everybody,' ordered Paul, as we got out of the bus in the yard outside the adega. There was indeed a hosepipe (occasion for horse-play afterwards involving Dow's Puckish London salesman, Tim Stanley-Clarke), which we took it in turns to apply to our feet, reducing the likelihood of a cheesy tone on the nose of the '87 vintage Warre (Bom Retiro goes into the Warre's lot). So, wearing progressively more from the ground upwards (bare feet, swimming trunks, then more conventional garb on the upper part of the body), we trooped inside the adega.

Twenty or so bodies, male and female, ranging from about ten years old to nearly seventy, stood in a large open stone tank, about six yards square and three feet deep. All were wearing shorts and with arms linked were performing a strange, slow-motion goose-step in what looked like a sea of blackberry jam. Our arrival had coincided with the end of the *corte* or cut, the really hard opening two-hour session of treading, which reduces the grapes from a solid mass into softish pulp, and the beginning of the *liberdade*, the free-for-all which takes the form of a dance. Some of the older treaders were doing the nearest thing to a waltz that is possible in three feet of jam, while the younger generation went for more individualistic modes of expression.

Well, the English bosses' party, that group of colonialist exploiters, or just mad eccentrics, could not stay for ever on the sidelines, attracting a few curious stares and a great deal of indifference. It was time to take the plunge. The sensation of entering a lagar, as these tanks are called, is hard to describe, at least in polite language. The stuff inside is lukewarm, slimy and deep purply red, and it reaches up to the inner thigh.

After a while, the atmosphere became quite merry (aided by generous tots of bagaceira all round), and one of the English party was emboldened to ask a nubile Portuguese girl (probably no more than fourteen) for a turn in the tank. Her reply of 'Fuck off!', in surprisingly idiomatic tones, cut through the accordion-playing, the slushing and the general hum with cruel precision.

The hosing-down afterwards was a prolonged affair, since half-trodden grape must is an immensely sticky and persistent substance. My toes were stained purple for a week afterwards. On the way back to Bomfim, Paul Symington explained that treading was by no means just a side-show put on for the benefit of visitors. 'Fourteen per cent of our total production is still made by treading in lagars. I would not say it was a better system than the modern one—we are obviously very happy with autovinification—but it is certainly an excellent system. The main disadvantage of the lagars is the lack of temperature control, which can be a serious problem in very hot vintages.'

Next morning we retraced our route back up the Rio Torto valley, and visited two other traditional quintas, Lajes and Macedos, where lagars stood full of the already trodden, fermenting must. At Lajes I noticed the traditional *ramos* or harvest garlands hanging from the adega walls. High up above the tiny, winding Torto river, Lajes was a place of rustic simplicity and peace. Orange trees and a profusely blooming Banksia rose grew outside the whitewashed farm buildings, while turkeys and pigs pecked and rooted in the yard behind. A couple of bare-footed children played with a mongrel of the small, curly-tailed type very common in the Douro. One of the children was a strikingly blonde little girl with blue eyes. 'You see quite a number of blonde children in the Douro,' said James Symington. 'The common explanation is the Scottish regiments who fought here in the Peninsular War.' The girl and her brother faced an eight-kilometre walk to school and back every day. I wondered how many days they did odd jobs round the quinta instead.

We returned to Pinhão by a different route, the high road which passes through the pretty town of S. Joao de Pesqueira, with fine eighteenth-century buildings decorated with carved stone escutcheons. There was also a modern school and a new shopping centre being built, welcome signs of new life in an area which can seem depressingly poor and moribund. From S Joao to Ervedosa, the land is too high to plant vines. Clumps of pine and cork-oak emerge from an undergrowth of gum cistus and Spanish broom. The cork-oaks, stripped of their bark every fifteen years, are as indispensable for the production of wine made to be aged in bottle as the vine itself. No synthetic substitute has been discovered, and the tree grows successfully nowhere else but the Iberian peninsula, especially Portugal. The Douro, however, is not an important cork-growing region: most of the world's supply comes from the Alentejo region near Lisbon.

From Pinhão we embarked on the final stage of our trip, a motorboat ride upriver to Graham's Quinta dos Malvedos. In the days before the dams, this stretch of the Douro was, for most of the year, unnavigable. Malvedos means 'bad ways'. Now boats provide the quickest as well as the most scenic means of transport. The 10-kilometre stretch between Bomfim and Malvedos is one of the loveliest on the river. One famous quinta follows another, on either side, vines in terraces descending right to the water's edge: Roeda, Romaneira, Roriz. The river bends in smooth curves; the water is glassy smooth. Apart from the single-track railway on the north bank, there is no sign of communication with the world outside the enclosed, enchanted valley. One has the feeling of penetrating territory which is both virgin, like the Amazonian jungle, and mysteriously cultivated, by unseen hands and in silence.

The house at Malvedos, looked after by James and Penny Symington, is more modest in scale than Bomfim, but has greater charm and character. The estate is a large one, 146 hectares, but until quite recently it produced more citrus fruit than grapes. The history of Malvedos had been more chequered than that of Bomfim, as James Symington explained:

'The Grahams started in textiles and dry goods in Oporto in the early nineteenth century. They had a huge textile factory in Oporto which employed thousands. There is still an area of Oporto called Graham. They got into port as a result of a bad debt in 1826, and continued with it as a relatively unimportant sideline, though their vintage port always had an impeccable reputation. After the Second World War the textile business went bust, as a result of terrible mismanagement, but the port side had been made a separate company in the 1920s. Eventually Ken Graham decided to sell the port business, including this quinta, in 1970, and we bought it. We did not have much cash then, so as soon as we had bought it, we decided to sell off Malvedos, which was not producing much port then. The buyer was a man from Pinhão: very fortunately we were able to buy it back in 1980.'

The Grahams' story has a further repercussion, which shook the

British community in Oporto in the early 1980s. John Graham, the youngest son of Ken, had been working for some years for Cockburn's when he decided to start up in the port business on his own. It caused considerable excitement, as the first new British port shipping firm to be founded for fifty years, especially as its founder was both a charming young man and a dedicated port shipper with a fine palate. The problem came with the name. When John Graham's first prototype labels appeared with the name Churchill Graham (his wife is a Churchill), and a neck label stating that he was 'recovering the old tradition of Graham's port founded in 1820', he received an immediate telephone call from James Symington.

The situation, complicated by the close friendship of the Grahams and Symingtons, became rancorous for a while, as lawyers were brought in by both sides. The result was that both the neck label and the Graham name on the front label were dropped. Many sided with John Graham as the underdog and felt that the Symingtons had used their greater muscle to crush a potential competitor. Paul Symington, who regards John Graham as his closest friend in Oporto, thinks there were faults on both sides. 'Johnny was incredibly naive, but we should have acted more quickly to defuse the situation.' He considers that the situation has now been resolved, however. 'Johnny is a dedicated man. He will still be here shipping port in twenty years' time—as I will be, I hope.' It seems fair to record that John Graham's firm, under the Churchill label, has quickly established a high reputation for quality. His Vintage Character is generally agreed to be one of the few on the market which justifies its name; his 1982 vintage (a year the Symingtons and most other shippers did not declare) is an excellent wine.

Sitting on the terrace at Malvedos after an energetic trek through the vineyards, it was easy to understand the chagrin John Graham must have felt at the loss of the jewel in the Grahams' crown. As darkness fell there was not a light to be seen looking west down the river, which shortly before, reflecting the setting sun, had finally taken on its eponymous gold.

'We love this part of the Douro,' said Penny Symington. 'We have bought a small property a couple of miles down from here, for our retirement, you know. Malvedos is wonderful, but it is a company house. I want somewhere where there is no staff and I can have the kitchen to myself.'

'There are no vines on the place at all,' said James. 'It is all the natural scrub, evergreen oak, cistus, aromatics, which is what we love best and will not change.' James looked far too young to be even contemplating retirement. He was buzzing with a new Symington project. 'We have recently taken a thirty-five per cent share in the Madeira Wine Company, which is owned by the Blandy family and has all the major brands. Madeira is an extraordinary place—if you think Portugal is colonial, you should go there. The wine production is very small: the total production of the island is smaller than that of any of the five or six largest port firms. But the wine is unique and ages astonishingly well. I am very excited about it.'

Darkness had fallen, supper, eaten out on the terrace, was finished. It was a warm night, scented with the leaves of grapefruit trees. A Scops owl was delivering its curious metallic bleep at regular intervals, like an amplified metronome. We were comparing the merits of two bottles of port, Graham's vintage 1963 and the single quinta wine of Malvedos, 1962 vintage. The Malvedos was lighter yet mellower, the marriage of brandy and wine complete, all harshness gone; beginning to fade a little, perhaps. The Graham's was a bigger, fuller wine, showing fruit, spice and even saddle-leather on the nose, still fiery on the palate. James Symington and I preferred the Graham: 'The most important thing about port is the fruit. The very old vintages are too dried up for me.' James left the table, lay down on a lilo and stared up in the starry sky, unpolluted by any sign of human life. 'Time to count satellites.'

The British in Portugal might be an anachronism, I thought, but with their mild eccentricity, their energy, their deep love of their adopted country, all expressed in the skilled production and selling of one of the world's strangest, greatest wines, they had earned some sort of right to stay. If revolution had failed to shift Symingtons, there was hope they might survive the more modern menace of corporate take-over.

Index

Index

Index